THE RIGHT WORDS AT THE RIGHT TIME

VOLUME 2

THE RIGHT WORDS AT THE RIGHT TIME

VOLUME 2:

Your Turn!

MARLO THOMAS and ^*new* FRIENDS

ATRIA BOOKS

NEW YORK   LONDON   TORONTO   SYDNEY

ATRIA BOOKS
A Division of Simon & Schuster, Inc.
1230 Avenue of the Americas
New York, NY 10020

First Atria Books trade paperback edition October 2007

ATRIA BOOKS and colophon are trademarks of Simon & Schuster, Inc.

For information about special discounts for bulk purchases,
please contact Simon & Schuster Special Sales at 1-800-456-6798
or business@simonandschuster.com.

Designed by C. Linda Dingler

Manufactured in the United States of America

10 9 8 7 6 5 4 3 2 1

ISBN-13: 978-0-7434-9743-5
ISBN-10:   0-7434-9743-0
ISBN-13: 978-0-7434-9744-2 (pbk)
ISBN-10:   0-7434-9744-9 (pbk)

THE RIGHT WORDS AT THE RIGHT TIME

VOLUME 2:
Your Turn!

EDITOR
Marlo Thomas

EXECUTIVE EDITORS
Bruce Kluger
Carl Robbins

CONSULTING EDITOR
David Tabatsky

For

The Children

of

St. Jude Children's Research Hospital

and

Their Parents

Contents

PART ONE

The Simple Stuff

PART TWO

At a Crossroads

PART THREE

Taking Chances

PART FOUR

Finding Yourself

PART FIVE

Survival

PART SIX

Friends & Family

PART SEVEN

On the Job

PART EIGHT

Love & Romance

CONTENTS

PART ELEVEN

Letting Go

Acknowledgments

I owe many words of thanks to all those who joined me in casting a giant net across the country in search of the perfect stories that would become this book.

To my husband, Phillip, who I can always count on for just the right words of encouragement (and the kindest words of critique); to my assistants, Ally McClure and Debbie Newman, whose talent for keeping me focused, on schedule, and *connected* (via email, fax, cell, *and* Blackberry) is truly an art form; to Judith Curr and Greer Hendricks of Atria Books, who shared the magic with us on the first volume, and who so enthusiastically urged us to re-create it in the second; and to the great support staff at Atria who kept the wheels turning throughout, especially Suzanne O'Neill and Hannah Morrill.

To our attorney, Bob Levine, and his associate Kim Schefler, whose unflagging support and uncanny attention to detail permitted us to keep our eyes on the prize (and the paperwork to a minimum). And to my treasured pal Kathie Berlin, whose giant Rolodex is exceeded only by the size of her heart.

To *Parade* magazine and Editor-in-Chief Lee Kravitz, who have championed the Right Words project since its inception, and who called on their loyal family of readers to tell us their stories.

To the team at FSB Associates—notably John and Fauzia Burke—who helped us in our nationwide search and pulled in a winning haul. To our intrepid band of readers—led by Paula Litzky, including Barbara Boulden, Arthur Morey, Caron Knauer, Katharine Thornton, and Gisela White—whose sharp eyes and impeccable instincts helped us to sort through close to a million words in search of the "right" ones.

To Julie Besonen and Buzz McClain, whose additional outreach yielded a special group of unforgettable stories that continue to enlighten and inspire us.

To Elizabeth ("Biz") Mitchell, for her sage editorial counsel and generosity of spirit.

To family, friends, and associates who graciously lent their time and assistance—each in their own way—in the making of this collection, including: Keith Hefner, Bell Chevigny, Greg Fagan, Kathryn Roth-Douquet, Paul Gilbert, Wayne Duvall, Jonathan Cooperman, Tracy Jensen, and Bridgette Kluger.

To the hundreds of others across the country whose stories ultimately did not make it onto these pages, but whose words nonetheless never failed to touch our hearts.

And to my editorial team, Bruce Kluger, Carl Robbins, and David Tabatsky, for the thousands of hours spent reading (and rereading); for knowing the joy of telling a story well—and whose company is reason enough to do Volume 3.

Foreword

I never saw the woman's face. I only heard her voice.

It was spring of 2002, and I was in the middle of a radio interview, talking about my new book, *The Right Words at the Right Time,* in which I had asked 108 famous people—people I admired—to write about the words that changed their lives. Halfway through the interview, a listener called the station and told a story that would stay with me.

Her teenage son had been in a terrible car accident, the woman said, and as she sat in the hospital waiting to learn his fate, two doctors prepared her for the worst.

"You have to know when to let go," said the first doctor, gently warning her that her son was probably not going to make it. The second doctor, believing that her child might pull through, cautioned her that, due to his injuries, he'd never be the same again. Then he added, "But life is precious."

Both men were telling the truth as they saw it, the caller explained, but their words couldn't have been more different.

"I sat there trying to decide which words I would hold on to through that night," she remembered, confessing that neither scenario was something she'd ever dreamed of happening to her son. "But in the end, I hung on to the words of the second doctor. Because life *is* so precious. And these were the words that gave me strength to endure the life trial that was to come."

The woman was so honest, and her account so moving. I'd been hearing stories like this ever since the book had come out. Everywhere I went, people were eager to tell me about the right words in *their* lives. In airports. At book signings. In countless, heartfelt letters sent through the mail.

That day in the radio station, I was reminded that we're surrounded by heroes everywhere—and I thought about how exciting it would be to assemble a new collection of right words stories, not from celebrities this time, but from everyday Americans.

Famous people have lots of opportunities to be heard. This book would provide a voice for everyone else.

The more I thought about the idea, the more I realized that the best way to find stories for the book would be to cast a net across the country—along both coasts and through the heartland. And so we did. We announced a nationwide contest in the pages of the paperback edition of *Right Words,* asking readers to search their memories for that vivid moment in their lives when words made all the difference. We set up a website for online submissions. We hung posters in hospitals and military posts, in schools and police stations and prisons. And *Parade* magazine, which had been a champion of the first book, lent a hand by soliciting stories from its readers.

It didn't take long for millions of thoughtful words to suddenly materialize around me—riveting, well-rendered letters, more than a thousand all together, from 30 states and three countries. Reading them late into the night was a joy, but choosing the 101 essays that would appear in this book was daunting. People didn't simply send us random thoughts that strung together a few memorable words from their past. They sent us their *stories,* pieces of their lives.

As I'd learned from the first book, the right words can transform us. They can challenge us at a crossroads; they can help us through times of sorrow; they can dare us to action. They can be spoken with love or shouted in anger. The right words can be funny words, thought-provoking words, words that prop us up when we think we can go no further.

And they can be found almost anywhere—in a poem or a songbook, illuminated on a computer screen, stitched onto a wall-hanging, or scratched into the dirt with a wooden stick.

Whether set in a small schoolhouse on the plains of Wyoming or in a Zen Buddhist monastery in Japan, each story we received sprang from the heart. For Michael Raysses of Los Angeles and Nebraskan Steve Martinez, the right words were spoken by strangers, one at a Starbucks, the other in an emergency room. Arizonian Susyn Reeve learned about human compassion, thanks to a chance encounter in a rainstorm. A teenage employee of Burger King grasped Floridian Tim Ciciora's hand and spoke two words that almost made a tough guy cry.

And for four special contributors to this book, words alone helped them extract a measure of hope from the devastating heartbreak of September 11th.

As the nights wore on and the stacks of letters grew, I became increasingly awed by the bounty of truth that surrounded me. I am a wiser person,

I think, for having taken the journeys so eloquently recounted in the pages of this book. And I'm thankful for the generous spirit of our contributors, whose strong and intimate and touchingly personal stories may help all of us to find our own right words.

Marlo Thomas

New York City
Spring, 2006

PART ONE

The Simple Stuff

"My mouth must have fallen open,
because he laughed and said,
'Yes, I do mean you. Really.'"

The Homecoming

Timothy Ciciora

Command Master Chief, United States Navy, Retired
Atlantic Beach, Florida

My ship, the USS *John L. Hall*, a guided missile frigate, had just returned from Desert Storm to its base in Mayport, Florida. As my fellow sailors and I walked down the pier, the first thing I saw was a 500-foot inflatable Budweiser beer can.

What the hell is this? I thought to myself. We had no idea what was going on stateside while we were overseas, nor any idea of what kind of reception was awaiting us. Suddenly, it seemed, we were the flavor of the month.

A giant crowd of families and well-wishers was there to greet us, but this didn't lift my spirits. I wanted no accolades or honors—I just wanted to get home. My master chief noticed my attitude.

"This reception is a lot better than the one I got when I returned from Vietnam," he snapped. "So keep it to yourself."

But after 12 years of service, I was sick of the Navy and thinking about getting out. I'd enlisted right after high school. Back in Chicago, I hadn't been the greatest student, and I knew there was more out there beyond my own backyard. I wanted to see the world and get a different kind of education. I wanted to be somebody. I wanted to do some good. Besides, McDonald's didn't offer a retirement plan.

But now I was at a crossroads. The last nine months had been long ones. We'd been sitting in Haifa, Israel, waiting for our six-month tour to end when the problem in Kuwait unfolded. Suddenly we were on our way to the Gulf. We accompanied the first carrier in years to go through the Suez Canal—right into the Red Sea and on to the Persian Gulf for a three-month extension.

On the way home, however, I began to think about my career in the Navy and soon grew distraught. Although I was a chief petty officer, I was having trouble advancing. I wanted a higher rank—more power, more prestige—but I had been passed over twice for promotion. So I was arrogant. If I couldn't advance, what was I staying in for? On top of all that, I was tired of leaving my family. I wasn't getting to watch my three sons grow up. I even missed my second son's birth. This would definitely be my final cruise.

Back at the pier, the carnival-like atmosphere raged on. Along with those welcoming our arrival were swarms of merchants, some with an arm slung around a sailor, all of them trying to make a buck. Above the crowd waved banners that read WE SUPPORT DESERT STORM.

I tore through the circus and made my way to the parking lot. Finally, I spotted my wife, Terri, standing by our car and grinning from ear to ear. Right away I felt a sense of calm.

My three boys—11, 9, and 7—were in the back seat, with their faces pressed against the rear window. The minute they saw me, they jumped out of the car and tackled me on the tarmac. I hardly recognized them—they'd grown so fast! We shared big hugs, though my youngest son was a bit hesitant. Like, *Who is this guy?*

As I slid into the driver's seat, Terri announced, "We're going to your mom and dad's in Indiana." This was good to hear. I hadn't seen my parents in eight years, and hanging out with my three brothers again would also be great. Besides, I needed to go somewhere inland, far away from the water, far away from those mammoth gray ships.

Even though I felt good about making the trip to Indiana, I was troubled during most of the drive. As Terri and the kids slept through the night, I had plenty of time to think. What kind of a job could I get on the outside? The last civilian job I had was as a delivery boy for a medical supply store. I didn't even know how to write a resume. But if I stayed in the Navy, didn't I run the real risk of being killed in action? A glance at my sleeping sons in the rearview mirror drove home this awful thought.

My mind buzzing, I didn't stop driving until we hit Chattanooga the next morning. Figuring this would be a good place to have breakfast, I pulled into a Burger King. It felt good to see the big orange and red sign. It was like a mecca to me. Overseas, they have American-style restaurants, but let's face it, the food just doesn't taste the same.

As my wife and kids groggily adjusted to the daylight, I walked inside and made my way to the counter. A teenaged girl stepped up to the cash register. She was tiny, with short brown hair, probably just out of high school. She took my order, and a few minutes later returned with my food. Just as I was reaching for my money, she spoke to me.

"Excuse me," she said in a timid voice. "Did you just get back from the war?"

I was still wearing my uniform. My hat was on the back of my head, my tie was undone, and I had a five o'clock shadow. But despite my rumpled appearance, my full dress of medals was obvious.

"Yeah," I grumbled, thrusting a twenty at her. I knew I was being an asshole, but I'd heard this routine before. Civilians always ask the same questions: "Are you a Navy Seal?" "Did you kill anybody?" "Did you blow anything up?" I didn't want to hear it, nor was I in any mood for small talk. I wanted to get my food, get out of there, and get home.

The young lady didn't take offense at my rudeness. Instead, she gently rolled my fingers back around the twenty-dollar bill in my hand. Leaning over the counter and planting a small kiss on my knuckle, she looked up at me and stared for a second, as if she was memorizing my face. Then she spoke one word.

"Thanks."

Did you ever feel like you suddenly owed the world an apology? That's how I felt at that moment. Here was this kid who had no ulterior motive, no agenda, no business deal to offer me. And yet she bought my breakfast for me anyway. Her register would probably come up short for that shift, and she'd have to make up for it out of her own pocket. But that didn't seem to matter to her. Unlike that throng back at the base, all of them jumping on the bandwagon, as if supporting the war was some sort of fad, this young lady's gesture had come from the heart. She was letting me know that she felt safe, that she knew someone was watching over her. When she spoke that one word, I didn't see just a girl expressing gratitude. I saw an entire nation saying "Thanks."

I suddenly felt like the Grinch feels when he discovers what Christmas is all about. For the first time in a long time, I felt like I had a purpose being in the Navy. It wasn't about money and rank or prestige. It was about raising the flag. We do what we do because no one else can or will do it. We fight so others can sleep at night. And I had forgotten that. So this sudden, unexpected expression of thanks from a total stranger hit me like a lightning bolt. I'd received many decorations over the years, but nothing could compare to the simple tribute she'd given me. It made me remember why I was here. It renewed my faith, not only in my military career, but in life, as well.

I was too choked up to respond to her. With a lump in my throat, and fighting like hell to get out of there before I started crying like a baby, I quickly made my way to the door. When I got back to the car, I discovered that the tears I thought I'd been holding back were now streaming down my cheeks.

"What happened," Terri asked. "Are you okay?"

"You know," I responded after a moment. "It really is true what they say."

"What is?" Terri asked, confused.

I then planted a soft kiss on my wife's forehead.

"Broiling *does* beat frying," I said.

There was no way I could've talked about it right there. So I just drove out of the parking lot. A single word from someone I didn't even know had transformed me. It changed my life, and my family's. I knew that I would be wearing my Navy uniform for a long time to come.

As I looked for signs to get back onto the highway, the road ahead of me seemed very clear.

A Beautiful Shade of Yellow

Jackie Sigmund

Business Owner, Independent Contractor
Charlotte, North Carolina

When my dad disappeared with my sister, it came as a total shock to my mother and me. Looking back, I shouldn't have been so surprised.

I was born in New York City, and spent most of my early childhood constantly moving among military bases in Germany, Austria, and Italy. Dad was an Army sergeant and a tough cookie. When he said something, you'd better do it. He had an explosive temper.

When we finally returned to the States and settled in South Carolina, Dad's verbal abuse of Mom continued and they finally separated. After that, things actually got worse.

Mom and I didn't have much money, my dad did very little to support us, and mom went from one job to another. The only possible escape would have been weekend visitations with my father; but Dad, who had always favored my sister, Janice, rarely asked me to come.

Then when I was 12, my father took my sister for the weekend and they never came back.

Days turned into weeks and months into years—and never a word. To be honest, I had mixed feelings, as Janice and I were not terribly close at the time. We were total opposites. She was a blonde, I was a brunette. She was the stern, older sibling; I was the kid sister, always being told what to do and what not to do. We resented each other's presence, and we constantly pushed our parents' buttons, vying for their attention.

Not long after they disappeared, Mom ran out of money and we were forced to move to Bed-Stuy, Brooklyn, where we lived in a small, railroad apartment with two other families. The place was cramped, and our only ventilation came from a window in the kitchen and another at the other end of the long and narrow hallway.

I was miserable. The soundtrack of summers on Stuyvesant Avenue was full of gunshots, alley cats, police sirens, and people arguing. Our only air-conditioning was putting a mattress out on the fire escape, and we often fell asleep in the sweltering heat, filled with fear and anxiety.

Naturally, this was a very rough time for my mother and me—no money and my sister gone—and yet Mom never let that get her down.

"I'm off to get a job!" she'd yell out in a cheerful voice most mornings. And even though she rarely came home with one, she never lost her spirit. We got by because all of us worked together. The kids would do whatever odd jobs we could find, and we always knew to bring our earnings to the table to share. If my mom was not working, her friend Sue, who shared the apartment with us, would help her out. And vice versa.

Sometimes the only way Mom could find work was through the barter system. She would take a job sweeping at the butcher's or grocery store in exchange for extra food. I always loved potato chips, but they were a luxury we couldn't afford—so Mom tossed beef fat into a skillet and fried it up into little chunks for snacks. I also remember thinking fruits and vegetables came in cubes, because when my mom would get leftover fruit she'd chop off the brown edges so they ended up looking like squares. I know this sounds like a "we were poor but we were happy" story, but the reality is, there were times I got very depressed.

One day, I was feeling especially desperate. Nothing mattered. I was tired of living in a two-bedroom tenement, sleeping three to a bed. I felt like there was no way out. I began longing for my earlier childhood days, when my father would take me on visits to the cotton farms of South Carolina. I loved the horses and played with the pigs and the chickens. I soaked up the farmers' love of life. They had nothing, but they were happy.

Dear God, I thought to myself in the prison of my Brooklyn apartment, *if I'm going to have nothing, just let me have nothing on a farm, where I can take my shoes off and run.*

My mom noticed my unhappiness and took me out for a walk. Everywhere we went, we were surrounded by trash, dirt, and depression.

"I hate my life," I told my mom. "There's no joy, just ugliness."

Mom didn't say anything, and we walked in silence for a few minutes. Finally she spoke.

"There really is beauty if you just take time to look for it," she said.

"Yeah, mom," I grumbled, staring at the tops of my shoes. "Where is the beauty in this godforsaken place?"

Mom's voice brightened. "Look, Jackie!" she said. "Is that not the most beautiful shade of yellow you've ever seen?"

I didn't know what she was talking about.

"Where?" I asked, looking up at her.

Mom took the toe of her shoe and moved a rumpled piece of newspaper on the ground. Beneath the paper was a plain yellow dandelion.

"Find happiness where you can," she said softly. "It's not just the great big whammo things. Look for the beauty of life in the small things, and you'll be the happiest person alive."

With that, she reached down, picked the dandelion, and slid it into my hair.

I knew right then that my mother's words would be with me for the rest of my life. And they have been. Whenever I feel down, I still look for a beautiful shade of yellow.

Jackie Sigmund

A Message in a Teddy Bear

Daniel Walisiak

Manufacturing
Naperville, Illinois

On that beautiful fall morning, my fiancée and I kissed good-bye as we left for work. We said, "I love you" to each other as we always did. We didn't know it would be for the last time.

The date was September 11, 2001. Susan worked on the 92nd floor of the South Tower in the World Trade Center in New York City. She was not only my fiancée. She was my best friend.

After both towers came down, I made endless attempts to find her. A few days after the attacks, family members were allowed to visit Ground Zero up close. As I stood along the fence, staring blankly at the ruins, I realized in my heart that she was gone.

Near the Family Help Center was a makeshift memorial with pictures of the missing posted on a wall. The long mural of faces seemed to go on for countless city blocks. I walked from one end to the other, examining every photograph. At one point, I spotted a large box filled with little teddy bears that people had left as gifts of kindness for family members of those who were lost. I took one and put it in my pocket.

Later that evening I noticed that the bear had a note pinned to it, written by a pre-K student through her mom. The little girl was named Demi Coon, and she was from Shawnee, Oklahoma. Along with her name and address she offered her prayers and sympathy.

I was so touched by the card that I wrote to Demi the next day, thanking her for her kindness. Along with my letter, I enclosed a teddy bear that I had bought for Susan a while before. Two weeks later, I received a letter back from Demi, which she had dictated to her teacher. Again I wrote her back, and before long, I was exchanging letters on a weekly basis with Demi and her classmates at Pleasant Grove School in Shawnee. They told me about their lives, and I did the same. Writing and receiving those letters kept me going through the impossibly long months leading up to Christmas 2001. Susan and I had planned to be married that winter, and my life no longer seemed to have purpose without her. I eventually moved back to my hometown of Chicago.

But the letters from the schoolchildren kept coming, and in February, I called the school and said I'd like to come meet Demi and her classmates in person. I knew this was an extraordinary thing to do, but I was still so lost and sad. My hope was that once I arrived and interacted with the children in a positive way, maybe I'd begin to feel better.

Demi and her teacher were waiting for me at the airport. As I walked down the ramp, Demi spotted me and smiled; then she ran forward and gave me a big hug as if she'd known me forever. I met her family that evening for dinner, and they were warm and gracious. The next morning, the school held a reception for me. It was overwhelming. Not only did all the children and faculty from the school attend, but so did many people from the Shawnee community.

After the students, their parents, and grandparents filed into the gym and took their seats, the pre-K class performed what they called their "Rise and Shine" program. They were adorable—singing, dancing, and reciting their parts. They brought tears to my eyes.

"Smile, Danny," all of the children said from the stage. "We love you."

I would hear these words again and again from those four-year-olds throughout the entire day—during the assembly, in class, after school on the playground, even as I boarded the plane to return home. Although they were total strangers, these kids expressed their love and joy in a way I had never known before. I hoped that spirit would stay with them for a lifetime.

Back in Chicago, I stopped for gas on my way home from the airport. The attendant greeted me with a cheerful, "How ya' doing?"

"Great!" I replied, noticing myself smiling in the reflection of the gas station window. It was the first time I'd done that since September 11th without feeling guilty. At that moment I knew that my life would go on.

I owe those children from Oklahoma a debt of gratitude that I can never repay. I made a promise to them that I would come back for a visit every year until they graduated. It has been almost four years since I lost Susan, and I've kept my promise. I cherish each visit more than the last.

Susan had always wanted to be a teacher. She was going to school to get her degree, but never had the chance to fulfill her dream. I am now convinced she had something to do with this whole thing. Just like those children, she continues to help me smile.

Dan Trafisiah

An Umbrella
to Remember

Susyn Reeve

Interfaith Minister and Spiritual Counselor
Camp Verde, Arizona

When I was 15 years old, my mom was hospitalized for two weeks, undergoing surgery for severe back pain. Because my two older sisters no longer lived at home, I was suddenly the "woman of the house." I desperately wanted my dad to think I was doing a good job, so I was very careful to be helpful and always do the right thing. That included making meals. Ironically, my dad, a quiet man, would have been pleased if I simply made him a peanut butter and jelly sandwich for dinner. But I wanted my mom to know that everything was okay on the home front, so I cooked.

One night while I was preparing dinner, I noticed that one of the burners on the stove didn't light when I turned the knob. *I'll ask Mom about this when I visit her tomorrow,* I thought to myself, figuring my dad didn't know much about anything in the kitchen.

The next day, Saturday, was chilly and rainy. Despite the bad weather, I decided to walk to the hospital. Once inside, I dried myself off and sat down to talk with my mom. As sheets of rain pounded against the window in her room, I told her about my week, the meals I'd been cooking, and how I was doing a good job taking care of Dad while she was away from home.

Then, casually, I mentioned that one of the burners on the stove wasn't working. My mom's reaction was immediate and scary.

"Are you trying to burn the house down while I'm here in the hospital?" Mom snapped. "Go home right now and ask the superintendent to fix the pilot light in the stove! Do I have to take care of everything myself?"

Furious and ashamed of myself, I stormed out of her hospital room shouting, "I'm trying to take care of things while you're gone! I'm never going to visit you again!"

I bolted into the elevator, tears streaming down my face. It was only when I got to the first floor and walked to the front door that I realized the intensity of the downpour. The rain had gotten much worse, and I had left my umbrella in Mom's hospital room. There was no way I was going back up there! So I stepped into the rain and began my walk home, crying all the way.

Within a quarter of a block, my clothes were already soaked through to my skin—and I had three more blocks to go. I felt so alone. Mom's hospitalization had frightened me, and I'd been doing my best to be helpful. But, once again, I obviously hadn't done enough! I was doing it all wrong! About a block from my apartment building, I noticed a man coming up the street, carrying an umbrella. He saw me, too, and hurried over.

"Looks like you're getting wet," he said to me. "Would you like to get under my umbrella?"

I took him up on his offer and we walked in silence. Less than a minute later we were outside my apartment building. I looked up at him.

"Thank you," I said. The man smiled at me, nodded, and went on his way.

It all happened in just a moment, but I have thought about it for more than 40 years. In the middle of my distress, a complete stranger had reached out to me and offered help. The gesture was small, the words few, and yet they had given me comfort when I most needed it.

I have tried throughout my life to extend my own "umbrella" when others have seemed in need. If this stranger could transform my despair with such a simple act of kindness, maybe I could do the same.

I walked into the building and saw our superintendent. I told him about our stove, and he went with me to take a look. Within moments, the pilot light was lit.

Susyn Reeve

Wisdom on Wheels

Maralyn Schwer

Self-employed Pastry Chef
San Francisco, California

When I was six or seven, my father taught me to ride a bike. It was scary to ride without training wheels, and like every other kid alive, I suffered many failed attempts. But my father never let me give up. He was the picture of patience, running beside me with his hand on the back of the seat, over and over, as many times as I needed him to. This helped me gain confidence.

Finally, I took off by myself down the sidewalk. I'll never forget the wind blowing against my face and the feeling of utter freedom and joy when I realized what I was doing! So what if I didn't know how to stop and eventually fell over? That didn't diminish the moment. My father's message was clear: Keep trying. It pays off.

About ten years later, my father gave a speech to my Hebrew high school graduating class, and that was still his message to all of us: persevere. Then in college, when I became familiar with the philosophy of the *I Ching,* I had to laugh to myself: The phrase "Perseverance brings good fortune" frequently appears in those ancient Chinese teachings. Did my father the cantor know how very Eastern he was? His words and deeds were so simple, yet they gave—and still give—me the confidence and optimism to get through many challenges. They've shaped my personal life and my worldview.

My father died 19 years ago. Shortly afterward, I saw a greeting card in a store, and on the front was a photo of a little girl on her bike with her father running alongside, his hand on the seat. Inside, the message read, "Thanks for sticking with me." I had to leave the shop.

But five years later, I found myself running next to my son as he was learning how to ride his own bike. At one point, his frustration became too much for him, and he wanted to quit.

"Keep trying," I told him, assuring him that the pleasure of the ride was well worth the effort. He believed me, and eventually he mastered his two-wheeler. Soon we were riding together.

I hope my son is learning that perseverance *does* bring good fortune. I know that's what his grandfather would have told him.

Maralyn Schwer

Confessions
of a Plain Jane

Jane E. Van Leuven

Research Director
Seattle, Washington

When I was 13, I figured it would be easier just to drop dead. I didn't know I had hit the customary angst of puberty. I thought it was just me.

Growing up in my family was like sharing a hotel with a few other guests you only saw at meals. My businessman father didn't have much interest in kids; he wanted to wait to see if they ever amounted to anything first. My attractive mother and her wardrobe lived in a social whirl. My older brother had his own life. So, I hid out in my room and read books.

Outwardly, my childhood seemed fine. I had lots of friends, got all A's, and was often class president. But I also weighed about 15 pounds less than everyone else and didn't even need a bra—at least not physically.

When the teen years hit, everything changed. In eighth grade, what I had—brains, grades, leadership skills—didn't count anymore. Looks did.

Now, I was just a skinny kid with braces, zits, and straight hair. A true Plain Jane. My family's word for me was "homely," and they said it a lot. My dad told me I should learn to take a joke.

One Saturday, my mother—in desperation—took me to get a permanent wave. When I was a kid, perms took all day. First, your hair was soaked in a solution that smelled like rotten eggs. Then it was wrapped in little bits of tissue paper, each clump rolled tightly around pink rubber rods. Next, you sat under a metal, conelike device that was part heat lamp, part hair dryer. And there you sat for hours until the perm "took." Finally released from this metal contraption, you'd watch as your newly curled hair was cut and styled, all while your body tried to cool down.

On this particular day, I was getting a perm because, that evening, my mother, grandmother, and I were going to a concert by the renowned pianist Roger Williams. His first hit recording, "Autumn Leaves," was already a classic. Williams had won world acclaim for his playing, and now he was performing in my hometown!

Out in the dark concert hall, I sat beneath my smelly curls, my hot pink cheeks still stinging, marveling at the beauty flowing from Williams's hands. When he played "Stardust," all of us in the audience were swept up in the power of his music.

As the evening wore on, Roger Williams's performance became more and more dominated by the man himself—his sincerity, his self-deprecating humor. After the last haunting notes of the final encore, it seemed as if the entire audience surged backstage to meet him in person.

My family was at the end of a very long line. While the musicians packed up their instruments and stagehands took down the set, Roger Williams sat at a card table in his shirtsleeves, looking hot and sweaty, signing autographs, and chatting with well-wishers. By the time we reached him, it was nearly midnight.

Taking a deep breath and timidly stepping to the table, I held out my program. Roger Williams sneaked a quick glance at his watch, looked up at me, and smiled warmly.

"Well, hello, pretty girl!" he said.

I was stunned. No one had ever called me "pretty" before.

My mouth must have fallen open, because he laughed and said, "Yes, I do mean *you*. Really."

Then with tears rushing to my eyes, I watched him sign my wadded-up program and turn to greet the others. Later, he asked my grandmother to send him the show's reviews and wrote her a personal thank-you note when she did. I still have it. That was 45 years ago.

That night, I went home, locked myself in the bathroom, and stared at myself in the mirror for a long time. I practiced my smile and whispered the words to myself very softly.

Well, hello, pretty girl.

Jane E. Van Leuven

Zen and the Art of Trying

DeMar Regier

Children's Author
Prairie Village, Kansas

It was the end of a grueling 24 hours in a Zen Buddhist monastery in Kyoto, Japan. Dehydrated from little to drink and eat, and exhausted from unfamiliar chores, my head was pounding, my stomach queasy. Throughout the day, I had washed the outside of a building in the early-morning chill, swept the garden, kneeled on the kitchen floor to peel potatoes and onions, carried bundles of heavy blankets from one residence to another, and spent hours in intense meditation. What little sleep I tried to get was spent fitfully tossing about on a blanket on a wooden floor. My beanbag pillow had not helped.

What was a slight, middle-aged woman from Kansas doing *here*?

As a graduate student of comparative religion and philosophy at Wichita State, I had wanted to experience, as much as possible, some of the disciplines of other religions. In particular, I dreamed of visiting a temple monastery to experience "Zen life" firsthand. So my husband and I made a trip to Japan.

When we landed, my brother, who was an academic in Osaka, informed me that I had an interview with Kosan, the head monk at Ryoan-ji. Even though I knew the chances of being allowed to visit were slim, I was elated. This was one of the most revered temples in Japan!

My audience with Kosan lasted three hours as he interrogated me about my sincerity. I sat in the lotus position throughout, pleading my case: I had done yoga for 15 years. I'd make do with the language barrier. I was on my own path of enlightenment.

After convincing Kosan that my intentions were serious, I was taken into the sanctuary for one more interview, this time with the temple's abbot. He was sweet and compassionate and went over everything, explaining the rigorous and austere life of the monastery. If I didn't get in, I figured, I could still savor this unique experience of drinking tea in ancient teacups in the most famous monastery in Japan.

Finally, after another two hours (in the lotus position), the abbot relented. I could stay at the monastery for a day and a night.

My first requirement was to remove my wedding ring and chain necklace, then exchange the clothes I wore for a heavy, black robe and straw sandals. Immediately my awkwardness was apparent. The dilapidated and stringy straw sandals kept slipping off; the oversized robe trailed after me. I had to walk slowly and cautiously. Not exactly a flying nun.

It didn't take long for me to realize that I was little prepared for the full impact of Zen discipline with its demand to purge oneself physically, mentally, and emotionally, in hopes of bringing a full awareness of each moment. In addition to the manual labor I was assigned, I was required to absorb other endless details: how to align my sandals neatly; how to brush my teeth without spilling a *drop* of water; when and how to bow, pass food at meal-time, and fold the bedding correctly; and how to splash cold water on my face before rushing off to chant *sutras* at four o'clock in the morning.

Because the monks observed a vow of silence, I spent much of my time on my own, scurrying along as best I could, my sandals scuffling beneath me. At all times, I had to remember to concentrate on each moment and to prac-tice frugality in every sense of the word—with food, drink, time, and speech.

Gykushu, the resident nun and my interpreter, explained the Zen life to me this way:

"Have no concern with physical discomforts such as cold, hunger, and pain," she said. "All is *Zazen*." (Translation: All of our tasks must be practiced with a complete calmness of mind.) I thought of these words as I sat in full lotus position throughout the three- and four-hour sessions of meditation. If even one small part of your anatomy moved, a monk would discipline you with a stick. (He did so with me because one of my thumbs wasn't perfectly placed.) By midmorning of the second day I was shaky, drained, and nauseous.

Finally, toward noon, I was given my final task: to iron a heavy, black cot-ton robe. I had to make it completely smooth, one painstaking patch at a time. By now, I had a crushing headache.

On my knees on the wooden floor, I pushed the old, lukewarm iron over and over the material, trying frantically to press out the stubborn wrinkles. But nothing helped, and the creases remained. Bending forward made my head throb and my stomach churn.

Please, God, I desperately begged to myself, *don't let anyone know I'm sick.* I was emotionally spent and ready to cry.

It was at this precise moment that Gykushu walked in. I leaned back on my heels, iron in hand, and raised my eyes to her. Seeing this small, serene woman with the shaved head and the caring black eyes, I smiled back wanly.

"Oh, Gykushu," I murmured at last, "I'm not doing a good job."

Gykushu knelt down. Leaning toward me and looking directly into my eyes, she declared firmly and softly, "DeMar, you must remember this: There is no good. And there is no bad. All that matters is how much you try."

I felt the tension leave my body. I realized that in wanting everything to be so perfect, so *good,* I had made myself sick.

When my time to leave the monastery had arrived—and when the ironing was finished—I took off the cumbersome robe and awkward sandals, collected my belongings, and told Gykushu and Kosan good-bye. They had been gracious, loving, nurturing. And so with head high—and stomach upside down—my 24 hours of monastic life came to an end.

Back home, as I've lived through the many busy years of marriage, work, graduate school, mothering, and grandmothering, Gykushu's words, *"All that matters is how much you try,"* have become my mantra. When ideas are vetoed, projects rejected, recipes flop, knowing that I tried keeps me unperturbed and even lifts my spirit. This has changed my life.

Guinea Pigs, Pancakes, and Why I Hate Nike

Ame Stargensky

Writer-Producer
San Diego, California

What do you call a spelling bee, tennis practice, a soccer fund-raiser, one dentist appointment, two sick guinea pigs, a three o'clock board meeting, and a full-time job? In my house that's referred to as Tuesday.

Being a single mom requires stamina, patience, and the power to reshape time itself. But, alas, it's no longer enough to be Super Mom. Every magazine cover now insists that we have firm abs, too—like a sort of Supermodel Super Mom. On the upside, I still *do* have the body I had at 20. On the downside, it wasn't so swell then either. In spite of my success as a mother, sister, daughter, friend, producer, writer, and school volunteer, there are three words that *really* bug me: "Just Do It."

I'll never forget the first time I saw that clearly over-caffeinated Nike commercial. It caught me off guard. I was in the middle of weeping on my sofa, having just survived a slumber party with nine little girls. They had managed to stop giggling by 2:00 A.M., and yet clamored for pancakes by six. Covered in flour, with inky circles under my eyes, I resembled something that had fallen off the back of a bakery truck.

And then there it was on the television screen: a parade of women, certainly my age, gritty determination plastered all over their perfect bodies. As they ran—over rocks, up mountains, across rivers—the sweatier and more alluring they became. Here was the kind of woman who might, in fact, be a mother, but who wouldn't know a carpool unless she could swim a hundred laps across it.

Then came the Nike logo and that booming voiceover: "Just Do It!"

I finished my doughnut, turned off the TV, and thought to myself, *Doing It is one thing, but must I Do It uphill, too?*

Why did I continue to care about this slogan so much? Because, frankly, I have no *time* to Do It, and the older I get, the less I want to Do It, anyway. Besides, it was always my understanding that Demi Moore looks the way she does so I don't have to. Sure, I have friends who rise with the sun to swim and run and cycle their way into tight jeans and jiggle-free miniskirts. I've tried, but I will never be one of them. I can't seem to carve out the time or my glutes. I have no hand-eye coordination, limited agility, and most important, a huge genetic disadvantage: Jews don't make the best athletes.

First of all, "Air Abramowitz" would never work on a sneaker. Secondly, we're not movers—athletically speaking. We tend to excel at wandering. In fact, if wandering were an Olympic event, you might see more Jews in sports. But you don't. Sure, we made a mad dash out of Egypt for the Promised Land, but the truth is, we were hoping the promise included a food court.

Frankly, I'd like to be less soccer mom and more hot soccer mamma, so

I joined a gym. I've never actually gone, mind you, but I still love telling people that I belong to one. It gives the illusion of Just Doing It with less risk of injury.

I wish I felt guilty about not carving out my own hard body, but I don't have the time. Instead, I am thrilled by my full life if not my fuller dimensions. Yes, my abs are more washing machine than washboard, and I've got cleavage that's large enough to be French braided, but I've finally decided that my magazine cover will just have to say, "Delicious!" If I'm going to take a big bite out of my life, then it's sure as hell going to include dessert. I guess that makes me more of a Super-Soft Super Mom. I don't look so good in the cape, but my daughter tells me I make a great pillow.

The more I think about Just Doing It, the more I realize I'm doing it all every day. So what do you call back-to-back meetings, Brownies, company for dinner, trumpet practice, guitar lessons, fall soccer, a new bunny rabbit, laundry mountain, two book reports, and a Margarita Night Out with the Girls? At my house we call that Just Doing Fine.

Anne Hargrove

Eye on the Road

Zev Saftlas

President, Empowerment Web Site
Brooklyn, New York

'm driving on the expressway one winter night. Suddenly my car starts to skid. I slam on the breaks—that makes things worse. Sliding sideways across the highway, barreling straight for the divider, I lose control of the car. I start to panic.

Then in a flash, I remember something I'd heard a motivational speaker once say. That guy, Anthony Robbins. Someone had given me a tape.

Did you ever wonder why so many cars involved in accidents wind up crashing into trees or lampposts? It's because the driver is aiming <u>not</u> to hit them.

The road's slippery, and the snow's making it worse. My hands grip the wheel tighter. For a second I'm blinded by the zigzag of oncoming headlights, and I can't see where I'm heading. This is bad.

You cannot <u>not</u> aim toward something, because by thinking about <u>not</u> hitting it, you're actually thinking about it. And that makes it more likely that you'll hit it.

The car's now tail-spinning. I'm definitely going to crash.

You can't aim for avoiding the negative. You've got to aim for the positive!

Bingo. I train my eyes on the other side of the highway and point my car at the clear lane. The back tires take hold, and the steering snaps into action. For the first time the car's doing what I'm telling it to. I head straight for the shoulder of the road and slide onto it, my foot riding the brake. Suddenly everything stops moving. I put the car in park, catch my breath, and take a look around.

I hadn't hit a tree, or a lamppost, or anyone else's car. I was safe.

When I think back to that snowy night, I don't even bother trying to figure out why I heard Anthony Robbins's words in the middle of a car wreck. Life is weird, I guess. But I did learn a big lesson behind the wheel of that careening car: Instead of thinking about avoiding failure, think about aiming for success.

I had aimed my car to a safe place, rather than trying to avoid a crash. Not a bad credo for life.

Aim for the positive. And, oh, yeah—while you're at it, buckle up.

PART TWO

At a Crossroads

*"The words whacked me
on the side of my head.
I knew she was talking to me."*

Forty

Ann Swinford, M.D.

Doctor and Radiologist
Ann Arbor, Michigan

I was always one of those people who saw the cup half empty—then promptly watched the water evaporate out of it. Time and again I had a million excuses for why I couldn't do something, why I shouldn't try, and why it probably wasn't worth it, anyway.

I grew up in Milwaukee, attended public school, and ended up at the University of Wisconsin where I wanted to major in marine biology. The problem was, studying whales at a landlocked school wasn't the best match. But genetics was: I attended a lecture on genetic counseling during my undergraduate work and was instantly hooked.

Now here's a science that can really help people, I thought.

I eventually got my master's degree—and a job—in genetic counseling; but over the years I began to feel stuck. I'd often thought about going to medical school—my science background and experience in the clinic certainly qualified me for it—but the cost was daunting, and as it was, I could barely pay my bills. So I pushed the idea away.

Frustrated and confused, I was talking one day to a physician whom I highly respected, a 63-year-old professor of radiology who had grown up in Latvia. Dr. Freimanis was a true gentleman—reserved and well mannered, in a Continental kind of way. He was the sort of fellow who always had something nice to say and could make you feel like a million bucks, even as he set a challenge for you.

"If I had it to do all over again," I said to Dr. Freimanis, "I would have gone to medical school."

"Why not apply now?" he asked matter-of-factly.

"Because," I replied, "by the time I finished medical school and my residency and my fellowship—*then* actually started my practice as a real doctor—I'd be forty."

"So?" he said cheerfully. "You're going to be forty anyhow."

That stopped me in my tracks. What an incredibly freeing idea. Here was one of the most accomplished physicians I'd ever known, not only saying, "Come along, be one of us," but also reminding me that time marches on, regardless of what we do or don't do with our lives.

I thought about Dr. Freimanis's advice over the next several months—not that I was able to avoid it. Every time I saw him he'd lean over and say, "So? Have you applied yet?" He was funny about it, gently but firmly nudging me along.

So I jumped in. I entered med school at 30, started radiology residency at 34, and finished my fellowship in breast imaging at 39. There were many sleepless nights along the way, but you can do that at any age. The bottom line is: I was a real practicing doctor at age 39—a year earlier than I had predicted a decade before.

And not a moment goes by when I am not thankful for the sage advice I received from Dr. Freimanis in the waning days of my 29th year. People often comment that doctors have an altruistic sense of wanting to take care of others; that we're always ready to say, "We will never give up on you." Well, Dr. Freimanis didn't give up on me; and because of him, I didn't give up on myself.

In fact, the lesson he taught me still applies to my life. I had gained weight during my medical training, and by the age of 45, I had given up all hope of losing it. That's when a friend told me, "Set a reasonable goal for your weight loss, give yourself some time, and try to get to where you want to be by the time you're fifty."

Guess what words popped into my head: *You're going to be 50 anyhow.* Over the next year, I lost 50 pounds and began training for my first 5K run.

As time goes on, I realize that age is just a number. That it's never too late to reach a dream. That life is measured in spirit, not in years. I can't wait to see what I'm doing at 60!

Ann Hufnagel MD

The Big Fix

Mary N. *

Accounting
Las Vegas, Nevada

H i, my name is Mary and I'm a compulsive gambler."

It was Christmas 1995. I had parked my car in a dark and scary lot at the end of Las Vegas Boulevard, the neon-lit casinos still visible in the distance. A long flight of stairs led me to a room full of faces and stories I can't remember.

I was in a fog—scared, guilty, broke, and deeply ashamed. I knew I needed help, but I was so lost in my own sickness that I actually expected Gamblers Anonymous to loan me money that very night.

Although I left the meeting that evening—not to return for another two years—a seed was planted in me, a glimmer of hope that I could be saved. But it wouldn't happen overnight—I wasn't ready.

*The writer has chosen not to use her full name.

I was totally consumed with gambling. If I wasn't *in action,* I was thinking about a way to *get into* action. I had no choice at the time. I did things I never thought I could or would do.

Absolutely nothing could keep me away from "the fix." When the compulsion hit, it took me over completely. I'd be vacuuming the floor one minute, and the next, the urge would be so strong I'd leave the vacuum cleaner right where it was, still plugged in, jump in the car, and go. My two sons, nine and fifteen, would cry and beg me to stay home, but I couldn't.

On a good night, I'd wait until the boys were asleep, then hit the casinos and stay out until five or six in the morning. On bad days, I'd drop off some fast food before racing off, leaving them on their own. Occasionally, I'd bring my sons along, deserting them in the arcade for hours with a fistful of quarters.

As a freelance accountant, I abused my flexible schedule to accommodate my gambling addiction; and even when I was at work, I was either trying to figure out how to cover the money I had lost, or thinking about the bets I would place with the money I had won.

I even tried quitting work altogether, believing that if I had no money, I'd have nothing to gamble with. Then I'd beg my boyfriend for 20 bucks just so I could go get the fix for one more night.

By the time I returned to Gamblers Anonymous two years after that first meeting, the constant pain of living with the disease had become too much to bear. I was skipping sleep, going for hours on end without eating, heavily dosing on coffee and cigarettes. I was letting people down left and right, but no one hated me more than I did. I was bankrupt in every way and beating myself up emotionally 24/7/365.

I truly believe my "higher power" led me back to GA, but even though I went to meetings almost every night, I still hit the casinos before or after, justifying it to myself by thinking, *Well, at least I'm going to meetings—so I'm trying, right?*

Then I met a man at one meeting who recognized my struggle.

"Nothing changes if nothing changes," Roger told me. Somehow in the midst of my insanity, I heard his words. Could I apply them? No. But at some deep level I understood them. I put them on my screen saver at work. Even while playing my favorite video poker machine, I repeated them to myself: *Nothing changes if nothing changes.*

I chased the fix for another year and ran into Roger again. "Nothing changes if nothing changes," he said once more. This time I started moving closer to arresting my compulsion to gamble. But after receiving my 30-day key chain at a meeting, I was back in the casino that same night. I didn't know how to handle success.

The final tipping point came one day while I was working accounts payable for a construction firm. When no one was looking, I cut myself a check, signed my boss's name, took it to the bank, and cashed it. Instead of paying my rent, I gambled half of the money away. That scared me. I knew I had crossed the line, violating not only my own morals but the law.

I immediately went to a meeting. The date was November 11, 2000— 11-11-00. Even the numbers were symbolic: four aces—a winner. I hoped that meant the same for me.

Roger's words were becoming clearer. It wasn't enough to *want* to stop gambling. I had to make changes if I wanted things to change. And I started to. I finally left what had become a dysfunctional relationship with my boyfriend, realizing that my gambling was only a *part* of our problem. I moved to a different part of town. I attended GA meetings at a different place and made new friends. I started implementing the tools of the 12-step program, like taking a different route home from work to avoid my favorite casinos, or calling my sponsor for help when I was having a bad moment.

The biggest thing I did was getting on my knees to pray. It wasn't a religious thing for me, but more like a spiritual cleansing. A miracle had happened. I had surrendered—and things started changing.

As I write this, it has been three and a half years since I placed a bet! I still attend meetings regularly, right behind three casinos, all within 100 feet of each other. Once in a while, people ask me how I can remain here in Las Vegas. My answer: It's the only place in the world with so much help available, with more than 80 meetings every week. Without such help nearby, I'm afraid I could return to my old habits.

When I think back to my gambling days, I realize that my real problem wasn't that I was running around trying to place a bet. Like most addicts, I was really running away from *myself.*

I also realized that I could make all the changes I wanted to on the outside, but that I would never be safe without changing on the inside, too.

Mary N.

Breaking the Chains

Leigh Anne Jasheway-Bryant

Writer and Teacher
Eugene, Oregon

A tattered old guitar book sits on the shelf in my bedroom. Some pages are missing, others look like they were once graced with spaghetti sauce and tears. And page 40 has been dog-eared so long that the crease in the paper is deeper than my laugh lines.

Someone else might have thrown the songbook away by now, and maybe I should have, given the fact that I don't play the guitar much these days, and when I do, the dogs hide behind the sofa and the neighbors turn up their stereo.

But I keep the book as a reminder, because there on page 40 are the words that helped me figure out something important.

When I was 32 years old, I found myself alone for the first time since I was 17. That's when I met the man who would become my husband. We were both brainy, nerdy types and had been drawn to each other like the social outcasts we were during our high school years in Abilene, Texas. After dating through four years of college, we got married, thinking we were old enough and wise enough to make it work.

Ten years later, when he decided it was time for him to go, I was devastated. Back then I couldn't see that I really wanted out as much as he did. I was more afraid of being alone than being miserable together. I couldn't see that together we were like gasoline and matches—fun to watch from afar, but a deadly combination up close. And I definitely couldn't see that the days ahead of me would be filled with more joy, love, and laughter than I thought possible.

Lonely and depressed in those first weeks on my own, I walked past a music store one day and wandered inside. I had owned a guitar for years, having received it as a high school graduation gift, but I'd only played it a handful of times before giving up. This was in no small part due to the fact that my husband had on several occasions informed me that, despite my longing to be a rock-and-roll star, I had no talent. And I believed him.

But that day in the music store, I decided I'd teach myself how to play my guitar. If not well, at least better. Maybe I'd never be Bonnie Raitt, but if I grew my red hair longer and could at least strum along with her albums, I'd still be able to live the fantasy.

I didn't choose a Bonnie Raitt songbook that day because it would have been too intimidating. Instead, I chose *The Eagles' Greatest Hits*. I made this decision for three reasons: I was familiar with their music, the chords in most of the songs looked simple, and it was a thin book and well within my budget.

When I got home, I wiped 11 years of dust off my guitar and shook a spider out of the sound hole. Then I opened the songbook and searched for just the right one. "Witchy Woman" caught my eye because it described how I'd felt recently, but it had complicated bar chords, so it was out. "Peaceful Easy Feeling" was what I was really after, but I could tell I'd have trouble with the notes. "Tequila Sunrise" just made me want to drink.

That's when I saw the song "Already Gone." How appropriate, I thought. I couldn't recall ever having heard it on the radio, but according to the book, it had only four chords. Perfect.

I started playing, strumming along well enough—that is, until I had to change chords, which took longer than it takes most real guitarists to change all their strings *and* their clothing. But I was having fun despite the challenges. The song began on page 37, but it was on page 40 that Jack Tempchin's lyrics suddenly jumped from the page as if they had been written just for me. I quit strumming and read them aloud:

I know it wasn't you who held me down
heaven knows it wasn't you who set me free
So oftentimes it happens that we live our lives in chains
and we never even know we have the key.

I was astounded. Somehow, I had made it to my thirties without realizing that the power to live the life I wanted rested in my own hands. I'd gone straight from my dysfunctional family to my dysfunctional marriage, unaware that the only one holding me down was *me*. I immediately began playing the song, performing it better than I've played anything before or since. I wasn't just playing someone else's music, I was playing my own life.

That was 17 years ago. I've had my share of tragedies and triumphs since then; people have come and gone from my life. But there's never a day that goes by that I don't remember that I possess the key to my own happiness.

Those words on that day made me a different person. In high school, I wasn't voted class clown—I was voted most likely to depress people. I used to sit in a closet and read Edgar Alan Poe and Sylvia Plath. These days, I write comedy and teach people how to find the funny in their lives. I've chosen this path because, for me, the ability to transform the things that go wrong in life—no matter how big or small—into something you can laugh at is one of the best ways of setting yourself free.

Every now and then I'll get out my guitar and play "Already Gone." I don't need the book anymore—I know the song by heart. I still play badly, but now I just laugh when I miss the chord changes.

Leigh Anne Jobleway - Bryant

Jumping the Tracks

Nicole Hanton

Domestic Diva and Part-time Preschool Teacher
Fairfax, Virginia

My childhood was not an easy one. I grew up in northern California with parents who were alcoholics and drug addicts. By the time I was a teenager, I had seen things most adults couldn't even fathom. My father beat my mother. My mother would drink so much at times, I thought she was dead. By the time I was ten, my parents had divorced. My seven-year-old brother and I stayed with our mom, whose drinking got heavier with each new bout of depression. I was living in a home without heat or hot water.

One night when I was 12, my mother was in another drunken rage, when she threatened to kill the cat. Terrified, I went to a neighbor's house, asked to use their phone, and called my aunt and uncle to come pick us up. Mom went into rehab after that, and Dad got custody of us. We'd been living with him for almost a year when something unbelievably bad happened: My father molested me.

So we moved back in with my mom, who tried to stay sober. By the time

I was 15, I was taking care of my younger brother, cleaning the house, and coping with my mother's addiction—but she wasn't holding up too well. On one occasion, I found countless bottles of cough medicine she'd hidden in the house.

Now, here's the remarkable thing about all of this: These horror stories are not what define me. They are merely stepping-stones to the person I am today. And all because of Lorry Divine.

I first met Lorry when I was in high school; she was the mother of my best friend, Melissa. Cheerful, interesting, and—most important to me—sober, Lorry was a wonderful mom who actively participated in Melissa's life. Her husband, Gary, was also amazing, a caring partner and a wonderful father. It's funny, until I met Gary, I'd always thought you had to be on your best behavior around dads. But Gary treated us all with kindness. He could be goofy and kind and stern and it was all okay.

There was no depression in Melissa's house, so naturally I spent a lot of time there. Here was the kind of stable life I often dreamed about. *So there really are normal families out there,* I'd think to myself.

As I got to know Lorry better, I began to open up to her and share my troubles. I'd cry to her and talk for hours on end. She'd listen carefully, never once speaking negatively about my parents. That really helped me. What she did do was bring me in and make me a part of her family. She even called me "Daughter Number Two."

But what was most amazing to me about Lorry was that she, too, had grown up with abusive parents. And not only did she survive, she *flourished.* That really helped, too.

One day Lorry picked me up to take me to her house, and on the drive over, she uttered one sentence that changed everything.

"You know, your life is like a train, Nicole," she said, "and you're riding down a certain set of tracks. But here's the incredible thing: Even though your childhood has gone one way, you can jump that set of tracks and follow your own tracks."

A silence hung in the air after she spoke, but the words remained in my head. A light had just clicked on. For the first time it dawned on me that I could make my own choices in life—choices that were different from my parents'. I had opportunities. I had a future. I had hope.

I pictured having a family and a home—not a house, but a warm and inviting and safe home.

I pictured having a husband who was my best friend and someone I could trust.

I pictured happiness with happy children.

Essentially, I pictured what Lorry had.

I don't know how it is for other people when they have a breakthrough like the one I had that day in the car, but for me it was a hopeful and enlightening experience. Not only were Lorry's words inspiring to me, but they were also a challenge. She knew I could do more with my life—that I could make different choices—so I almost felt like it was now up to me to prove her right.

And I did. During my senior year, I applied to college and was accepted. Through grants, loans, scholarships, and more hard work than I'd ever done, I became the first person in my family to graduate from college, earning a bachelor's degree in social work.

I began to work for a rape crisis center and child protective services where every day I would meet children who were enduring the same kind of hardships I'd grown up with. And with each one, I shared Lorry's invaluable words about the train tracks of life—and how we can jump them—in the hope that these kids would draw the same inspiration from them as I had.

And just like in my fantasy, I got married to a man who truly loves me and tells me so every day. He is a wonderful person and my best friend; and we have been blessed with two beautiful children. Ours is a warm and supportive household, and I am forever grateful to have had the chance to give my kids the childhood I never had.

Because I did it. I jumped my parents' tracks and followed my own. Just as Lorry told me I could.

Nicole Hanton

The Clock

Joan Mueller

Wine Grape Grower
Tucson, Arizona

There are three things usually associated with teenage imprisonment and boredom: Latin, 11th grade, and an IBM school clock. But in my case, the three came together to mean freedom. The driving force behind this transformation was Miss Vancavage, better known by her students as "The Vanc."

Miss Vancavage was the perfect image of a Latin teacher. Short and stout, sensibly dressed, and forever in black, sturdy shoes, The Vanc peered at her students through dark, piercing eyes. She spoke through thin, pursed lips, never raising her voice to her students. Yet somehow the class was terrified of her.

For me, Latin was a nightmare. By the third year it was all about translations, translations, translations. Most nights I went to bed without completing the day's homework, but as I slipped into sleep, The Vanc would appear before me: I'd be sitting at my desk, staring down at the text, my heart beating a thousand times a minute, those sturdy shoes slowly clacking the floor as her slitted eyes scanned the room seeking the next victim.

"Please don't call on me. Please don't call on me," I'd pray.

"Joan, read the next passage," The Vanc would command.

I'd open my mouth to speak but only squeaks came out. The harder I tried, the squeakier I sounded. I'd wake up in a panic, dreading the day to come. A living nightmare.

Now the clock.

Long before PCs were known to the world, IBM made clocks and sold them to schools across the country. One hung on the wall in every one of my Framingham, Massachusetts, classrooms. At the start of each school year, I'd enter my new classroom filled with anxiety, and, not knowing what to expect, I'd nervously scan the room, seeking something familiar. That's when I'd see the IBM clock—always there, always the same, staring down at me with the same big, bold, black numbers, its steady hands sweeping around the circle, ticking away the time.

Over the years, while classes droned on, I'd spend many hours staring at that clock. The second hand intrigued me the most. There was nothing unusual in its job; like all second hands, it made its loop in exactly one minute. What fascinated me was the *way* it made its journey. It was a jerky journey. The hand would land on a number, then pause ever so slightly before jumping onto the next—each tiny move accompanied by a distinct clicking sound.

Jump. Click. Pause. Jump. Click. Pause.

This went on 60 times a minute, for all six hours of the school day. It certainly wasn't the most exciting thing in the world, but watching it gave me comfort. By the 11th grade, I once calculated, I had accumulated 45 million clicks in my head.

But Latin class was where I acquired the most clicks. After all, each second I watched click by was one second closer to escaping the horror of becoming The Vanc's next victim.

One day in Latin, I was doing my usual second-watching, when cutting through the clicks, I heard that voice.

"See that second hand ticking off time?" hissed The Vanc. "Every time a second is ticked off, it is gone forever. And you will never be able to get that second back."

The words whacked me on the side of my head. I knew she was talking to me.

The Vanc was now standing over me. As instructed, I looked up at the IBM clock on the wall and watched the second hand making its slow, jerky journey from number to number.

Jump. Click. Pause. Jump. Click. Pause.

My old, faithful friend appeared the same, but suddenly I was seeing it differently. All those seconds, minutes, hours that I had wished away . . .

For the first time, I wanted to grab the second hand and send it spinning backward to collect all the hours I had wasted. I wanted that time back.

I felt empowered. In a matter of seconds The Vanc had changed the course of my life. The IBM clock would continue its orderly clicking. But I could choose *how* to spend the time it measured.

Twelfth grade would be different. The first thing I did was change my schedule to exclude Latin IV, despite the many adults who told me I was making a big mistake. It was no mistake. I took the courses I wanted—

courses that made me forget the clock on the wall. My grades improved, and so did the rest of my time in high school.

Funny, I never really liked Miss Vancavage, but hers is the lesson I will always carry. She threw a lot of Latin words at me, and I don't remember any of them. Just the ones about the clock.

Joan Mueller

Busted!

Ann Pierce *

Restaurant Manager
New York, New York

When I was a kid I shoplifted—mostly nickel-and-dime stuff, like candy bars. It's not like I didn't know it was wrong. It was *very* wrong. Stupid, too. But at the time—and despite a decent upbringing—I was more interested in the candy than the morality. And I was never caught.

That is until a lifetime later, when at the age of 25 (yes, old enough to know better) I got seriously busted. I was driving cross-country with my friend Carole and by the time we reached Las Vegas, I was sick of the disco music we'd been playing in the car. I went into a record store and browsed through the cassette tapes. Everything seemed outrageously priced, so I decided to create my own little buy-one-steal-one deal.

I was a poor, struggling artist, waitressing for cash, and planning to move

*The writer has chosen not to use her real name.

west on a hope and a prayer. In those days, I didn't have the luxury of charging my whims on a credit card. I owned no plastic.

I took one tape to the counter—*Maze Featuring Frankie Beverly*—and put a Crystal Gayle tape in my pocket. (I rationalized this second choice by telling myself that Gayle was a one-hit wonder, and that I certainly wasn't going to spend my hard-earned money on *her*.) The way I figured it, since I was buying a tape, who would suspect I'd be stealing one, too?

Then I walked out the door, right through the metal detector.

Bing! Bing! Bing! I was so dumb I didn't even realize at first that the alarm was sounding because of me. But once it hit me, I went belly-up. I've never been good at lying, and here I was caught red-handed. So I stopped right in my tracks, threw my hands in the air and announced, "All right, you got me!"

A dorky young guy took me to a back office and called the police. Somehow I managed to stay cool, even when the cops escorted me out of the store with my hands cuffed behind my back. My car was parked right next to the police cruiser, and as I went past it, I caught a glimpse of Carole in the front seat. She looked completely stunned. I signaled for her to follow us to the police station.

When we entered Clark County Jail, I immediately spotted a group of guys shackled together. A chain gang! Here I am, this white-bread, Midwestern girl from Ohio—wearing green army pants, a work shirt, no bra—and they're staring at me like I'm white *toast*.

As the sergeant took my mug shots, reality kicked in. I suddenly became very frightened. I kept thinking, "Please tell me this is not happening," like I was stuck in a bad dream and couldn't wake up.

I thought back to when I was 12, and my family lived in India. At my school, we had a canteen where students could buy things and put them on a tab. I went crazy. I bought notebooks with Hindu deities on the front, wonderful pens, and tons of chocolate (they have great chocolate in India). I ran up a huge debt, and when my parents found out, they were furious. I had to pay off the bill with my allowance and birthday money.

Clearly I hadn't learned my lesson, because here I was in trouble again, but this time I was busted for real. I was overcome with humiliation and guilt.

I was placed in a holding cell with a group of women who were charged with prostitution. I was relieved. I'll take hookers over a chain gang any day. At first I kept to myself, but as the hours passed, the number of hookers in the cell grew to about a dozen. I started talking to one of them, and eventually confessed what I'd done.

The quintessential tough chick, she listened to my story with a blank expression, and then matter-of-factly said, "If I can't afford it, I don't need it."

That got my attention.

If only I'd had her advice a few hours earlier, I wouldn't be where I was now. What kind of idiotic arrogance made me do something like this?

I wanted to make a phone call, but the hookers wouldn't let me. They had a routine, and being a rookie, I wasn't part of it. That was just as well. I would have hated to call my parents. They would have been so disappointed in me—but no more disappointed than I was in myself. So all I could do was count on Carole being out there somewhere, working to get me out.

She was. By the end of the day, she managed to come up with the $400 bail, and I was released that night. When my case came up in court the next day, the public defender told me to plead nolo contendere to a misdemeanor. I paid a $50 fine and Carole got her bail money back.

Although I'd just as soon forget the shame of that whole ordeal, I've never forgotten the words my cellmate-for-a-day told me. Until she said, "If I can't afford it, I don't need it," I was no more a grown-up than the kid who stole those candy bars. It took a dumb crime, a smart hooker, and a day in jail to teach me that it's so much easier to live an honest life.

And something else: If you can't afford to do the time, you certainly don't need to do the crime.

What I Found on the Couch

Dan C.*

Social Worker
Petaluma, California

D on't be an asshole."

It had been my understanding that the discourse Freudian psychoanalysts exercised with their patients usually toggled between "Mmm-hmm" and "Why do you think that?" So to say that I was surprised by the "asshole" remark is an understatement. It was, however, the beginning of my new life.

For many years I had been going absolutely nowhere. Armed with a master's degree in theater and a fair bit of stage experience, I'd moved to New York in the fall of 1983, toting along my metaphorical tap shoes and allegorical greasepaint. There I joined a small band of friends from college who had also followed the dream of fame and fortune (or at least of making a living in show biz).

*The writer has chosen not to use his full name.

For a while, life was fun and exciting: auditions, rehearsals for self-produced showcases, hanging out. But as drummer Levon Helm of The Band noted in *The Last Waltz*, New York is an "adult portion," and I found I didn't have the stomach for it.

Faced with mounting rejection and a dwindling bank account, I returned to my comfort zone of odd jobs and alcohol to soothe the hurt. A typical evening consisted of a six-pack or two of the cheapest beer in the supermarket, along with whatever out-of-the-box dinner was available.

In the spring of 1984, I began working at an eastside restaurant. As an actor, I made a great manager. But the real pull was the booze: The food and beverage industry is a wonderful haven for an alcoholic; not only was my drinking behavior tolerated, it was encouraged. With free-flowing drinks, a chilled beer mug always at hand, and easy connections for cocaine and marijuana, I had found a *new* comfort zone—and it was *very* comfortable.

Soon I was supplementing the alcohol with two or three grams of cocaine a week, and life was either terrific or spinning completely out of control—depending on when you asked me. Alcoholics have many things in common, one of the most typical being a penchant for nurturing resentments better than a mother bear nurtures her cubs. After a couple of years at the restaurant, I decided I wasn't getting the respect or the salary I deserved. As a result, my relationship with drugs and alcohol intensified, as did my sense of despair about where my life was headed. A trusted co-worker referred me to a therapist she had known since her childhood. So off I went to figure out my life.

My therapist was a trained Freudian analyst, and I was on the couch from day one. I liked this—there was something freeing about just talking and not having to look at the person I was addressing. From the beginning, my analyst focused on my use of drugs and alcohol, and she laid down the law: If I drank or used within 24 hours of an appointment, our work would be terminated, as it was a waste of her time and my money.

I remember feeling a strong sense of relief that, for at least one night of the week, I wouldn't have to drink. But how would I manage on the other six? I did my best that summer, trying not to drink, or drinking in responsible ways, or at least trying to control my habitual use of alcohol and drugs. Needless to say I wasn't very successful. Every time I thought I had my problem under control, it reminded me who was really in charge.

I remember a night in Hawaii, literally leaning against a street lamppost, like a drunk in a cartoon, too smashed to move. I remember only parts of an evening later that summer in New York, walking home from a restaurant with my cousin and her friend, falling in and out of memory blackouts long enough to smash a glass in the street and embrace my cousin's friend a bit too fondly.

Finally I'd had enough. I held my breath and *just didn't drink* for about two weeks, despite my therapist's continued urging to attend an Alcoholics Anonymous meeting, where I could receive support and not feel like I was doing this on my own.

One morning on the couch, I announced that I had not had a drink or a drug in about two weeks and that I was feeling really good. Furthermore, I said, since I had managed this feat solo, I would forego Alcoholics Anonymous, as this would make my triumph that much more meaningful. I concluded my little speech and waited to hear my therapist respond with unconditional support and enthusiasm for such a brave and smart decision.

"Don't be an asshole," she said.

This was not what I wanted to hear, but exactly what I *needed* to hear. Her point was that I knew nothing of *not* drinking, and that the good folks at AA *did*—and they could help me with that.

Not entirely convinced but now desperate, I agreed to go to a meeting that night. On my way there, a New York summer rainstorm kicked up. Dutifully, I trooped the five blocks uptown to the church where the meeting was scheduled, only to be greeted by a sign on the door that read, CHURCH UNDER CONSTRUCTION, NO AA TONIGHT. At first I believed this to be a sign that my unassisted efforts at sobriety were being blessed by God (this was a church after all). But as I marched home, soaked from the knees down, I remembered, "Don't be an asshole"—and everything it implied.

No, I really *didn't* know anything about not drinking, and I was beginning to understand that if I stood half a chance at pulling this thing off, I needed help.

Two nights later I entered my first Alcoholics Anonymous meeting. I listened to others talk about their own struggles to make rational sense of an irrational relationship with alcohol. In my heart, I knew I was in the right place.

At the end of the meeting, we joined hands and, as is custom, recited together, "Keep coming back—it works if you work it." I decided I would. And I've continued coming back and working it for nearly 19 years—one day at a time.

Dan C

Prison Saved Me

Dax Xenos

Artist
Austin, Texas

I remember clearly the day I was arrested. Thirty cops, guns drawn, swarmed around the plush living room where we had set out the cocaine.

"If you go for a gun, I'll kill you," one of them said. He pushed the cold, blunt muzzle of his weapon against my temple.

Go for a gun? I didn't have a gun. I wasn't a criminal. I was just a guy with some cocaine, having some fun. That's the way I thought back then. Drugs do that to you. They are that seductive.

I was 30 years old and had never been arrested for anything. I came from a good family and had a good job. A little cocaine was icing on the cake. This was the late 1970s, when sex, drugs, and rock-and-roll were the hip trend. Everybody did it. Then people starting dying, and it wasn't fun anymore. I had gotten caught up with a fast crowd and ended up on the fast track to prison.

"Sixteen years," the judge said. Life, as I had known it, was over.

The prison environment was a culture shock, to say the least. An upper-middle-class guy thrown into the belly of the beast had a lot of growing up to do. A lot of soul-searching and getting priorities straight.

Prison was ugly, boring, and oppressive. It was a bad place filled with bad people who had nothing to lose. My standoffish attitude didn't play well with hardened convicts. I knew about the finer things in life without having worked my way up. Now I was at rock bottom and the view wasn't pleasant.

I was depressed and lonely. Everything I'd owned had been stripped away by legal fees and repossessions. My so-called friends fell out of contact. I had deeply hurt my family. I was alone without love or hope and blamed everyone else for my situation.

One day, as I was returning from working in the fields, I passed an old, black convict in pressed white clothes sweeping up the run. He sized up my exhaustion in a glance, stopped sweeping, and said:

"I was unhappy because I had no shoes, until I met a man who had no feet."

"What?" I replied.

"Things could be worse," he said.

"How?" I asked. "I've got sixteen years."

"With good time, you'll parole out in three," he said.

"Three years?" It still seemed an eternity.

"You could be dead. You could have a life sentence."

The look in his eye tweaked something inside of me. He was right. Things could be worse. I *could* be dead. I *could* have a life sentence.

Suddenly, the inmate adage, "Do your time, don't let your time do you," made sense. Circumstances don't forge character; your reaction to them does—and that part, you *can* control.

I started using the time to read—novels, religion, philosophy, law—and saw that everything had a measure of truth to it. With my attitude change came an acceptance of responsibility for what I had done. No one made me do the cocaine. No one was to blame for my situation but me—not my friends, my parents, or my upbringing, not even the criminal justice system. Only me.

"That which does not kill me makes me stronger," Nietzsche said.

I began to reflect. I had lived a privileged life, and now I needed a good dose of humility. I'd never really considered the poor and the underprivileged people of the world who were now my neighbors. Prison is a great equalizer. Everyone showers in the same stalls and eats the same food. You find out who you are behind bars.

Another thing I learned in prison was about dealing with people at their most basic level. The Golden Rule—"Do unto others as you would have them do unto you"—is the prevailing axiom, and one that has immediate karmic consequences. You leave people alone and they leave you alone. You get into other people's business and you might get a shiv in the ribs.

With my head clear from plain food, hard work, and a total abstinence from drugs or alcohol, I began to write again. I rediscovered my passion for words and became editor of the prison paper, winning some awards and encouragement along the way.

Just as my fellow inmate had predicted, in three years I made parole. After my release, I landed a writing job and have since published many articles and stories. I've written documentary scripts for programs that tell the truth and dispel illusions.

Today, I am married and have two children, four dogs, and a home in a nice neighborhood. I work hard every day and appreciate the privilege of being a free and creative individual who's trying to do something positive for the world. Life is good.

Going to prison saved me. It forced me to reevaluate my life, to put everything in the right perspective.

"I was unhappy because I had no shoes, until I met a man who had no feet." Amen.

PART THREE

Taking Chances

*"I remember listening carefully to the whole poem,
but the last words are the ones that
would become forever engraved in my mind."*

My Perfect Mess

Nancy Roman

Finance
Litchfield, Connecticut

I had a rotten fifth grade. Although I made good grades, worked hard, was quiet and mostly obedient, Sister Saint Therese du Divine Coeur hated messy. And I was *so* messy.

Sister Saint Therese made us fasten our winter boots together with clothespins, line up our book bags neatly in a row under the windows, and cover our textbooks with brown paper. Plain, blank brown paper. Months into the school year, we still weren't supposed to have a single doodle on any cover. I was ten. I don't think I need to elaborate.

I also never remembered to bring a head scarf to wear on confession day. So once a month, I confessed with a Kleenex bobby-pinned to my head.

But in Sister Saint Therese's eyes, my penmanship was her purgatory. Her handwriting was like the Declaration of Independence. Mine was the way desperate people scrawl on bathroom mirrors when they've been kidnapped.

At Saint Anne's School, composition was the most important subject. That was fine with me. I was a wonderful storyteller, and I knew it. But in fifth grade, our monthly essays became ordeals. Because our stories didn't only need to be beautifully written, they had to be beautifully *written.*

Each student would write a first draft on "practice paper"—cheap grayish sheets from the communal tablet. We would bring our essays one at a time to Sister. She'd look them over, correcting our spelling and grammar as she clicked her teeth. Then from her desk drawer, she would hand us our black-and-white-speckled composition book. The paper in the book was stapled to the center, so unlike spiral notebooks, if you tore out a sheet, the composition book tattled on you. Talk about leaving a paper trail.

Once we were handed our books, we were supposed to turn to the next blank page and copy our finished essay. With a fountain pen.

Giving me a fountain pen was like giving a toddler a bowl of spaghetti. No matter how careful I was—how deliberately I formed every letter— something would always go wrong. An *a* looked more like a *d,* an *m* always had one too many humps, the line that crossed through the *t* in "the" always crossed through the *h,* too. And don't get me started on the ink blots and the smears. (I challenge each of you with a ten-year-old to look at your child right now and picture him with an old-fashioned fountain pen in his hand.)

So I'd turn in my story riddled with smears, blobs, shaky letters, and mistakes, all of which I had tried to fix. Sister Saint Therese would be furious.

"Mother Mary would weep!" she'd cry, holding up my open book for all the class to see. Sister Saint Therese du Divine Coeur was a serious humiliator.

That's when I'd get a Black Ticket. These were small pieces of paper about the size of a Band-Aid, black felt on one side and white on the other. You wrote your name on the white side and deposited the ticket in the Black

Box, which sat directly in front of the statue of the Blessed Virgin. I think we were supposed to be offering up our sins, but for the life of me I never understood why Mary would want our sins in the first place.

At the end of every month, Sister Therese would open the box and read the names one by one. How we dreaded hearing our names come out of that box. A ten-ticket count was very bad. Once you accumulated that many tickets, you had to write your name in the Black Book. This could be considered the hotel registry for Hell. And I got booked. Repeatedly.

The school year is an eternity when you're ten. And when most days include at least one moment of mortification, they crawl like Palm Sunday's high mass. But the Blessed Virgin must have known that no child should be a nervous wreck forever, because when I got to sixth grade, my teacher was Sister Regina Marie.

Like all the nuns at Saint Anne's, Sister Regina was strict. She looked to be six feet tall. Her habit stopped just short of her ankles, so you could see her thick black stockings and heavy-soled shoes. She had big hands with knuckles like my grandfather's.

In Sister Regina's class, we marched like West Point cadets. Slouching was lazy, and laziness was a mortal sin. She had little tolerance for fidgety boys and less for giggly girls. And she liked science way too much for my tastes. But all of this was okay with me, because with Sister Regina there were no Black Tickets, no Black Box, no Black Book—and no black-and-white-speckled composition books.

For our essays, Sister Regina had snow-white paper with the palest of blue lines. And she sold us (at cost, I hope) special ballpoint pens.

"These pens are one hundred percent guaranteed never to leak," she said. "You will never get a glob of ink at the tip to mess up your papers." I bought one right away, and when my grandmother gave me 50 cents for running an errand, I bought a spare. I knew a bargain when I saw one. Still, the thought of putting that glob-proof pen to that immaculate sheet of paper was too much to bear.

When Sister Regina announced our first essay assignment of the school year, I was expecting it to be "How I Spent My Summer Vacation." Not so. Instead, we were told to "describe something beautiful."

On my walk to school each day, I passed a tree that looked like any other for most of the year—except at autumn, when it turned the most brilliant red. So I wrote about the red tree and how it always caught me by surprise. Since I liked telling stories more than describing things, the story was about a tree that decided, quite deliberately, to stay green as long as possible, letting all the other trees go first, the better to startle everyone by turning every single leaf to crimson over the course of one night.

It was a pretty good story for an eleven-year-old, once you got past the thesaurus overload. (I had a tiny green book called *Little Book of Synonyms*, and I applied it liberally.) My tree was *fiery, ruby, crimson, scarlet, vermillion, blood-drenched like a rose, a beet, an apple, a sunset.* I was in vocabulary paradise and delighted with my essay.

But I had to write the finished version on that pristine paper. With a death grip on my special pen, I was overcome with fear. The tears came, and I cried all over my white paper.

Sister Regina came over to my desk. She leaned over me from her great height.

"What in the world is the matter with you?" she asked.

I looked away. I could hardly answer. "I'm afraid I will make a mistake," I whispered.

"So what?" Sister Regina said.

So what?! So what if I made a *mistake?* I suddenly felt like I was the star of one of those catechism filmstrips, like the one where Saint Paul gets knocked off his horse. Because at that moment, angels began singing and the clouds parted and the sun shone down on my ruby tree. A teacher had actually said *"So what!"*

Sister Regina leaned in closer, her veil providing a small, private space for the two of us.

"Look," she said quietly, "we all want everything we do to be perfect, but sometimes it just doesn't turn out that way, because we aren't perfect. If you aren't satisfied when you're done, and you think you can do it better—not perfect, just better—well, then, just do it again. You can do it as many times as you like."

I've had many wonderful teachers who have guided and inspired me. But Sister Regina Marie's kind words at that moment have meant as much to me as anything I have heard before or since.

In those few words, I learned one of the most reassuring lessons of life: that you don't have to be perfect. You only have to satisfy yourself. And there is no limit to the number of chances you get.

I'm *still* messy. So what?

Nancy Roman

Facing the Music

Kathleen Muldoon

Educator
San Antonio, Texas

Disabled. Crippled. Handicapped. Amputee. These were just a few of the labels ascribed to me when, following a devastating illness and long hospitalization, I left the hospital at age 23 on crutches, with one leg amputated and the other encased in a metal brace.

As strange as it seemed to my friends, the labels and stares of others didn't bother me. After all, I'd survived a nearly fatal health crisis. And while not pretty, my prosthesis—a mass of metal hinges and straps that extended from the floor to a pelvic harness—took me where I needed to go.

Although I adapted fairly well to the new hardware—not to mention this whole new way of life—there was one thing I really missed, something that I was a little embarrassed to share with anyone. I wanted to dance.

Dance had always been an important part of my life, dating back to when I was a little girl and my grandmother taught me Irish folk dances. I cannot claim ever to have been a natural-born dancer, but only to have always loved it. As a child of the rock-and-roll age, I loved the freedom of dancing to a steady beat—twisting, gyrating, leaping, twirling—sometimes in sync with the music, often not. As a teen, dating *was* dancing. That's what we did.

After my hospitalization—and after the "new me" had mastered walking again—I did try to dance in the privacy of my apartment. But I soon learned that with no feeling in my remaining foot and, of course, none in my artificial limb, I'd lost all sense of balance. My physical therapist explained that I no longer had *proprioceptive ability,* which is knowing where my body was in relation to space. I didn't understand the concept; all I knew was that when I watched my new version of dance in the mirror, I looked like a wooden toy bobbling on a stick.

My solution was to stop watching myself in the mirror, but not to stop dancing—which I did whenever I heard one of my favorite tunes on the radio. The only parts of my body that moved were my head and hips, but in my mind, all of me was dancing.

Social events, however, became torture for me. I hated sitting on the sidelines as others danced joyfully, but I didn't want to make a spectacle of myself. I tried tapping my fingers, bobbing my head, but it wasn't the same. I wanted to be out on the dance floor.

One evening I was invited to a friend's anniversary party, and I found myself desperately trying to think of an excuse not to attend. I knew there would be dancing. Tears filled my eyes as I flashed back to a vivid scene from my childhood. Gran was teaching me the polka, and we were giggling wildly as we whirled around the tiny kitchen in her apartment.

But then I suddenly remembered something else: the hand-stitched sampler that hung on her wall. When Gran had immigrated to America from

Ireland, she'd brought with her several of these samplers, each one bearing an Irish saying. One of my favorites had been about dance. It read:

DANCE AS IF NO ONE'S WATCHING.

SING AS IF NO ONE'S LISTENING.

AND LIVE EVERY DAY AS IF IT WERE YOUR LAST.

I grabbed a piece of paper and wrote these words down. My spirits soared. Maybe I could dance at the party, I thought. But would I?

Casting my fears aside, I went to the event. As the band struck up a lively waltz, I felt a tightening in my stomach. People trickled onto the dance floor. I watched them for a while, took a deep breath, then excused myself from the couple who'd brought me to the party. I approached Paul, a young man I'd dated in my former life.

"Paul, would you dance with me?" I asked.

He hesitated for only a moment.

"Well, sure," he said. "but you'll have to show me how we're going to do this."

I hadn't thought about that! I looked at the other couples as they swept by us. A waltz wasn't exactly like the twist, where you can face your partner and each do your own thing.

"Put your hands on my shoulders and lead," I said finally, sounding like I'd done this every day of the week.

And we began to dance. Paul led slowly and I did my best to follow, careful not to trip him up with my crutches. I stumbled a few times, and I soon learned that I definitely could not move backward. But I pressed on, allowing myself to get lost in the music and in Paul. I quit caring about how I looked and what other people thought, and instead just danced—*as if no one was watching.* I wasn't graceful, to be sure. Yet I felt good and happy and, most important, I was having fun.

By the time the music stopped, Paul and I were both out of breath but smiling. And, yes, some people were watching. And they applauded.

That night, I sent up a prayer thanking God that Gran had so painstakingly stitched such wise words on that sampler so many years ago. Today I imagine Gran looking down from her corner of heaven, smiling and applauding, too—because I haven't stopped dancing.

Kathleen Muldoon

Bottom of the Ninth

Marlon LeTerrance

Entertainment
Memphis, Tennessee

The moment I heard the whack of the bat I knew there was no escape. Panic and fear spiked through me. I wanted the moment to fade away, like a dream does when you can't quite remember its details.

As the baseball sped toward me, I could hear the crowd erupt in a roar of anticipation. The outcome of the North Carolina Little League Championship game was suddenly on my shoulders. In the millisecond it took for the weight of this realization to sink in, I understood I wasn't prepared for the outcome. It was the bottom of the ninth inning. The bases were loaded. The score was seven to six, with only one out. A flawless catch and double play would win the game. I'd be hoisted up in the air by my teammates and declared a hero.

These were intoxicating possibilities. But as the ball rumbled toward me, I knew I wasn't ready to be celebrated. There was too much at stake, and being successful meant taking too big a risk. The consequences seemed unbearable. If I dropped the ball or let it get by me, we would lose the game. I didn't want that responsibility. I just wanted to be with my dad in the backyard, where it was okay to make mistakes and laugh a little, too.

I could imagine my father somewhere in the crowd, confidently nodding his head. He believed I could play first base far better than I ever imagined. Every weekday, exhausted from his long shifts working with juvenile delinquents, he'd invest countless hours teaching me fundamentals. Throughout the evening, we'd relentlessly practice the art of fielding ground balls and catching pop flies until he was certain I had it all mastered. I'd reluctantly fumble through all the correct motions, more scared of the ball hitting me than I dared to let on.

"Don't be afraid," my father would say, winding back his arm to throw me another lightning-fast grounder. "You can do it. Trust me."

As I crouched into position, he'd smile, offering encouragement when I missed and nonchalantly pointing out my mistakes. When I would somehow get the ball to land safely inside my glove, he'd laugh and shower me with praise for not giving up. "See? I told you," he'd say proudly. "Just believe in yourself."

His support was bottomless. "Always keep your eyes on the ball," he'd advise. "As long as you can see it, your glove will catch it." No matter how many times the ball got away from me, my father would always say, "You can do it," as if he knew something I didn't.

This time, though, my father was wrong. The ball was storming toward me way too fast to follow with my eyes. My right leg wobbled to the side as I attempted to move in on the ball, leaving me dangerously close to falling. My glove felt loose and heavy, and it was difficult to crouch into position. I wanted to close my eyes, stick out my glove, and just hope the ball landed there.

My dad knew how much I hated ground balls—they have a way of bouncing in unpredictable patterns. He never accepted the idea that human beings have natural limitations, believing that all things were possible as long as you worked hard enough and believed in yourself. In his eyes, the game of baseball was merely the starting block for the lessons he felt I needed to learn. In fact, he would tell me that life was a lot like catching a grounder. If you keep your eye sharp, never letting your attention drift from what's important, then you will triumph.

As a kid, I think he assumed I was smarter and more talented than I actually was. There were many times when I would cry out in frustration, "I can't. I can't do it!" But Pops never allowed me the luxury of that excuse. He was convinced that the more a person gave up on some things, the easier it became to give up on all things.

As I forced my eyes to follow the ball, it took its final hop toward me, blasting up from the ground like a missile.

I wanted badly to follow my dad's advice, but how could I focus on the ball when all I could hear was a bullhorn announcing my failure? The ball was moving too fast and bouncing too high. I felt powerless. With family and friends cheering for me, how could I face them if I dropped the ball? Teammates were analyzing my every move. What excuse could I offer them if I messed up?

I was about to make my desperate attempt at catching the ball when I noticed something horribly wrong. In the middle of its last bounce, the ball was veering away from me, wickedly to my right. There was no way I could catch it now.

It was over. I could hear the players from the other team racing to claim victory. I never wanted to play baseball again.

You can do it. Trust me.

I'm not sure if my father actually yelled from the stands, or if the words just floated into my mind. Either way, I heard them—and suddenly, everything became unnaturally silent. Time paused in mid-stride. I drifted into a peaceful, dreamlike state. Amazingly, I could now see the ball with magnified clarity. I became fascinated by the small dents and scuffs on it, markings I'd never noticed before. The threading was perfectly stitched, lending a hypnotic effect as it rotated in the air. Nothing else mattered. Not the crowd. Not the double play. Not the victory or the loss. I watched the ball with a relaxed sense of appreciation. It had suddenly become too beautiful to let it get away.

Every muscle in my 11-year-old body sprang into action, fully prepared for whatever conclusion fate had in store. I wasn't afraid anymore. I now understood what my father had been telling me. The ball could be caught. And I could do it.

I dove for the ball, believing.

Everyone Is Shy

Julie Knapp

Editor
New York, New York

From the age of 9 to 14, I went to five different schools, so I was always the new kid. My family moved around a lot, and the first day at each new school was terrifying. I was painfully shy and gawky and spent a lot of time keeping to myself on the playground, or sitting alone at the lunch table. Not a lot of fun. I was also really tall for my age, even towering over the boys. I felt like a giraffe on display.

On my first day of third grade in Edwardsville, Illinois, I was particularly nervous and took my time getting ready before school. I kept changing my clothes, finally deciding on a faded red-and-blue plaid cotton dress. I thought it looked okay and wouldn't make me stand out too much.

As my mother sat me down and brushed my hair into pigtails, I confessed my dread to her. I remember her response was matter-of-fact, but tough.

"Everyone is shy," she said. "Don't think you're the only one."

"*You're* not shy," I replied.

"Of course, I'm shy," she said. "I just hide it."

I was shocked! My mother had a weakness? Impossible. She was confident and assertive with shop clerks and waiters, and her laugh was so loud I sometimes got embarrassed. She had a much bigger personality than all the other mothers.

As she finished braiding my pigtails, my mother turned me around and looked me straight in the eye. "Here's what you do," she said. "When you get to school, look around for another girl who's standing alone, then walk up to her and be friendly. Ask her questions."

"What kind of questions?"

"Her name, which teacher she has, nothing complicated."

The elementary school was just a couple blocks from our house, so my mother walked me there, gave me a pat on the head, and left. I stood there rigid, convinced as always that everyone in the schoolyard had all the friends they wanted and wouldn't give me the time of day. While I waited for the bell to call us into class, I saw a girl about my age leaning against the brick wall, all by herself.

Okay, I thought, *here goes.* I walked up to the girl, smiling, introduced myself and began asking her questions, just as my mother had instructed. She told me her name was Kathryn, and she answered all of my questions. She appeared so grateful that I was showing an interest in her that she took my hand when the bell rang, and we walked into the school together.

I had an instant friend. And soon, one friend led to another. That school year was one of my best. I found out later that my mother had stayed around and spied on me that morning, and she was so proud to see what I'd done that she started crying.

As we moved from Utah to Minnesota to Arkansas, I'd give myself a pep talk each time I started at a new school (it never stopped being hard); and by the end of the year, when my parents were ready to move us again, I had made lots of friends. It was always wrenching to leave them behind.

My mother's method of fighting shyness worked so well that I became a braver person because of it. "Everyone is shy" became a kind of secret password for me—when I moved to New York City to live on my own; whenever I started a new job; even when I went to parties.

A few months ago, my boss needed me to attend a gala dinner for work. I went by myself, dressed in a long gown, and wearing heels that put me over six feet. When I walked in, I felt that old attack of shyness. Seated at a table of strangers, I remembered my mother's words and introduced myself to each one of them. Before long, we were all laughing and engaged in conversation.

It was like being back in the third grade again, only this time I was at the fun table.

Bull Ahead

Donna Surgenor Reames

Registered Nurse
Pine Mountain, Georgia

I was always an indecisive person. This goes way back to when I was a little girl, growing up in the small Georgian town of Pine Mountain, just outside of Atlanta. Back then I would spend ages at the candy counter, staring through the glass window at all the colorful selections, sometimes taking so long to make up my mind that I didn't buy anything at all.

Indecision would continue to plague me for years, keeping me from being as whole as I could be. Whenever I was confronted with life's bigger questions, I became paralyzed, afraid of making the wrong choice. In fact, I'd be so busy weighing pros and cons and rights and wrongs, that I usually remained right where I was—stuck and unsure.

I certainly didn't get this trait from my parents. My mother was extremely organized and decisive; and my stepfather, a military man, was also very structured. Sometimes my mom would tease me about my indecisiveness, saying, "Are you sure you're my child?"

One summer just before I graduated from high school, I was sitting out on the front porch swing with my boyfriend, Vince. Six years my senior, Vince was everything I wasn't. Where I was dreamy, he was focused. While I usually wavered, he was extremely disciplined. Vince was like a rock, always stable, never in crisis.

We'd become friends when I was 16, and he was a ranger at the state park, a job he'd been determined to get since he was a child. Vince was like that about everything. He never hesitated or second-guessed himself. Even his house was focused. He lived with his dog, his bike, and with nature. He represented the kind of pure strength and deliberation that I didn't have.

Most important, he made decisions easily and aggressively, quickly zeroing in on whatever choices he thought would best affect his personal and professional life.

That night on the porch, I was wrestling with whether or not I should stay home for college or go away to a better, more challenging school. On one hand, I was only 17 years old and afraid of moving six hours away from my home. I was so connected to my mom. She was a separated, single mother at the time, and she didn't have much money. I'd been working to help pay the bills.

But on the other hand, I also knew that going away to school might be just what I needed—a place where I could do new things, make new friends, and discover all sorts of opportunities that I never knew existed. Should I follow my heart or follow my head? I was surely at a crossroads.

Vince listened carefully, then suddenly leaned forward, and looked hard into my eyes.

"Sometimes you just have to bull ahead," he said, reaching out to take my hand. "If you make a mistake, you'll learn from it. If not, you'll benefit from it."

Bulling ahead isn't easy for an indecisive person, but I took Vince's advice and went to college, returning home for monthly visits. For the first time in my life, I had made a strong decision, and it not only solved a specific problem, but gave me a real peace of mind. Vince was responsible for that. And over the years, his advice has come back again and again, each time making a world of difference in my life.

For instance, after I got married (not to Vince, ironically) and everyone told me I was too old to become a mom, I made the decision to try anyway. It would take several years and lots of expensive infertility workups before I would realize my dream of motherhood. But the part that would have ordinarily hung me up—the decision to jump in with both feet—was no longer a hurdle, as I bulled ahead just as Vince had told me to.

When I was tired of my nursing job and wanted to make the crazy leap into writing at a newspaper—something I'd never been trained to do—Vince's words escorted me into that newspaper office.

"Give me three months to get my bearings," I told them, "and if you don't like me you can fire me." Not only did they hire me, but I ended up winning awards for many of the stories I turned out for them.

And when I gained 35 pounds in my last pregnancy and a local radio station sponsored a ten-week fitness challenge, I swallowed my pride (they showed applicants' "before" pictures on the internet!) and jumped right in. I pushed myself to get to the gym every day, always repeating Vince's words in my head like a mantra, "Just bull ahead, just bull ahead . . ." Ten weeks later, I won the competition, having shed nearly 15 pounds. My self-esteem soared. Once again, Vince's words reminded me that decisions were meant to be made.

I don't know where Vince is today or what he's doing, but I'll tell you this: If I was back on that porch swing with him right now, I would have no trouble deciding what to say to him. I'd just bull ahead and thank him from the bottom of my heart for helping me to change my life.

Donna Surgenor Reames

The Juror

Christine Ducey

Business Owner
Oceanside, California

A few years ago, I was selected for my first jury duty. After listening to the court officer's opening-day pep talk—all about the importance of community, responsibility, and justice—I was pretty moved. I really wanted to be a good juror.

The case involved a young man who had been charged with assaulting a policeman. The defendant had been outside his home, blasting his boom box, and neighbors had complained about the noise. When the police arrived on the scene and confronted the defendant, a struggle ensued, and he wound up kicking an officer.

The defendant's innocence or guilt would depend on whether he'd aggressively assaulted the officer, or had done so in self-defense. Because he did not speak English, we were instructed to listen only to the court interpreter.

At the end of the opening remarks, I confess I was fairly sure that the defendant didn't stand a chance. But as the trial progressed, it began to look more and more like the police had used excessive force. By the time the judge sent us off to deliberate, I strongly believed that this was a simple case of self-defense.

Once behind closed doors, the jury foreman—against the advice of the judge—immediately called for a vote. We were divided, with the majority electing to convict. This didn't exactly soothe the tension in the room, and our deliberations after that became contentious and angry.

The debate lasted several days, as we continued reviewing the testimony. One of the key elements in the transcript—and one that convinced several jurors that the defendant was guilty—was how he had changed his testimony during the final round of questioning. According to the transcript, he had answered three times that the police had treated him roughly; but the last time, he said they had not. I couldn't understand why he would have changed his response.

One Hispanic juror finally revealed that, in Spanish, the defendant had not changed his story but, rather, the translator had misinterpreted his words. A heated exchange erupted, with everyone reminding this particular juror that he was supposed to ignore all Spanish testimony. At this point, the jury room became even more emotionally charged.

Those few jurors who had been on my side now wanted a conviction. Only the Hispanic juror and I were holding out, and we were getting terrible pressure from the others to reverse our opinion.

The tension continued to build, and I felt increasingly isolated. As I tried to explain my position one last time, one juror began yelling at me, accusing me of being a bleeding-heart liberal who was more concerned with protecting a minority than considering the facts of the trial.

As we left the courthouse for the day, the Hispanic juror confided to me that he could no longer take the pressure, and despite what he believed, he was planning to change his vote.

Now I was totally alone. As I drove home, I became overwhelmed. The trial had been draining, but the emotional torment of trying to stand my ground against ten—and now, it seemed, eleven—other jurors was too much to bear. I felt physically sick.

On the morning of what was certain to be our last day of deliberations, I woke up in a panic. I knew that the pressure on me to change my mind would be enormous. I began wondering if I could force a mistrial and dreaded how it all might turn out. A man's freedom was at stake.

Just before leaving for the courthouse, I got a call from my good friend, Kris. Because the judge had repeatedly admonished the jury not to disclose any information about the trial, I told Kris only about my deteriorating emotional state.

"I don't know what I'm going to do!" I said into the phone, over and over again.

For a second I heard only silence on the other end of the line. Then Kris said, "I know exactly what you'll do. You'll do the right thing."

That's all I needed to hear.

By the time I arrived in the jury room, I had decided that I didn't care anymore how angry the other jurors had become with me. I was determined to stick by my convictions. And I did. When the final roll was called, I was the only dissenting juror, and a mistrial was declared.

As we entered the courtroom to inform the judge of our decision, the jury foreman whispered to me, "What makes you think you're so much smarter than the rest of us?" What he obviously didn't understand was that I never considered my opinion any better than his—or any other juror's, for that matter. I only knew what I believed to be true, and just as Kris had predicted, I did what I thought was the right thing.

Case closed.

Christine Ducey

The Right Road

Debra Cheehy

Homemaker and Children's Author
Manassas, Virginia

Near the end of my sixth-grade year, my family and I moved from a small, one-horse town in Illinois to a bigger city just an hour away. I liked our new life—our neighborhood was older and more established, and we lived in a house instead of an apartment—but I had one problem: Overnight, I became the dreaded "new kid" at school.

Being the outsider is never fun. You eat lunch alone in the cafeteria, you're excluded from cliques, and people look at you like you're an alien. At the time, Twiggy was the top model, and all the other girls dressed in mod clothing, with hoop earrings and Peter Pan haircuts. My hair ran down to my waist.

Feeling awkward and alone, I longed for the security of my old friends back home. I tried the best I could to fit in, but the clash of personalities between me and my new schoolmates became dreadfully apparent the day Mr. Bergin, our beloved English teacher, gave the class a writing assignment.

"I want you to write a report about the person you would most like to meet—and *why*," he said. "It can be about anyone you choose, as long as they're still alive."

An immediate buzz filled the room as my classmates began whispering to one another about the possibilities. I listened closely, and over and over the same four names echoed through the room: Micky, Davy, Peter, and Michael—otherwise known as the Monkees.

At that time, the Monkees were everything. They'd started as an invention for American TV—a clever, comic version of the Beatles—then quickly became all the rage, appearing on everything from fan magazines to talk shows to lunch boxes. The cool kids never missed an episode of *The Monkees* after school, and collecting their records was an in-crowd requirement.

After Mr. Bergin announced the assignment, I sat in my seat wanting to join the rest of my classmates in their enthusiastic chatter, but I just couldn't get excited about meeting the Monkees.

Besides, I already knew who I wanted to meet: James Cagney.

A box office star of my parents' generation, Cagney had always been my favorite actor—I simply adored him! To me, he was the perfect embodiment of a movie star. I never got tired of his films, whether he was having a gunfight in one of his gangster movies, or smashing a grapefruit into Mae Clarke's face in *The Public Enemy,* or tap-dancing across the stage in *Yankee Doodle Dandy.* I even tried to imitate one of his famous scenes by dancing down a stairway in my own home and wound up falling down the steps and breaking my foot in two places!

Back in the classroom, I was daydreaming of my imaginary meeting with Cagney when the bell rang and snapped me back to reality. I headed home, singing "Yankee Doodle Dandy" all the way.

Just as I got inside the door, the phone rang, and when I picked it up I heard the familiar voice of my best friend from back home. Cindy and I had been inseparable since second grade. I told her about my English assignment, and—no surprise—she blurted out her vote.

"Oh, that's so easy," she gushed. "Davy Jones! That's who I'd want to meet!"

Ugh, I thought, *not Cindy, too.*

"So which Monkee are you going to write about?" she asked.

"Think about it, Cindy," I said. "Who do you *think* I'd pick?"

The line was silent for a moment, then Cindy moaned.

"Oh, no!" she said, "You wouldn't! Not *James Cagney!*"

Although Cindy had never understood my infatuation with Cagney, she'd come to accept it. But she also knew what was socially acceptable—and unacceptable—at our age. Listening to the latest music was cool. Following the newest fashions was cool. Short actors from another era were definitely *not* cool!

"Debbie," she said gently, trying to tell me what I already knew, "if you write about James Cagney, everyone is going to laugh at you. You have to reconsider this."

I finally relented, agreeing that I would write about Davy Jones.

After we said our good-byes, I decided to get to work. I took out a piece of notebook paper, wrote my name, grade, and subject in the top right-hand corner, and began my report:

"The person I would most like to meet is Davy Jones from the Monkees," I wrote slowly, "because . . ."

Because, . . . because . . .

I stopped writing. Tapping my pencil to my head in an effort to bring forth the words—any words—I immediately grew frustrated. Try as I might,

I could not think of a single reason why I would want to meet Davy Jones, or any Monkee for that matter. I slammed my pencil down.

"I can't! I won't!" I blurted out to no one in particular.

As I crumpled up my paper, I thought about my predicament. I knew I wanted to fit in and be liked, but was writing about Davy Jones really the way to go about it? What bothered me the most was that it wasn't the truth. It was not the real *me*!

With renewed determination, I took out a fresh sheet of paper and began to write:

"The person I would most like to meet is James Cagney because . . . because . . ."

And then the words flowed. I wrote about the way Cagney danced and spoke his lines and about how he could scare you or make you laugh or make you cry. Most important, I wrote about how I *felt* when I watched him on the screen—which was wonderful. Finally finishing my essay, and satisfied that I had included everything I wanted to say, I placed the report in my English book and went to sleep, rather pleased with myself.

Two days later, Mr. Bergin called the class to attention. Taking a report from the stack of paper on his desk, he made an announcement.

"Debra Thomas," he said, "would you please come up to the front of the class?"

I heard him speak the words, but I was frozen. *This couldn't possibly be about the report*, I thought. *No way.*

I felt the color rushing to my face as I slowly stood and walked to the front of the classroom.

"There are twenty-nine reports here," Mr. Bergin said, "and they all express the same desire: to meet one of the Monkees. Debra is the only student in this class who wanted to meet someone else. Debra, please read your report."

Taking the paper from him, I lowered my eyes and began to speak, my voice soft and unsteady.

"The person I would most like to meet is . . . James Cagney."

Glances were exchanged, and I could hear giggling throughout the room. By now my cheeks were burning and tears stung my eyes, but I continued reading. Before long a feeling of calm came over me. The more I read, the better I felt. I *had* wanted to meet James Cagney. It was true! I meant every word that was on that paper.

As I finished my report, Mr. Bergin quieted the class and put an arm around my shoulders.

"A-plus!" he said.

When I took my seat, Mr. Bergin reached for a book on his desk. Opening it to a marked page, he told the class, "I would like to read a poem to all of you. It was written by a man named Robert Frost, and it's called 'The Road Not Taken.'"

I remember listening carefully to the whole poem, but the last words are the ones that would become forever engraved in my mind:

> *Two roads diverged in a wood, and I—*
> *I took the one less traveled by*
> *And that has made all the difference.*

That day, Mr. Bergin gave me the courage to follow my heart. And whenever I do, I always find that road.

Debra Chal"y

PART FOUR

Finding Yourself

*"I immediately took the words to heart.
After all, my mother had said them,
and Mama never gave bad advice."*

Coffee with Sam

Michael Raysses

Writer and Actor
Los Angeles, California

When I stared into the mirror on that hazy Los Angeles summer morning, I was struck by the eyes staring back at me. They were lifeless and dull.

Seized by the notion that my life had become nothing I recognized nor wanted, I was hit with the cold realization that this was certainly not what I had planned. I'd moved to California from Indiana to pursue an acting career, and though I'd had modest successes, none of it seemed to connect me to anything else. All it had led me to was this moment—holding down a nine-to-five job, preparing to angle my way through rush-hour traffic, and yearning for a cup of coffee.

I continued to wrestle with this realization as I drove to work, when suddenly an old man appeared, crossing the street in front of me. I hit the brakes, the tires screeching their protest. As startled as I was, the old man barely seemed to notice how close he'd come to becoming roadkill. He was dressed in a dark suit and black fedora, more fitting for a Chicago winter than a midsummer morning. I shook my head at his carelessness.

Parking my car, I ran into Starbucks. As I got in line, there he was again—the man I'd almost hit—standing right in front of me. I wanted to say something to him about being so negligent, but he turned to me first.

"Hello," he said with warmth and familiarity, almost as if we were old friends. I felt disarmed, instantly regretting having had any ill thoughts about him.

When he got to the head of the line, the old man ordered a cup of coffee.

"Tall, grande, or venti?" the clerk asked. The man looked perplexed.

"Just a cup of coffee, please," he answered. And in one of those moments that make you wish for a simpler time, the clerk recited the very same inane litany of choices. Watching this was torture, so I stepped up and ordered a large cup of coffee for the old man. When he finally got what he came for, he exited the line, toasting me with a look of relief and gratitude.

As I poured cream into my coffee, I noticed that he had taken a seat on the patio, and that I would have to pass by him on my way out. I looked up at the clock—I was running late—but as I left the cafe and went past him, I stopped. I heard myself ask if I might join him, not even knowing why. He gestured to a chair and greeted me like he was expecting me the entire time.

Sitting down, I finally got a good look at him. His suit was shiny from too much wear; his shoes clung to his bare feet with what little life they had left in them. The light blue shirt he wore beneath his coat was missing a button directly over his chest. His expressionless face was rimmed by a thick gray beard, which gave way to his eyes, two deep pools of blue, an oasis in the desert of his countenance. I hadn't really seen his face until I saw his eyes.

His name was Sam. He was 72 years old and had suffered a stroke sometime in the last two years. He was Jewish and from Germany. He'd been married twice, with children from his first union. They were all adults now.

As we talked, his words seeped from him like water from a dam that didn't want to burst. Yet the more that trickled out, the greater the cascade. Listening to him talk, I was struck by a paradox: He was dressed shabbily, but he presented himself regally. Even when he became animated, I could detect him trying to maintain an air of decorum.

Without prompting, Sam began to talk about the very things that had weighed so heavily on me that very morning. He spoke about his past and how it didn't match up with his present. He didn't even bother to mention his future. In fact, the more he spoke, the more passive his voice and manner grew, until by the end of our conversation, he was talking as though his life were over, and he was now merely marking the days. During the time it took to finish my coffee, Sam had changed before my eyes. He now appeared worn smooth by sadness and resignation.

Getting up from the table, I asked Sam if he needed a lift; he accepted a ride to a cross-town bus stop. As I pulled over to drop him off at the curb, he sighed.

"Would it be okay if I tell you something personal?" he asked.

"Sure," I said, thinking he was going to say that he knew it was me who had almost hit him earlier that morning. But instead, he tattooed me with a stare.

"When I look into your eyes," he said, "I see the eyes of one who can do anything. But, Michael, I also see one who is blind to all that he has already done."

I would like to say that in the ten years since I met Sam that hot summer morning, my life has been transformed; that his vision propelled me to reach the potential he saw there. But that would be a lie neither of us could tolerate. What I can say with complete assurance and eternal gratitude, however, is that ever since that day, whenever I stare into the morning mirror, I see a glimpse of what I imagine Sam saw that day. And for the briefest instant, I believe it, too.

Michael
Reysses

What Mama Said

Thomas Kennedy

Prisoner
Pollock, Louisiana

The year was 1968, and I was living in a rural farm community in Louisiana. It was a most turbulent time for blacks and one of the ugliest eras in American history. But this is where I first heard the words that would help shape my young mind.

The words came from my mother, a beautiful woman with cinnamon-colored skin and a loving soul. Mama was my first teacher. She had me so academically prepared by the time I started first grade, I scored nothing but A's. Best of all, she taught me to read, and I loved reading because it opened whole new worlds to me.

I'll never forget my first day of school. It was a humid September morning, the air thick and damp as it is only in Louisiana in the waning days of summer. Mama decked me out in new clothes she had ordered from the Sears, Roebuck catalog, and even she wore her Sunday best. She held my hand as we proudly marched off to the school one street over. We walked slowly so our clothes wouldn't stick to us. The slow pace didn't help to calm my nerves, and as we walked, I remember trying to figure out how I could free my hand from Mama's clammy grip. I was a big boy now and I couldn't let my friends see me hanging onto my mama. They would laugh at me.

The mothers of all the first graders stayed in the classroom for the first period. When it was time for them to leave, some of the children began to cry. Not me. I rejoiced at the freedom (only I did so inwardly, ever careful of Mama's feelings). But before she left the room, Mama left me with these words:

"Be the best at whatever you do."

Be the best at whatever you do. I immediately took the words to heart. After all, my mother had said them, and Mama never gave bad advice. I quickly became my teacher's favorite student, my hand always raised, the answers to her questions always on my lips.

Even at this young age, I knew that being the best at what I did could reap great rewards. Sometimes on our Sunday drive, our family car would detour through the white neighborhood—only in the daytime, though—and my mama's eyes would light up when she saw those giant houses. I often thought to myself that if I were to excel in school, I'd be able to buy Mama a home like that someday. She deserved one.

The next year, 1969, integration came to my hometown, 15 years after the Supreme Court had decreed segregation unconstitutional. Our teacher, Mrs. Willie Mae Dixon, looked depressed on that freezing December day as she announced this to our second-grade class. Strangely, she hadn't appeared this sad even when she'd told us about the death of our hero, Martin Luther King.

It wasn't until the next semester, when we would be bussed to Oak Grove elementary—a "white school," as we blacks referred to it—that I understood why Mrs. Dixon had seemed so concerned. For the first time in my schooling, my teachers weren't on my side. In fact, it seemed as though they liked me better when I wasn't so smart and proud. Before long, my best work was only a so-what, and I wasn't encouraged to do better. So rather than strive to be the best, I stopped trying, and my grades declined.

It's funny how words said with just the right intonation can have such a profound effect. My teachers weren't outright calling me stupid, but their manner implied it, and I felt every bit of it.

In the schoolyard, things were less subtle. I was called ugly things—cruel and racist names. Sometimes Mama's words prevailed, and I rode above it all. But a lot of times my fist did the responding. Before long, my desire to excel went from the classroom to the sports field, and I became a prep school star athlete. And with the help of a Pell Grant, I enrolled at Northeast Louisiana University (now the University of Louisiana at Monroe).

I knew that my talent lay in the game of football, and that my 6'2", 220-pound frame was an impressive calling card. So that first spring semester, I walked onto the tryout field with 100 other young men who also thought they were good enough to play at this level. Once again I took Mama's words with me. They'd always been my motivating force when the odds were stacked against me. Now they were my battle cry.

Of all the walk-ons, I was the only one to make the final cut. But I wasn't content with just being on the team. Only the starters had a real chance for the next level—going pro, the big bucks—so I set my sights on the number one spot. This time, my goal eluded me. By the end of the spring season, I was the third-string tight end. Still, my talents landed me on special teams my first season, and I earned my letterman jacket before some of the others who had been zealously recruited. I was on my way.

That following spring, a friend of mine from Los Angeles visited me at school. Like a number of families from our small town, his family had made the migration from Louisiana to L.A. I had even lived there myself, on and off. By now, my friend was a success. He was driving a brand-new Cadillac at 19, and jewelry was draped around his neck and wrist. When you're black and poor, money defines success, no matter how one comes by it. So I didn't question the source of his sudden wealth—it was none of my business. Besides, my future was set. I would be playing in the NFL in a couple of years, and when that happened, he could come and see *my* new toys.

By the time the next spring season ended, I had worked my way to the second team and was breathing down the neck of the guy in the number one slot. The moment he faltered, I knew, I would step into the role that would catapult me to stardom. After the last game, the head coach invited each player into his office at the stadium to evaluate our spring performances and recommend a training regimen for the summer.

As the coach's secretary escorted me into my session, I was optimistic and expectant. With the spectacular performance I'd had that spring, I knew he would talk mostly about elevating me to a full scholarship. But what he told me that day would ultimately determine my future.

"We're moving you to third team linebacker," he said.

I was stunned. When I asked why I'd been moved down instead of up, the coach explained that in order to save money, he was promoting a white guy who was already on full scholarship to second team. This way, he wouldn't have to put *me* on full scholarship.

In other words, he could continue to get my services for a little bit of nothing.

As I drove away from the stadium, I was heartbroken. I'd worked so hard to make my way to second team, only to get a demotion.

Rather than lie around depressed for the summer, I packed my things and took off for Los Angeles to visit family. Not long after I got there, I could feel the tug of the streets. Within a few days, I was selling drugs. I only wanted to make enough money to buy some new clothes and maybe a new car in which I could return to school, my world back on course.

But I never made it back to school. Late that summer, I was arrested for possession of cocaine and sentenced to six months in jail. After a subsequent arrest in 1991, almost a decade later, I was sentenced to life in prison for distribution of cocaine. I'm expected to die in here.

I could go on forever about the injustice of my sentence—a life term for violating only prohibition laws, not committing murder. I could talk about how preposterous it is to inflict such a severe punishment on someone, especially in a country where drug use rises every year.

But the bottom line is: I got myself here. And now I must make the best of this.

When I held my mama's hand on the way to school those many years ago, this was not where she expected me to end up. She encouraged me to be the best, and I was for a while. Then I messed it all up.

The good thing is, Mama's words are still my driving force as I write this. Maybe I'll be a writer. Maybe through perseverance and dedication to this craft, I will find some way to make Mama proud of her oldest son again. I have to believe I can.

Thomas Kennedy

The Ride Home

Mike Sackett

Business Owner
Glen Arm, Maryland

After 23 years running a machinery-design business, I was burned out and depressed as hell about what I'd done with my life. I went to a shrink who tried to put me on drugs. I told him to get lost.

All three of my older sisters were artists. That was my dream, too. But I was raised in an Irish-Catholic family, where boys looking to become men didn't talk about wanting to be an artist or writer, much less actually making a career of it.

So one day, when I heard that a local Girl Scout troop was looking for a face painter, on a whim I volunteered my services. I also face-painted for some inner-city schools. The kids loved it so much, I thought it might be a great way to cheer up children who really needed it. So I called a local hospital that treated kids with cancer, and they welcomed my offer. I intended it to be a one-shot deal.

On my first day in the wards, I paused outside the playroom of the children's surgical unit and gulped a handful of aspirin. My chronic back pain was acting up. Then I pushed through the door, my paints in hand.

"Hey, Mister, will ya' paint my butt?" shouted a little boy with a softball-sized swelling on his neck. I shot him a mock glare that only succeeded in giving him a case of the giggles.

As I squirted paints onto my palette, children immediately began lining up beside my table. Those too little or too weak to walk rolled up in wheelchairs pushed by their parents or one of the hospital staff. Some wheeled over their own IVs on casters, clutching at the poles that held their drip bags, like tiny shepherds wielding their staffs in a school nativity play. Most were bald.

This would be tougher than I bargained for, I thought.

"Hi, sweetie, what's your name?" I said to a shy little girl. Her mother smoothed what remained of her daughter's strawberry curls, her eyes blotted with mascara and tears.

I took the little girl's hand in my palm. It was tiny and white, plump at the wrist, like a baby's. A swatch of gauze covered a purple bruise from the IV needle that was inserted in the back of her hand.

"A pretty girl like you should get a pretty picture, don't you think?"

She nodded. Her skin was as pale as sifted flour.

"Marie, tell the nice man what you want," her mother said.

"I already know what she wants," I said, smiling. "A pink rose, right *here!*" I patted the back of her hand. "Then I'll paint green leaves right *here,* and put a ladybug right . . . *here!*" I wiggled a finger into her armpit. Marie's giggles rang in my ears like wind chimes.

In the next ward, another little girl chose Ariel, the Little Mermaid, complete with her fiery red hair.

"My name ith Ariel, too," she said.

"Really?" I responded, painting streamers of seaweed across her cheek.

"Yeth," she answered in a mouse voice. "My hair uthed to be red."

I swallowed. "I'll bet it was beautiful," I managed to whisper.

I wandered into the hallway, my back pounding. The suffering I was seeing among these children was already more than I could bear—and I had three more wards to go. Slumping against the wall, I peeked in at my next patient, a little boy with a foot-long zipper scar across his head. I groaned, and my eyes filled with tears.

"Boy ain't dead yet, mister!" came a voice from behind me. The words hit me like a brick, and I felt a rush of anger that someone had been watching me.

"Who the hell are you?" I asked, turning around to the voice. The man addressing me was not a part of the hospital's medical staff. He was a grizzled old janitor who could have passed for Gabby Hayes.

"Think that long face o' yours is gonna help these kids?" he asked, with a touch of West Virginia twang. "Better think ag'in. You gotta save your tears for the ride home."

And then he was gone, with his mop and bucket.

Save my tears for the ride home. I knew right away that the old bird was right. Five minutes later, the boy with the zipper scar and I were laughing so hard that the floor nurse had to come in and ask us to keep the noise down.

After that day, there was no turning back. Gradually, I discovered that I'd been sacrificing part of who I was by spending my life in a profession I didn't love, and that my pursuit of material success could never give me what I needed. What I found in these wards could.

For 12 years now, I've been coming to this hospital and making these kids smile and laugh—not all of them, but enough to remind me why I keep returning. Once a month, I shut down my machinery business and pack up my face paints. I only want one thing: to see every one of these children get out of this place and go back home where they belong.

Even after all this time, I still mist up on the ride home. Mist up? Hell, sometimes I cry like a baby. But that's okay. By the time I pull into my drive-way, not only are the tears gone, but so is the pain in my back. Freedom from pain—a feeling of peace will give you that.

Through
My Daughter's Eyes

Beverly Tribuiani-Montez

Homemaker
Brentwood, California

I felt inadequate growing up: chubby, never pretty enough, bent on perfection, feeling like I always needed to be better. My mom pushed me so hard to be the best, not realizing that usually made me feel the worst. As a result, I spent a long, long time looking in the mirror, never seeing someone I liked.

Then one day all of that changed when I met for the first time a beautiful, passionate, and confident woman—myself.

I didn't make this transformation by reading dozens of self-help books or through weekly visits to a therapist (though that couldn't have hurt). I learned more about the kind of person I wanted to be from my three-year-old daughter, Jessica.

It was a hot summer day and Jessica wanted to go swimming. I had a horrible headache and was feeling sorry for myself, having not yet lost the weight from my last pregnancy, eight months before. I was on mommy overload and had no energy left to go outside and play. I couldn't see any light at the end of the tunnel.

After an hour of Jessica begging me to at least try on my bathing suit, I agreed to take her swimming. She sat on my bed, watching me try on two or three old bathing suits.

"That one's *beautiful,*" she said, so sincerely.

"Oh no, this one is still a little too tight," I replied, turning to look at the back of my thighs and then back to my paunchy stomach hanging over the seam. I was horrified.

"I like that one the best!" Jessie said, nodding her head for added enthusiasm.

"Yeah, I guess it looks okay," I said halfheartedly.

"But how does it *feeeeel,* Mommy?" she asked.

I smiled at her attempts.

"Well, it feels pretty good. Let's go swim."

We ran out the back door, and Jessica immediately jumped into the pool, begging me to jump in after her. But I like to get in the slow way, so I began inching my way in, toe first, then my ankle.

"Jump in, Mommy!" Jessica squealed.

I was so hot, and knowing that I would have to start dinner soon, I figured, what the heck, and cannonballed into the water. Jessie was delighted that I hadn't followed my normal routine, and she swam over to me splashing and kicking. She gave me a big hug.

"How do you feel?" she squealed again.

"*Cold,*" I stammered, laughing and trying to catch my breath.

Jessica giggled and splashed around me some more, then threw her little arms around my neck.

"How do you feel *now?*" she asked.

"I feel great!" I said with the enthusiasm I knew she was waiting to hear in my voice.

"See, Mommy?" she said, smoothing my hair away from my face. "You *do* look beautiful."

There was something about her voice and the look in her eyes that told me she was telling the truth. Her truth. I became extremely conscious about who I am in my daughter's life. In that single moment, I never felt more beautiful.

I climbed out of the pool and cannonballed in all over again. But this time, I left the old me standing behind on the deck—the me I never wanted her to know. I felt young and happy again, cutting loose in the water with a new freedom.

Jessica wasn't old enough that day to consciously select her words. She had no agenda, no ulterior motive. She spoke straight from her heart. Her love was unconditional. She accepted me for who I was.

I caught a glimpse of the way Jessica saw me, and I understood how awful she would feel if she knew how bad I felt about myself. Beauty isn't always something that you see; it's also something that you feel—laughing out loud, dancing with gusto, holding hands with someone you love, reaching your goals, running through the sprinklers, taking chances, loving completely, singing along with the car radio, sharing your life with someone, knowing your kids think you're funny, and cannonballing into a pool. These things are beautiful. They make me *feel* beautiful.

As a high school teacher, I was always very positive, telling my students that anything was possible, that everyone has gifts to be embraced. As a mother, I have tried to teach both of my daughters that "beautiful" is not an adjective, but a verb. I've told them how precious their little bodies are, how awesome it is to exercise their minds, how a smile can change someone's day.

Until that day at the pool, I hadn't been practicing what I preached. Although I'd always been a cheerleader for others, I was never one for myself. Not until my three-and-a-half-year-old showed me how.

Beverly Tribuiani-Montez

On the Same Ground

Tena Zapantis

Customer Account Manager
Clinton, Massachusetts

My 12-year-old son, Nick, is crazy about baseball, but unbelievably, we'd never visited Fenway Park in Boston. For most baseball fans, that might be understandable. But we live just an hour away—there was no excuse. That's why I'll never forget our first trip there.

The magic happens from the moment you first enter Fenway through its old concrete archways. Handing over your ticket, you head down a few ramps and through a darkened tunnel. When you finally pass through that last doorway, the sensation is nothing short of amazing. The smell of sausages and oversized hot dogs. That enormous green lawn. Suddenly you're Dorothy in *The Wizard of Oz*, going from her gray home in Kansas to the Technicolor world of Munchkinland.

Seeing it on TV is nothing like the real thing, and for Nick and me, it was a hypnotizing experience. We felt like we were in a dream—a dream I could get addicted to.

As we sat in the stands, facing the giant wall in left field—the famous "Green Monster"—I began to wonder if all the other fans were as moved as I was by the spectacle before us. The sounds of the cheering as each player was introduced were overwhelming. Our seats weren't great, but you could see the whole park; and even though it was one of the coldest nights that spring, we barely noticed.

But there was another reason we'd made the trip to Fenway that evening, and that would be Pedro Martinez. We are regular churchgoers, but for my son the word "worship" doesn't mean pews and prayers. It means Pedro. Nick pitches for his Little League team, and to him, Pedro is king.

I don't mind this. In fact, just like Nick I get a real kick out of watching Pedro point up to the sky as he leaves the pitcher's mound. Gesturing to a higher power is a great example for my son. It's worth an hour in church on a Sunday anytime.

But witnessing the adoration in my son's eyes as we watched the warm-ups also took me back to a place I hadn't been in a long time. I was nine years old and I, too, had a hero. Her name was Dorothy Hamill, and she was an Olympic figure-skating champion. I knew everything there was to know about Dorothy. I was glued to the television set every time she appeared. I read books about her. I got my hair cut like her. I even had a Dorothy Hamill doll. Convincing my mother to sign me up for ice-skating lessons, I decided (at nine!) that I wanted to be just like Dorothy.

I remember one day in particular. I was in the kitchen with my mother, going on and on as usual about Dorothy Hamill. I was quite the Chatty Cathy. My mother was a quiet woman and not one to give advice. That's why I was stunned when she interrupted my babbling with an unexpected comment.

"Just remember, Tena," she said, "Dorothy Hamill walks on the same ground as you."

It didn't sink in at the time, and sure enough, as I got older my infatuation with Dorothy ebbed. But now, a quarter century later—and only two months after my mother passed away—her words came back to me as I watched my son watch Pedro trotting onto the field to stretch.

Nick was jumping up and down wildly, screaming at the top of his lungs, flush with excitement—so I spoke to him in silence.

He walks on the same ground you do, Nick, I thought, wishing he could somehow hear me, but not wanting to spoil his excitement. Finally understanding what my mother had meant all those years ago, I wanted Nick to know the same things:

That while it's great to have a hero, he should never undermine his own worth by comparing himself to someone else.

That our differences are what make us special.

That a Cy Young Award does not make a man great.

And that no achievement, no position, no accomplishment in life puts anyone higher than anyone else.

I turned back to watch the action on the field, thinking of all the things I should tell my son. But instead, I just sat in my seat, smiling. And in my mind's eye, I saw Nick, on the field next to his hero, standing on the same ground.

Tena Zapantis

P.S. Not long after I wrote this, two important things happened: The Boston Red Sox won their first World Series in 86 years; and Pedro Martinez left the team to join the New York Mets. Not surprisingly, my son's hero lost his shine.

"Well, Mom," Nick told me when I asked him how he now felt about Pedro, "it's like your favorite book. You can only read it so many times before you get sick of it."

I guess my 12-year-old is learning that most profound of life lessons—that all of us, even sports heroes, are human. And whether we're on the field or in the stands, we're headed in our own direction.

More Than Feet and Inches

Ruthie Just Braffman

High School Student
Bala Cynwyd, Pennsylvania

It was no wonder I wasn't looking forward to entering ninth grade! High school is well known for being a battleground, where everyone seems to be going through awkward physical changes, emotional mood swings, and low self-esteem. For me, height was my nemesis. I had always felt insecure and out of place as one of the taller members of my class, standing a head above the other girls and stooping at the back of the line to avoid sticking out.

I especially hated being around large groups of people, like during the social hour after services at my synagogue. Once the prayers were finished, I would leave as quickly as I could, just so I could avoid another well-meaning congregant squealing, *"Ruthie! Look how tall you're getting!"* Ugh.

My grandfather would watch me grow increasingly uncomfortable, but he didn't laugh at my self-consciousness or try to console me. Instead, he'd admonish me.

122

"Stand straight, stand tall," he'd say, as I unsuccessfully tried to shrink myself. And each time I'd sheepishly comply. Even at 15, I understood that his advice was about more than just feet and inches.

My grandfather grew up in war-torn Europe. When German soldiers occupied his hometown, the beautiful and thriving city of Tarnów, Poland, he defied them and eventually wound up joining the Soviet army to fight for his country's freedom. "Stand straight, stand tall" meant something else back then.

I trusted my grandfather more than anyone in my childhood; and whenever I was afraid of something, he would tell me stories of his life.

After the war, he boarded a boat for America; and on January 27, 1947, he stepped onto the dock of Pier 86 in Manhattan. He was hungry and suffering from seasickness. Alone in a new country, he was frightened about his future. Still, he marched head-on into the hustle and bustle of the streets of New York, and soon met other European immigrants, each of them trying to find their own way. If they could do it, why couldn't he?

"Stand straight, stand tall," he'd remind himself.

At first my grandfather refused to enter an American synagogue. He was angry with God for the loss of his entire family back in Europe. *What's the point of praying?* he asked himself. *Who is listening?* But soon he began to long again for the beauty of Judaism and the comfort of the Jewish community. He felt his faith returning. When he walked into synagogue that first time, he walked in proudly.

Standing straight and standing tall.

Thanks to the help of a loyal and trusting friend, my grandfather acquired a jewelry booth on Canal Street, the heart of the busy diamond district in New York City. He once told me how nervous he was on that first day of work, not only trying to learn this tough new business, but also a new language. To his surprise, the men in the neighboring booths—who could have taken advantage of him—offered their help and advice. Within months, my grandfather was commanding his spot behind his counter, selling diamonds and cultured pearls as if he'd been doing it all his life.

Stand straight. Stand tall.

In later years, my grandfather would escort both my mother and her sister down the aisle at their weddings. As he stood with each of them beneath the chuppah (the wedding canopy), he thought about their new beginnings and the adventures and journeys they would experience together. He also thought about the children who would one day carry on his family name.

I am so proud to be one of those children. Listening to my grandfather's remarkable experiences has changed the way I view my own life. His advice to me has become much more than a challenge for me to improve my posture. It tells me to be proud of who I am.

"Stand straight, stand tall," my grandfather said. And I do.

Ruthie J. Braffman

Saved!

Ted LoRusso

Playwright
New York, New York

W e are all children of God," said Reverend Donald Dipper, who paused, pointed a fat finger at his gathered flock and added, quite loudly, "except for the homosexuals among us. They are a cancer on the fabric of society."

Usually whenever Pastor Dipper bellowed about people being a cancer on the fabric of society, emphatic "Amens!" and "Hallelujahs!" ricocheted off the sanctuary walls. But that Sunday morning I didn't feel like shouting along with them. I was too terrified. Squirming nervously in my pew, I was sure Pastor Dipper was talking about me—and that everybody knew it.

I was being outed by my minister.

How did he know? Yes, I was struggling with my sexuality, but it was a secret storm—I'd spoken about it only to one friend. Could that person have told on me? Was it because I looked different—them in their prim Sunday best, me with my long hair, platform shoes, elephant bell-bottoms, and rings on every finger?

Or maybe it was just obvious to Reverend Dipper that I carried a torch for Timmy Jones.

I had met Timmy one year earlier in 1973, during our senior year high school production of *West Side Story*. He was a Shark. I was a Jet. Mortal enemies on stage, we were fast friends backstage. Timmy was lean, athletic, handsome—a blond, sun-soaked god. I was awkward, pale, a blob. I couldn't believe he was my best pal, and I feared our friendship would end when the play closed. But at the cast party, Timmy pulled me aside.

"Would you like to come to church with me this Sunday?" he asked.

Church seemed an odd place for a first date, but rarely had I been asked out, and never by another guy.

"Yeah, sure, what time?" I said.

That Sunday morning I waited at the curb in front of my house. In my fantasy, Timmy pulled up in a red Cadillac convertible, top down, shirt off. I hopped in the front seat, took off my shirt, and suggested we skip church, drive to my uncle's cottage, eat lunch by the duck pond, and go skinny-dipping.

Timmy pulled up, but not in a convertible. He arrived in a brown station wagon. He was sitting in the front seat between his parents. His overfed younger brother took up most of the back seat. I squeezed in next to him, and off we all went on my first date with Timmy.

I had never been to Timmy's church. Walking into the pristine sanctuary, I pummeled Timmy with questions. What do we do? When do we stand? When do we kneel? Timmy instructed me to sit, listen to the word of God, and follow along.

I sat, one ear attuned to God's word, both eyes on Timmy. At the time, my church-going habits were pretty much like those of most kids my age: zone out during the liturgy, and do what everyone else does. So at the end of Pastor Dipper's lengthy sermon, when people began filing up the aisle to the altar, I stood and followed the lady in front of me.

What I didn't know was that Pastor Dipper had just asked if anyone in the congregation wanted to accept Christ as their personal savior. Before I knew it, I had inadvertently given my heart to Jesus.

One year later, I was still there. I wasn't exactly connecting with the services, but the people were nice, coffee and doughnuts were served, and I liked being the new kid—the kid Timmy introduced to Jesus.

Best of all, my friendship with Timmy blossomed. We were inseparable. We went on church hikes, sang in the choir, carried matching denim-covered copies of the *Living Bible*. And though I never did convince him to go skinny-dipping, every Sunday, without exception, we sat together in church.

That is, until Dipper's damning sermon. The following week Timmy muttered something about there not being enough room for me and my bell-bottom pants in the same pew, and he sat with his family. After the service, he told me our friendship was on hold until I straightened myself out.

There was nothing to straighten out. Dipper was right. I was a cancer on the fabric of his church. Jesus and Timmy were not my boyfriends. I was excommunicated.

What hurt the most was not feeling vilified in church that day but being betrayed by my best friend. What's funny is, even though Timmy was the only person I'd told about my struggle with my sexuality, he never knew that he was the one I secretly desired. Or did he?

I suppose it doesn't matter. I gradually stopped being born-again, and after some soul-searching and a weekend at the Continental Baths in Manhattan, I became a devout homosexual instead.

I was repeating Dipper's fateful words to a therapist at a cocktail party recently, when something profound occurred to me. I should be grateful to Reverend Dipper and Timmy Jones. Had they not spurned me or called me out, I might still be there, living a lie and married to some poor girl named Dee Dee. Their words, though painful, were liberating. Despite everyone's best efforts, I was saved.

Ted Johnson

By Any Means Necessary

Ron Rey

Playwright, Actor
New York, New York

As a young black teen growing up in Brooklyn in the 1970s, I often felt silenced by my own self-doubt. Living in a white establishment that seemed bent on suppressing my growth and survival, I didn't have the knowledge to cope with the harassment and targeted abuse. So I blamed myself.

I grew up in a household with an absentee father; my mom was the family's driving force. I didn't have what all boys needed in order to deal with life's issues: a positive male role model. So I eventually gravitated toward those who gave me a sense of belonging, without paying heed to the consequences.

Perceiving society as purposely designed to ensure my own failure, I rebelled, falling in with the usual suspects, like gangs, dealers, and pimps. I collected money for the neighborhood number runners, making the rounds and intimidating those who couldn't pay up. But at the end of the day, these activities just gave me a false sense of vengeance.

I perceived society primarily in racial terms—and with good reason. For example, one day while waiting in the train station for my mother to arrive home from work, I was approached by a couple of policemen, who clearly looked suspicious of me. Despite my calm explanation for being there, they didn't believe me. I was guilty by reason of color. As one of the cops started flipping his book open to write me a summons for loitering, my mom came up the steps just in time to stop him. It wasn't only his abuse of authority that made me angry—he seemed to be pissed off that I was telling the truth. To this day, I still don't welcome the sight of policemen.

Luckily, I was also heavily into sports during that time, so in spite of having no father around to support me, I somehow managed to stay out of any serious trouble. I saw how the people around me—the gang members, the number runners—were always on pins and needles. Unable to trust anyone, they were consistently high-strung. I also knew that, even though I enjoyed the rush of our adventures, I couldn't continue to subject myself or my family to that type of lifestyle. And yet I wasn't strong enough to pry myself away from them, and there was no immediate alternative available to me besides sports—and sports weren't financially viable.

It wasn't until I was exposed to Malcolm X's autobiography in the summer of 1977 that my life started changing for the better. I'd be in the park playing basketball, and my friend would begin talking about Malcolm. The more he spoke, the less I wanted to play and just listen.

For the first time, I began to feel a real connection to a man worth role-modeling. Malcolm X said:

"We want freedom by any means necessary. We want justice by any means necessary. We want equality by any means necessary."

I was captivated. Yes, the words were inflammatory, and they probably scared the hell out of the white establishment. But to me the words "by any means necessary" were most vital. They gave me strength and foresight. They helped me to see our so-called system for what it was (and still is): one that will only bring failure to those who are weak enough to follow its design and manipulation.

Meanwhile, Malcolm's transition from unlawful activities in his younger days to cultural leadership later on resonated for me, because I understood that such a change required extreme discipline. Even though the mainstream media portrayed him negatively—suggesting that he was looking forward to killing white people, particularly members of law enforcement—I understood his message as one of defending our right to a life of fulfillment. The fact that he was true to his wife, his children, and the people who followed him showed me that, for any man to start a journey in which he leads others, he must first have a platform to stand on, and that he must maintain that position without wavering.

My own journey was a struggle at first. I severed my ties with the gangs and surrounded myself with people who embraced a better lifestyle. I began engaging in community activities that were positive and gratifying. I became an after-school tutor. I volunteered for block association clean-up projects. And though I was a teen father, I became a responsible one, spending quality time with my daughter. I completed high school, went on to college, and after graduating became an associate financial planner, working my way up to stockbroker.

But before long I knew that creating more wealth for those who already had it would never give me the same satisfaction as helping those who really needed it. So I started working as a counselor with at-risk youth who were perilously on the road to self-destruction. I'm proud to say that over a 13-

year span, I was able to redirect quite a few of them and even saved one from committing murder.

Why was I effective? Because my experience had taught me to know theirs. I often shared Malcolm's words with them, and explained what those words had meant to me. To these kids, I was living proof that as a young black teen, you must first learn from your mistakes; and then as a man, you must be there for others to keep them from making the same mistakes. I didn't pass judgment, but I did preach Malcolm's words.

"'By any means necessary' doesn't mean arming yourself with a gun," I'd tell them. "It means arming yourself with discipline, community pride, education, and financial freedom."

Malcolm's message still rings true for me today. I remain convinced that as life presents its greatest challenges, good men and women will move righteously—"by any means necessary."

PART FIVE

Survival

*"Words, all by themselves,
are so powerful and so life-changing.
That one word saved my life."*

A Silent Night in Vietnam

Stephen T. Banko III

Public Servant
Buffalo, New York

For me, Christmas was always in the music.

From those innocent days in grade school—where the nuns drilled the words of every carol in Christendom into our brains—until today, I have always found great delight in the songs of Christmas, in the power of their message and the unbridled joy they bring.

My most enduring memories of Christmas still sing to me. The holiday seemed so much simpler back in the South Buffalo of my childhood, when the annual pageant was followed by a cup of ice cream, some Christmas cookies, and an hour-long carol sing. It didn't matter to anyone that puberty had rendered the male voices in our chorale more akin to a pond full of bull-frogs than to the Vienna Boys Choir. The real essence wasn't in the voices anyway. It was in the hope and promise of the words.

Less than a decade later—half a world away from the well-scrubbed faces of my grade-school friends and a lifetime away from those sweet class-room sing-alongs—I would spend a far different Christmas under the strange spell of carols and morphine. I was a patient at the Air Force hospital in Yokota, Japan. That was the good news. The bad news was that precious few of my fellow troopers in the Seventh Cavalry had been that fortunate. After five hours of furious combat, I had lost virtually every friend I'd had in Vietnam. And now I was on the verge of losing both my leg and my sanity.

I'd been inducted into the Army on April 20, 1967. I was a typical draftee, expected by my family to go, with no questions asked. It was a rite of passage.

But I felt conflicted. I was the only one among my friends in our conservative Irish-Catholic community who thought the war was a bad idea. Living in Buffalo, near the crossing into Canada, I had walked over the famous Peace Bridge on many occasions to play hockey. I could've easily walked into Canada to avoid the draft and never once looked back. But I didn't. I went because that's what I was supposed to do.

Although I wasn't anxious to ship off to 'Nam, I was happy to leave the stateside army with its polished shoes and mandatory haircuts. That kind of discipline wasn't for me. A change of venue was appealing even though I had no idea what would happen.

We arrived in Vietnam in January 1968. I was a sergeant E5, an infantry squad leader in charge of 12 guys. Most them were 18 or 19 years old; I was 22. Compared to them, I'd been around. I often regaled them with stories from back home. Their favorite ones were about my Florida spring-break escapades. I had to tell those over and over.

But my guys also came to me with their personal problems. I became a lot more than their commanding officer. I was like a big brother, a father, and a teacher all rolled into one.

By the time we survived our first two battles, we had all become very close. I now had my justification for being in Vietnam: to protect these kids, to keep my men alive. As a sergeant, I made this my mission.

On December 3, 1968, the 368th North Vietnamese Army battalion ambushed our unit in a small clearing near the Song Be River. The first bullet entered my leg at 11 A.M., instantly breaking it. The second bullet hit at 2:30 P.M., two and a half inches away from the first wound. By then, all the medics in our unit were dead. They were usually the first to go, the bravest of the brave. I'd used all of my bandages on the other men in my unit, so the only thing I had to stop the bleeding in my leg was elephant grass. I bound my knee with it, and the bleeding eventually stopped. But my leg became horribly infected.

Only three guys from our unit of 12 survived. And from the rest of our platoon—40 guys I'd come to know really well—86 percent died that day.

My whole reason for being there was gone. I had failed the very boys I'd promised myself I'd protect, and I had serious survivor guilt. My kneecap had been shot off, I had shrapnel wounds and burns all over my body, but worse than anything, I was eaten up by the memory of those boys. I was emotionally devastated.

Through four operations, doctors struggled to save my leg and give me some semblance of hope. Although my universe had been turned upside down by the annihilation of my unit, I was uplifted by the care of the nurses at the 34th Evacuation Hospital, who were slowly working me back toward health. They had become my friends and were planning a picnic for us on Christmas day.

Then once again, my world spun crazily out of control. I was abruptly sent off to Japan where a new team of orthopedic surgeons would try to save my leg. My stretcher was loaded onto the airplane with the other wounded. We were stacked four high, and the plane was uncomfortable and noisy. I felt totally adrift.

When I finally arrived at this strange, new hospital at Yokota Air Base, it was nighttime. I was in a lot of pain. I was also frightened, not knowing if I was about to become an amputee. It was December 24th, Christmas Eve.

I was despondent. This wasn't just another day on the calendar for me. Our family always opened gifts on Christmas Eve, and yet now I was alone in the starkest, bleakest sense of the word.

I began to think about my life and how fate had landed me in this strange place. I was angry about what I'd endured in the jungles of Southeast Asia. There was no magnificent glory to losing a limb. This entire war experience was not the great romantic crusade we'd been led to believe it would be.

My feeling of isolation grew. The patients were not talking to each other, and the nurses didn't speak with us either. The only sound was the American programs playing on the overhead TV. I remember watching *Bonanza*. The Cartwright family was speaking Japanese. Everyone on the ward was fixed on that singular flickering image.

I became aware of the music just after *Bonanza* ended. Piped in over the PA system, it had begun quietly at first. Then it seemed to get louder. Finally, the songs began to fill the room like a gentle blanket of snow.

"The First Noel." "It Came Upon a Midnight Clear." "Hark! The Herald Angels Sing."

Bit by bit, the carols began to restore a tiny measure of familiarity to this very different environment. I could almost believe in "Joy to the World," and for a second I thought I could smell the fresh-cut fir trees of my youth.

Just then, I noticed a barely audible moan coming from the bed next to me. I'd been so absorbed in my own agony that I was oblivious to the fact that others were enduring the same pain, if not worse.

I looked over at the neighboring bed. The soldier in it was covered in plaster from the top of his head down to his knees. The only openings in the enormous body cast were cutouts for his eyes, nose, and mouth. His arms were plastered all the way to his wrists, with metal rods holding them away from his body. Slowly, I became aware that the Christmas songs I'd been enjoying—with their messages of hope and love and triumph—were being steadily punctuated by the sounds of pain and suffering throughout the ward.

I looked again at the man next to me. While others in the room screamed out in anguish, he could barely groan. I couldn't imagine what kind of horrible trauma had left him this way; what terrible pain was engulfing his body; what hopes and dreams of his may have been crushed by the brutality of his injury. As bad as I thought I had it—my leg shot to pieces, the burns and wounds, the fevers—I was lying next to a guy who had it worse than I did. I had to stop feeling sorry for myself.

I listened to the Christmas music, so full of hope and love. I knew my two Silver Stars and Purple Heart wouldn't mean anything to that kid. I wasn't even sure what they meant to me anymore. I had to do things in combat that haunted me. I had killed people.

My mind was wrapped around all kinds of thoughts, most of them not very good. At moments like this, the mind can't save you. Only the heart can.

Before long, the nurses came through the ward with sleep and pain medications. Just as they dimmed the lights, the beautiful strains of "Silent Night" descended on the room, closing out Christmas Eve 1968.

Silent night, holy night . . .

Suddenly, my pain and loneliness didn't seem so important. I asked the nurse if she could move my bed a little closer to the man next to me. She gave me a quizzical look, but complied.

I reached out and took my new friend's hand.

All is calm, all is bright. . . .

No words were spoken. None were necessary. That's the saving grace of music. Music speaks to the heart in ways that words can't. And in that moment, it spoke to me clearly. It told me I could still make a difference in one soldier's life.

For the first time that Christmas season, I believed I might leave Vietnam with enough humanity intact to start over. For the first time in a very long time, I really wanted to.

After a few seconds, I felt a gentle tightening of the hand in mine.

For me, Christmas will always be in the music.

Stephen T Banks

Bitter or Better

Judith Grace

Church Secretary
Hoffman Estates, Illinois

M y third pregnancy ended with an extremely difficult cesarean delivery of my son, and he died six days after his birth. The loss was devastating.

Throughout my pregnancy, I had been so up, so positive, so happy—all of which intensified the depression I sank into after my child's death. My sadness was compounded by the fact that my previous pregnancy had ended in miscarriage. This time I had been so sure everything was going to be fine.

In the following months, I didn't bounce back. My usually buoyant mood vanished, and I began to see the world as little more than a reminder of my crushing loss. I remember so clearly seeing a woman in church I casually knew. We had both been pregnant at the same time. When I found myself face to face with her and the beautiful triplet sons she'd given birth to, all I could think about was that *my* son, Nicholas, was in a cemetery plot. I actually felt physical pain, like I was going to die at that very moment from a broken heart. My grief was that staggering. A bitterness was growing inside me that I could not control.

One day, I got a call from Sylvia, a former neighbor of mine who I hadn't spoken to in a few years. Ever since childhood, I'd had great respect for Sylvia; she was a deeply caring person. She called because she'd heard about what happened, and she wanted to know how I was holding up.

Sylvia clearly heard the bitterness in my voice and in my soul. I was still so hurt and angry. I kept asking her, "How did this happen? Why did this happen? And why me?" Then Sylvia said something that made me weep. And I kept weeping even after I hung up the phone.

"Whenever something hurts us in life," she said, "we have a choice to make: We can become bitter or better. It's really up to us."

Bitter. Or better.

Almost immediately, those words began to carry me through my days. Rather than focus on my sadness, I knew I needed to respond to my loss by managing my hurt. I needed to control the anger I felt. I needed to *heal myself.* It wasn't easy work, but I set my mind to it, and each day I felt a little better.

Sylvia's words not only helped me through this wrenching episode in my life, they would return time and again through countless other ordeals in the coming years: when my beloved son-in-law died tragically in a car accident at the age of 22; when I suffered through the long-term aftereffects of childhood family traumas; when my husband and I divorced after 30 years of marriage. Each time I was given the choice of being consumed by tremendous grief and anger or seizing the power to choose the type of person I wanted to be. And each time I chose better over bitter.

It's been three decades since Sylvia first uttered those words to me, and I continue to pass them along to others, almost like a gift. I have come to learn that bitterness is like a soul cancer that spreads quickly, and that it can devour us bit by bit. Choosing to be better is the only antidote.

I have lived both sides of the bitter-better divide, and I can say with all my heart: Better is better.

Judith Grace

Within My Reach

Pius Kamau, M.D.

Thoracic Surgeon and Writer-Columnist
Aurora, Colorado

I was born and raised in tropical Africa. As a child, I walked barefoot among arid jungles and vast savannas. I imagined one day building bridges, just like the ones my family and I crossed as we traveled back and forth through Nairobi, from our ancestral home in the highlands near Mount Keyna, to Mombasa, where my father worked.

But when I was 14 years old, my life took a dramatic turn. My father, who had tuberculosis, became disabled and had to return to the Kikuyu homeland to be with the rest of our family. I was left in Mombasa on the Indian Ocean, living with an uncle. I went to high school for a year, but had to drop out when I couldn't pay for my tuition. I needed a job, so I began working as an orderly in a provincial hospital, cleaning bedpans, serving food, and mopping floors.

I'd had no concept of what happened within hospital walls, nor had I ever considered the possibility of a medical career. But six months into my job, I began taking care of a man who had been stabbed in the abdomen. He was in serious condition and required an immediate operation. I remember being amazed when I learned from the nurses that the procedure would allow his intestinal injuries to heal. My teenage mind was curious and impressionable. I asked many questions about the surgical process; I cheered the patient on, wishing him well each and every day. I cleaned him regularly, took away his contaminated dressings and linen, and proudly watched him recover. I felt like I'd played a role in the miracle of saving his life.

That's when I found myself actively dreaming of one day becoming a surgeon. I couldn't think of anything more magical than the ability to perform procedures that could save lives. That would certainly be better than building bridges, I thought.

Although the idea of becoming a surgeon was like wishing for the moon, fortune smiled on me: I was admitted back to my high school in Nairobi when my father agreed to finance my education by selling one of our two small farms. Given this second chance, I worked harder than ever before in my life. I had a tremendous amount of catching up to do and rededicated myself to my studies.

I finished school and was admitted to Strathmore College, a multiracial university in Nairobi. As a pre-med student studying physics, chemistry, and biology, I was at the cusp of realizing my ambition for a medical career. But tragedy struck. I was on the college rugby team, and one night after a match 120 miles away in Nakuru, I was involved in a terrible car crash. Four of us were in a Volkswagen Bug. We were driving up a hill and around a bend in the dark, and our driver, one of my professors, didn't see a disabled truck parked on the side of the road. We plowed into it and our gas tank exploded.

Flames shot up everywhere. My friend and I managed to get out of the blazing vehicle; but the driver and another white professor of ours died in the fire.

While my friend sustained only minor injuries, I had extensive burns and broken bones. I was taken to Nairobi Hospital—which was ordinarily a whites-only hospital, catering to Europeans—where I underwent a series of surgical procedures. I was in the hospital for four months. My first doctor there, an English surgeon, showed little interest in my future or in me. He performed a procedure that left me with a claw hand, on which one finger had to be amputated.

I was heartbroken. I watched my ambitions of becoming a surgeon rapidly disappear, receding like a ship over the horizon.

Fortunately, a team of doctors from America was visiting our national hospital, which catered to black Africans. I showed them my hand, and the lead plastic surgeon, Dr. Michael Wood, said that he could help me. He agreed to operate.

After the surgery, Dr. Wood came by to visit me. I was nervous. Knowing that the purpose of the operation had been only to repair my hand—not restore my dream of becoming a doctor—I asked him a question timidly, practically in a whisper.

"Is there any hope I can ever become . . . a surgeon?"

Dr. Wood was quiet for a long time. Then he looked over the top of his glasses, directly into my eyes.

"There are no guarantees in life," he said. "Remember, your hand is only an instrument of your mind."

His words breathed new hope into me in a time of despair, and they rekindled my passion for becoming a surgeon.

I began to use my mind to see beyond my limits. I created a rigorous rehabilitation program, choosing guitar as my therapy. I wanted to prove to myself that, with nine fingers, I could still do what any other person could do with ten. My hero was Django Reinhardt, the legendary guitarist, who had lost the use of two fingers himself as a boy. My guitar soon became a lifeline.

Today, I am a surgeon in America. Despite my former injury, my hand functions normally, and I am not at all limited in the procedures I can perform. But surgery is more than just removing or fixing an organ—it's also about compassion. I deeply love and care for my patients. I understand the horror of their pain because I have been in the inferno myself. I hurt when they hurt.

And always, I remember to tell my patients the same words Dr. Wood spoke to me so long ago. I remind them that recovery is always within their reach, and that the key to their dreams lies not in the dexterity of their fingers, but in the power of their minds.

A Single Word

Janice Ann Nelson [*]

Speech-Language Pathologist
San Jacinto, California

I grew up in North Carolina during the 1950s and '60s, an era of both relative innocence and amazing social change. In 1967, I was 13 years old and what I considered a normal junior high school student. I had good grades and good friends. My family lived on a farm, and I had a horse named Lady that I adored riding every weekend along with my best friend and her horse, Beauty. My friend came from a family with an extensive history of alcohol abuse. In contrast, I believed my home life was more stable.

Living out in the country, being raised in a household that adhered to devout religious precepts, I was isolated from much of the outside world. I was rarely allowed to be on the telephone with my girlfriends for more than three minutes at a time, especially if my dad was at home. And most of my knowledge of sex was from dirty jokes that were tolerated—and even

[*] The writer has chosen not to use her real name.

encouraged—within my family of four brothers and no sisters. I didn't even know what necking was.

My dad had firm rules at home and equally concrete consequences for any sort of disobedience. In our strict religious community, men were revered as the family leader, and not to be defied. Period. For example, in the fifth grade I got two F's, so my father grilled me in history and math every night, whipping me with a yardstick if I didn't know the answers to his questions. I got all A's the rest of the year. His rules worked for him; they justified his actions. But as tough as he was, he was predictable—and I have always relied upon predictability.

All my life I had adored my dad. He was big and affectionate. He liked to show me off at family gatherings, picking me up and holding me over his head for everyone to see. I loved the smell of cigarettes that permeated his clothes and hair, even the slightly perceptible line of grease under his nails.

Most Sundays, my brothers and I went to church with our mother, and sometimes Daddy came, too. Our church was a simple three-room building, nestled atop a wooded mountain. During one service, our branch president (the congregation leader) said a word that was new to me, yet was also somehow familiar. I didn't know how I knew the word exactly, but somewhere inside of me an alarm went off. I had a gut feeling it was a very important word and I couldn't wait to know its meaning.

I anxiously waited for church to end. As soon as I got home I pulled our huge dictionary from underneath the television and took it into my room. I found the word and stared at it. As I read and reread the definition my heart raced, and its meaning grew sharper and clearer. The word was *incest*.

I guess it started when I was in kindergarten. My father would have me parade around the house naked. The touching started when I was nine or ten, the kissing not long after. I remember my dad kissing me full on the mouth in front of the whole family at the dinner table, as if I were Mama, or a girlfriend. No one said anything when it happened, nor did they seem to notice my discomfort and embarrassment. It was probably too dangerous for them to admit to seeing it. My dad would tell me that this making out would help me to be the best wife I could be someday; and that he was teaching me. He told me that a lot.

Any time I was alone with him, something would happen, and as I got older, the action progressed. Never to intercourse—but to oral sex, which was just as bad, or worse. It happened everywhere: at home, in the car, in his bedroom, in the barn, in the parking lot of the grocery store. Behind the church.

Up until then, I had always thought my life was normal. Now I knew better. But I was bright enough to know that if I ever told anyone, Daddy would go to jail. Then how would we live? Who would replace the salary of a bank vice president? My mother was a housewife at the time. She wasn't conscious of what was going on. She had a certain naiveté about her. Beginning in third grade, I had a sense she was jealous of me. She yielded totally to my father so I knew I couldn't go to her to protect me. I even once asked her to tell Daddy to stop kissing me. She laughed.

When I told my father about the word I'd read I didn't address him aggressively. I pleaded. I said our relationship had to change immediately. Uncharacteristically, he did not argue or disagree or coerce. I had expected a battle, a full-fledged war. Or that he would rape me. But I stood my ground. Now that I had the facts, I knew I had a reason—a real honest-to-goodness reason—for it to stop. What we had been doing was wrong.

After confronting my father, I never allowed myself to be alone with him. Not in the car or in the house. Every time he came into my room to try to make out with me, I told him again that it was wrong. He kept trying and I always said no. Finally, he stopped. In fact, we eventually stopped having any kind of normal connection. He would not hug me or even look at me anymore.

Ending this secret relationship was the hardest and best thing I ever did for myself. I loved my father, yet he hurt me more than anyone else ever could have.

Years later, a therapist would tell me that my brothers and my mother had probably looked the other way in order to protect themselves. There was a lot of denial in our house. But I believe my mom never knew and still doesn't, so why tell her now and put her through that grief? Dad's been dead for nearly 30 years. He was diagnosed a manic-depressive, became addicted to prescription drugs, and committed suicide by overdose in 1977. He was 51, I was 23. In a note, he said that he'd lost all hope for life.

I never said anything about my abuse to anyone until I told my roommate in college. That's when I really found out that what was normal for me was not normal for others. My brothers only discovered the truth a long time after our father died.

The whole experience over all those years has taught me to be more compassionate. It helps me at work, identifying kids with their own serious problems at home. It helps me to be a better person, although I would rather have learned that another way. And now, for the first time in over 20 years, I can sleep.

Words, all by themselves, are so powerful and so life-changing. That one word saved my life.

A Serious Case
of the L.I.D.s

David Parker

Artist
Stratford, Connecticut

You know how people come and go in your life? Well, I can tell you from experience that, for those of us who have been injured or become disabled, chances are most people just *go* from your life. This is a story about someone who didn't go away.

Five years ago I fell down a flight of stairs and cracked my neck. For the first few months after the accident I was able to get around without too much trouble. But then my condition started to deteriorate, and I had my first surgery. Today I get around with a walker, but mostly I am confined to a power chair.

Robert Messore and I met a few years before my accident. Without a doubt the most gifted guitarist I have ever known, Robert knew that music was a passion of mine, and much to my surprise, he offered to give me guitar lessons. We continued them for a short while after my accident, but as my condition worsened, I had to put the guitar aside, along with my dream of playing it even half as beautifully as Robert did.

But Robert never forgot me. That summer, he came for a visit and, as always, brought along his guitars. He played for nearly two hours. After that, he would call every so often, just to check up on me. Robert was one of a handful of people who treated me the same way after the accident as he had before.

About a year went by and I hadn't heard from Robert in a while. One night I wasn't doing too well. I was feeling in a dark mood and suffering from what I call L.I.D.—Loneliness, Isolation, and Depression. I discovered that the best way to handle L.I.D. was by finding something to focus on. So I logged on to my computer and typed Robert's name into a search engine. I found a link to a local radio station and clicked on to an archived show called *Profiles in Folk*. That night, I listened to my friend play his music. While it played, I searched around the site and found Robert's song list. It was number six that took me by surprise. The composition, an instrumental, was called "Take It From Dave Parker."

On most radio shows, the artist and the host banter in between the songs, and I was fascinated to hear what Robert had to say about this particular song. So I double-clicked on "Take It From Dave Parker."

The words I heard that night allowed me to look at myself from a totally new perspective. When Robert spoke about me, he described a man who was instilled with hope, determination, and spirit. This was quite different from the way I had been seeing myself lately.

"Dave is always looking forward," Robert said of my condition, "almost as if he's decided, 'Okay, that didn't work. So what's next?'" Robert's words made me realize that maybe I could find that part of myself that he still saw, but that I had lost sight of.

A few months later I got a phone call from Robert. He asked me about the software I used to make music, because one of his students was recovering from a stroke and was feeling frustrated. In the course of our conversation I mentioned that I was having an informal house concert in a few days, and invited him to attend. Robert said he would be there with his guitars in hand, and he was. That night he played "Take It From Dave Parker."

Robert had the humanity to see the person inside my body. He showed me that true friends don't eliminate you from their lives, even if your disability makes them uncomfortable. They stand by you. They take the time to see you for who you are.

Robert's kindness helped me to realize that, although my life may never return to what it once was, it can be so much more than what it had become. The important thing is to keep putting one foot in front of the other, even if that's all you can do. And who knows, when you're not looking, someone might even name a song for you.

The Poem That Reached Through Time

Diana Michael

Health Care, Author
Coon Rapids, Minnesota

When I was 16 years old, I was raped by a classmate. I had a crush on this boy, so when he invited me to visit his apartment to see his new motorcycle, I was thrilled. But once I got there, he baited me into the garage and held a knife to my throat.

What made it even worse for me was that I lived in a very strict home. Our whole house revolved around religion. We had a prayer kneeler in the upstairs hallway where I was sent to say penance. I was taught that we were all born to suffer and to offer our suffering up to God. I thought everyone else believed as we did.

After the rape, I felt so guilty. Not only had I lost my virginity, I thought I had lost my soul. Sometimes I wished I'd let him kill me. That way, I would have gone straight to heaven as a martyr. I didn't tell anyone about the rape. I didn't even tell my twin sister. But the shame ate away at me until I began to feel suicidal.

One night I decided to take an overdose of my mother's barbiturates. I was gagging on the pills and having difficulty swallowing them, so I turned on the TV to distract myself. The comedian Steve Allen was on the screen in the middle of a sketch, jumping into a vat of Jell-O. Suddenly, I started to laugh—and couldn't stop laughing. I watched until I fell asleep. When I awoke early the next morning, the TV was still on.

Not long after that, my father bought me Allen's out-of-print autobiography, *Mark It and Strike It,* for my birthday. Inside was a poem Allen had written when he was a 17-year-old boy in Chicago's Hyde Park in 1938. Before I knew it, the words had sped 26 years through time to a desperate girl in St. Paul, Minnesota.

> *He takes a pencil from the leather jacket*
> *and writes a note of farewell.*
> *Suicidal and full of immature maturity . . .*
>
> *. . . Sadly troubled,*
> *he ran away into himself and spoke*
> *but rarely to his people . . .*

Further into the poem, Allen addressed my deepest concerns, the conflicting messages of religion. Immediately, I didn't feel so alone, knowing that this television legend had once felt the same despair that I was feeling. Steve Allen had not only literally saved my life by jumping into a vat of Jell-O, he was now helping me through his words.

Page after page, I learned more about him and how much he had overcome: Steve Allen's father died when he was 18 months old. His mother was a vaudeville performer who often left home for long stretches on the road. As a result, Allen was cared for by his aunts.

I understood the loneliness he felt as a teenager, his inability to connect with his mother. His life story helped ease my shame.

Shortly after reading the book, I wrote Steve Allen a letter.

"Don't get your hopes up," my dad said. "He gets thousands of letters."

But Steve Allen did write back, beginning what would become a lifelong correspondence. The first of his 33 letters to me was written on December 28, 1964. Eerily, his last letter was dated the same day, December 28, 1999.

Thirty-five years after I read his life story, Steve Allen wrote the foreword for my own autobiography, which included his letters. My book, too, is out of print, but maybe someday a troubled teenager will read this story, all about a poem that reached through time. And then, perhaps, the right words will save another life.

Diana Michael

Chew Your Water

Terrie McKenna

Nurse
Redwood City, California

D r. Death walked into the examination room. His real title was Director of the Cancer Tumor Board, but considering the news he was about to deliver, he was more Grim Reaper than medical specialist.

"Find homes for your children and get your papers in order," he said, explaining that my cancer had progressed in the worst way possible. I'd been diagnosed with five tumors in my neck that had been there for more than a year. It was all so ironic. Here I was, a nurse, working in the ER and surrounded by medical experts. But I was so busy taking care of everyone else, that I forgot to pay attention to myself.

Even before meeting Dr. Death, I knew I was in trouble—ever since that first call from my own doctor. When I heard her speak the words, "You have cancer, we need to talk," my heart fell into my stomach. I looked at my three kids and knew I needed to go outside. I remember lying in the driveway, curled up in the fetal position behind my car. I didn't need to hear another word from my doctor after that. She had lost me at "cancer."

After somehow managing to make my way back into the house, I went to my room and began making calls. It felt like only seconds had passed before three of my friends were standing there with me.

Still in a state of shock, I prayed that I could explain my diagnosis to them without losing it. No such luck. Once I heard my own voice make the announcement, it was over—the tears flowed. We clung desperately to each other, as if, God forbid, we would all drown if one of us let go.

My poor babies, now hearing this horrible noise, came running in, utter fear on their faces. We pulled them into our arms. My oldest daughter, then 13, started to scream, "Mommy, please don't die, *pleeease.*"

Looking back, I wish I could delete that scene. I watched three little lives scarred that day. And even though I knew there would be more tears to come, I swore to myself that my children would not be subjected to them. I tried to get on with my life.

It was around this frightening time that I attended a conference on Eastern medicine and met Dr. Lee, a Chinese instructor-physician who held my attention like a magnet. After class, he offered to give me an acupuncture treatment. This became the luckiest day of my life. As he inserted a cluster of needles into my arms, he kept staring at me.

"You smile all the time," he said quietly, "but your aura is very sad." I rambled on about being a single mom, having three kids with a deadbeat dad, long shifts at the hospital, endless guilt, wah-wah-wah. I was a basket case.

Before I could go on he stopped me.

"You do everything too fast," he said. "You need to stop that now."

He went on to tell me that the things I was doing in my life were all okay, but that I needed to do them in moderation. "If you do not learn this," he said, "the lessons will be repeated until you do. So pay attention."

I knew right away what Dr. Lee was referring to. Whether you study the Bible, the Koran, Taoism, or any number of life philosophies, one common theme is that life's greatest lessons are destined to repeat themselves if you don't learn from them the first time. The truth was, I wasn't paying attention to very much in those days. I was on complete autopilot.

"If you remember to breathe," he continued, "your health will be so much better."

Breathing? That sounded too easy. Then I realized that I *didn't* breathe properly. You must extend the abdomen fully as you inhale, and exhale until it returns to its normal position. I had been doing just the opposite.

But Dr. Lee's final words of advice were the ones I've never forgotten.

"Chew your water," he gently admonished.

At the time, I wasn't sure exactly what Dr. Lee had meant, but I knew it had everything to do with slowing down and finding peace within myself. I would later learn that Gandhi once talked about "chewing your water and drinking your food," but that had more to do with digestion. In this case, Dr. Lee was telling me to reconnect with the things I did every day, even if I was just driving my car, eating a meal, or cleaning my kids' room. Somehow, I needed to flip a switch in my brain and begin living my life in a whole new way.

"It's no wonder that the tumors are in your neck," Dr. Lee concluded, removing the last needles from my arm. "Your head is not connected to your body. You are two different people."

When my acupuncture session was over, Dr. Lee reminded me to cooperate with my doctors, and this encouragement made it easier for me to accept the brutal treatments I was about to face. I trusted him when he told me I would be fine.

The experimental treatments I eventually received in the hospital were effective, but I truly believe I am alive today because of the divine intervention of my Chinese guru. I call it a miracle.

As a nurse, I appreciate the conflict between Eastern and Western medicine, but no matter how a disease may be treated, the power of love and positive thinking are undeniable.

These lessons will stay with me forever. Stop. Listen. Breathe. And remember: Chew your water.

Jerrie McKenna

Nobody Dies Here

Bob Lenox

Musician
Berlin, Germany (via Brooklyn, New York)

In 1981 in a small town in Pennsylvania, I met a well-dressed man with a Polish accent who said he was a Count. A strange claim, to be sure, but why should I have doubted him? His whole manner was European in style, as he strolled down Main Street like royalty from another place and time, tipping his hat at passing ladies and gentlemen in a fashion of Old World elegance.

However, as our conversation went beyond initial formalities—as he tried to regale me with images of his big car, his big house, and his big money—I could sense something behind his bravado. I could sense the pain there. As we got to know each other better, I understood the reason.

At the age of 12, with World War II in full rage, he was taken from his family's chateau, beaten by the German SS, and sent off to Auschwitz. The cruelty he was subjected to there quickly took its toll: Within a year, he had lost his hair and thought he was going blind.

"One night I was lying on my bunk," he recalled to me, "when I suddenly screamed, 'I'm going to die, I'm going to die!' Just then an older man in the upper bunk pulled back the straw mattress, stuck his face over the edge of the bed, and said to me, 'Nobody dies here.'"

The Count told me those words saved his life.

I didn't get it. Millions of people died in the concentration camps during World War II. What did the old man mean, "Nobody dies here?"

It would take me nearly two decades to find the answer. I was living in Berlin. My wife went to work one night, and after feeding our three-year-old daughter dinner, I decided to start a little home improvement project. I was climbing down from a ladder when one of its rungs suddenly broke, sending me reeling backward onto a wooden chair. I actually heard my ribs crack and could feel one of them piercing into my lung, which promptly collapsed. As I lay on the floor I realized fairly quickly that I couldn't breathe. The lights grew dim. I felt a peculiar rush run through my entire system. I was chilly and hot at the same time.

I saw my life in Los Angeles and New York pass before me. I saw faces with names and numbers randomly appearing from my past. I heard a voice—a soft voice—saying, "Sleep. Go to sleep. You've worked hard enough. You've lived hard for more than fifty years. Sleep."

I wanted to sleep deeply at that moment, to slip into a place without pain. But then I saw a vision of the man in the top bunk bed who spoke to the Count. It was as if I'd actually been there and heard his words myself. *Nobody dies here.*

In an instant, I understood the deeply personal nature of survival, and how in my case, it was actually within my grasp. Fighting off the voice in my head that was telling me to sleep—and with what little breath I could muster—I raised myself just enough to see into the next room, where my little daughter was watching a cartoon and laughing, oblivious to what had happened.

"No, not here," I whispered. "Nobody dies here."

Somehow, I managed to crawl out the door to my neighbor's house, gasping for air. The next thing I knew, I was in the hospital, where doctors brought me back from the brink. My life had been saved.

A few days later, I asked one of my doctors if I could have died from the accident.

"Very possibly," he said, "had you not fought to stay awake and hung on to your consciousness. But you came to the right place," he added with a smile. "I'm the doctor responsible for everyone's care. And nobody dies here."

I couldn't believe it. He used those very words—the same ones the Count had spoken to me so many years before. In that moment, returning from the brink of death, someone else's right words had saved me when I needed saving most.

Doing the Thing You Cannot Do

Carole O'Hare

Homemaker
Danville, California

Losing my mother, Hilda Marcin, on September 11, 2001, still doesn't seem real to me. Although I knew she wouldn't live forever, my wish for her was a quiet and quick journey from life, without pain or suffering. Instead, this gentle and loved lady suffered a violent and horrific death. She was a passenger on United Flight 93, which crashed in rural Pennsylvania. Knowing the kind of person she was, I'd like to think that she was calm and peaceful in those final minutes of her life, and that her consoling manner was a comfort to those around her.

On September 11th, my mother was moving from New Jersey to California to live with my husband and me. She'd just retired in June (at 79!), and we'd been planning her move for a year. Since her death, my grief has been compounded by the constant reminders—on TV and in the newspapers—of the horror of 9/11.

Thankfully, I am left with countless, treasured memories of my mother's decent and long life. She loved a good party, had a bountiful sense of humor, was strong of heart and mind, and took everything—both the ups and downs—in stride. Over the years, she'd frequently recite a quote to me, a line spoken by Eleanor Roosevelt, a woman to whom my mom often looked for inspiration.

"You gain strength, courage, and confidence by every experience in which you really stop to look fear in the face," Roosevelt said. "You must do the thing you think you cannot do."

Growing up, I saw how these words spoke directly to my mother's character. But now more than ever, I, too, understand the importance of "doing the thing you think you cannot do." I know the emptiness of missing someone so deeply that some days you cannot imagine your life moving forward. I know how hard it is to accept the loss of a loved one to a violent act. And so I reflect back on Eleanor Roosevelt's quote as my mother might have done, knowing that the only way to overcome the grief I still carry is by facing it head on with strength and confidence. I do this by remembering the things I miss about her the most.

I miss her vibrant smile.

I miss watching her cook and sew.

I miss the way she dressed up for dinner, even if we were only going out for a burger.

I miss her voice and talking with her every day, even though we lived three thousand miles apart, and the way she ended each conversation with, "Love you, honey."

I miss our peanut-butter-and-jelly picnic lunches, sitting down by the bay, playing Scrabble, and walking along the water.

I miss taking her to the driving range, where she'd watch me hit golf balls and yell "Good shot!" even when the ball dribbled two inches in front of me.

I miss the soft touch of her fingertips as we held hands while saying the Our Father in church every Saturday night.

I miss greeting her at the airport when she came for her summer visits. I always felt sad when she left again; we'd cry and hug at the airport, and I'd watch her walk through the gate, thinking, *Will I ever see her again?*

When Eleanor Roosevelt said that strength and courage can be gained by looking fear in the face, she was speaking about people like my mother.

These days I try my best to look fear in the face, too. I write a newsletter for the Flight 93 families, which keeps us connected and helps me to cope. And on those tough days, I remember something else my mom used to say: "Life is for the living, Carole. Go do it."

Carole O'Hare

15 Minutes

Katie Adair

Homemaker
Foxborough, Massachusetts

I know now I am not unique. I'm not the only one whose world has been shaken by some unexpected event. But when you go through a life-altering experience, you really believe you are alone.

One day, I was a stay-at-home mom, rushing to pick up one of my three children from basketball or gymnastics and worrying about the right color to paint my front hallway and trying to be a good leader for my daughter's Girl Scouts troop. The next, I was diagnosed with breast cancer, out of the blue, at age 40.

Cancer? It was definitely not on my personal radar. The diagnosis stopped me dead in my tracks. In a single moment, the misguided delusion that I was invincible was completely shattered. My background as a psychiatric nurse helped me understand my situation intellectually; but the emotional realization of being the patient this time—facing cancer from the other side—was crushing. It felt like a death sentence.

Initially, I told only my husband and several close friends, who had babysat for my kids while I was getting this supposedly routine exam at the doctor's office. Telling my children would be much more difficult: My son's first communion was coming up in a few weeks, and I didn't want to ruin that. But how could I keep such a thing to myself?

I couldn't. Before long, my oldest daughter began to notice something was wrong. I was constantly on the phone with doctors, going for lab tests, and clearly distracted. Finally, my husband and I sat down with our children and told them the news. We promised not to lie to them any more, and did our best to keep everyone focused on helping Mommy simply get rid of her sickness. Luckily, kids don't track such things the same way we do.

Freshly diagnosed—and preoccupied with my new occupation of cancer patient—I tried to be strong for those closest to me. My mother had recently discovered she had lung cancer, and that seemed more than enough for her to handle, so I waited almost six weeks before I told her and my dad. I also needed to continue being strong and positive for my kids, my husband, and my friends and family.

But I couldn't escape the grief I felt at the loss of my health. Along with my everyday worries, there were moments when this new fear of the unknown became overwhelming. I would think about the impending surgery and about the chemotherapy and radiation treatments looming ahead of me. These thoughts would often strike in the stillness of the night, or during quiet days when my family was out of the house.

How do I live my regular life, I wondered, and deal with this new stranger at the same time?

That's when a dear friend gave me her simple words of wisdom. I'd had one of my sleepless nights and could barely think straight. I was feeling sad and frightened and wondering how I could get through the day ahead. So I spoke to Janis.

"Just take some time for yourself each day," Janis advised. "Allow yourself to worry, to cry, to grieve, but do it for a specified amount of time—like fifteen minutes, or a half hour, or even an hour. Get it out. Then put it aside for the rest of the day."

The words seemed so simple and practical. Janis, whom I'd known since our oldest children were toddlers, had given me permission to feel what I was feeling; but even more important, she'd given me permission to return to being myself during the other moments of my day—to be a mom, a wife, a daughter, and a friend. I had forgotten how to do that.

Before Janis spoke those words to me, I hadn't realized how much I'd been longing to get back to being just me—me without the cancer. It had seemed impossible to think of one without the other, and now Janis had freed me from my own demons, if only for a piece of each day. Of course, I still had my moments of sadness and fear, but now I felt like *I* was in control of *them*, not the other way around. I started embracing—not fighting—my feelings.

As my hair started falling out, I bought a fantastic wig and started getting all of these great comments about my "new hair." Funny, it *was* better than my own; and when I told people the truth about my cancer, they were shocked. But I knew I was going to beat it.

Three years have now passed since that April day when I was first diagnosed with cancer. Ironically, the closer I came to death, the more I learned about how I want to live. Looking back, I realize what I needed most was time to grieve, to come to some kind of acceptance about having cancer. In the midst of it all, a compassionate friend threw me a lifeline to help me through those rough waters.

There are days when I fear my cancer will return, and those thoughts can be overwhelming if I allow them to be. But thanks to my friend's words, I now know that with each new day also comes 15 minutes—to grieve, to think, even to cry—before going back to the business of celebrating my life.

Katie Adair

PART SIX

Friends & Family

"My husband didn't just say these words when times were tough. He also said them at moments of triumph."

The Well

Charlie Riggs [*]

Writer
Madison, Wisconsin

can't believe it!" Kathy announced, draining the last swig of tequila from her glass. "Not even in our fifties, and we're officially orphans! Just call me Annie."

"The sun'll come out tomorrow. . . ." chimed in Rachel, singing in her best pre-adolescent orphan voice. The two of them burst into laughter—and then tears. Only 11 months apart, my older sisters always seemed to be in sync.

Earlier that afternoon we'd buried our mother. She'd died in her sleep a few days before, exactly three years and a month after our father's death. Now, five hours, dozens of stories, and one bottle of Jose Cuervo later, we were still trying to sort it all out.

I hugged Kathy and Rachel tight, and didn't let go until their tears

---

[*] The writer has chosen not to use his real name.

stopped. It hurt me to see them in so much pain, but there was another reason I needed to hold them close. I didn't want them to see that I *wasn't* crying. I didn't feel like crying, either.

By the time I was born, my mother had grown tired of parenting. She wasn't an unkind woman, or even what some might characterize as a neglectful parent. She was just bored, I suppose. Formerly an artist of some renown, she'd stopped painting when Kathy was born, then gave up sculpting when Rachel arrived. When I came along, her career was officially a thing of the past. I remember playing hide-and-seek with my sisters in her little abandoned art studio off the garage, a small, dank room cluttered with folded up easels and dried lumps of clay.

But when I turned five, things began to change. With her three children in school, my mother started to paint again—then sculpt, then exhibit. Soon she was back on the circuit. If she wasn't holed up in her newly renovated studio, she was attending gala openings and seminars around the country. Between her and my father, whose law practice was thriving, they brought in enough money for plenty of child care.

As a little boy, I wasn't bothered by this. Mom came and went—that's all I knew. I guess that's the difference between children and adults. When we're small, we're better at settling for less.

The older I got, however, the more I began picking up little clues to the short shrift I'd been given as a child—things I'd seen all my life but never really noticed: the silver, framed portrait of Rachel in a cowgirl outfit, riding a pony at her fourth birthday party; home movies of Kathy's ballet recital, with all the relatives in tow. Somehow our family shelves lacked any real documentation of little Charlie's childhood, yet I managed to shrug off the personal injustice of it all. It was easier to look the other way.

Two days after my mother's funeral, I went to her home to box up her belongings. My sisters and I had been doing this in shifts, and my assignment was the attic. Sitting on the floor among six decades of memories—vintage clothing, cracked pottery, half-finished canvases—I discovered a crate stuffed with my sisters' and my old school papers.

Beneath a stack of yellowing folders were three scrapbooks, each bearing the factory-engraved title, *Baby's First Seven Years.* My mother had filled out Kathy's to the letter, chronicling everything from her birth weight to her first words to her first communion. Rachel's baby book was a bit leaner, though it still held an ample supply of photos and the occasional report card. Mine had been barely cracked open. Other than a page of scribbled birth stats and a wallet-sized snapshot of me as a newborn, the only memento tucked into the pages was a white envelope containing a lock of my hair. On the front, in my mother's handwriting, were the words, "Charlie's first haircut, November '67."

I stared at the envelope for a long while, and to my surprise, my pulse didn't rise a single beat. Just as I had done when I first learned of my mother's death, I simply sighed. Then I went back to sorting through her belongings.

But as vacant as my heart felt at that moment, my mind buzzed with persistent thoughts of my mother's life and death. Why had I felt nothing at her passing? How could I sit in that attic and hold in my hands undeniable evidence of her indifference to me, only to feel the same indifference in return?

Then guilt set in. Where was the sadness and longing? Was I a bad son? Had I been wrong for not doting on my mother during those last months, when she'd grown so ill. Kathy and Rachel had cared for her daily. Why hadn't I?

The next morning I scheduled an appointment with my therapist. I'd been seeing Dr. Copeland on and off since my father's death, but after a while I'd begun to think of my sessions with him as a self-indulgent luxury. Now I really needed to see him.

"How are you doing?" Dr. Copeland asked with a warm smile as I settled into my chair. "Are you okay?"

"Yes," I said flatly, "and that's my problem." Then I unloaded. I spoke about my discovery in the attic. I talked about my childhood. I wondered aloud about my mother's true feelings for me. I described the guilt I felt about not shedding a tear at her funeral and how I didn't feel the loss I thought I was supposed to.

Dr. Copeland sat back in his chair and thought for a moment. Then he leaned forward.

"The well's only as deep as they dug it," he said.

I said nothing.

Only as deep as they dug it.

"Look, Charlie," Dr. Copeland continued, "your mother, for better or worse, dug the well of love and feeling the best way she knew how. The fact that it's not as deep as you'd like it to be isn't your fault. The guilt isn't yours, either—*she* did the digging. Now your life is about digging your own well for someone you love, one that can be as deep and lasting and beautiful as you want it to be."

Dr. Copeland stopped talking and let the words sink in. Before I could form a response, our session was over.

I took the long way home that morning, winding through the farm country where our family used to go on Sunday afternoon drives when I was little. I rolled down the window to let in the spring air.

The Boy at Ground Zero

Paul Keating

Computers and Technology
Ashland, Massachusetts

My two boys miss their grandmother. So do I.

My mom, Barbara Keating, was aboard American Airlines Flight 11 on September 11, 2001. She was returning home to California after her annual summer visit with all of us. The night before she left she tucked her grandsons in bed and kissed them good night.

Three painful weeks later I went to New York City to visit Ground Zero.

Following the instructions of the Mayor's Office, I took a cab to the New York City Bereavement Center. National Guard Humvees blocked off the area, and soldiers and police officers were placed at every intersection. Those who weren't immediate family members weren't allowed past the first checkpoint. I had to leave my camera, show positive ID, and provide a special record number. I said I had no idea what a record number was. The guards told me that all relatives were issued one, and without it, I couldn't enter the site. They seemed dumbfounded that I was a relative of an airline victim, as they obviously hadn't encountered many "plane people."

My contact at the Mayor's Office finally got me through, and I was issued two passes to be worn at all times. One said FAMILY and the other, W.T.C. But instead of writing my record number on the pass, they wrote PLANE. I was an outsider in a club no one wanted to belong to.

Past the first checkpoint I saw a woman wandering around, carrying a big poster of her missing daughter. The sight was sad, and I couldn't think of anything to say to her. Did she really think her daughter was still alive? Would I believe the same about my mom, if I didn't already know she was dead? The disbelief I felt during those days that immediately followed September 11th was hitting me all over again.

After passing through more checkpoints and more walls of photos and flowers, we came to the main building. I was stunned. The interior had to be at least 200,000 square feet. Inside was a large family area with phones, internet access, counseling, religious support, and a free cafeteria. Representatives from the Police Department, the Fire Department, Social Security, and the insurance industry were everywhere. The Red Cross provided most of the manpower, and the Mayor's Office was in charge.

I was escorted to the back of the facility and given explicit tour instructions for our short trip down the Hudson River to Ground Zero. We were provided with flowers or a teddy bear to leave at the ad hoc memorial we would visit along our way. Accompanied by Red Cross counselors, a priest, and two Coast Guard chaplains, we walked to the boat, escorted by guards from the New York State Police.

Seeing that I was alone, the head of the Red Cross contingent, a man named Paul, became a special friend to me that day. He had lost family in the

Oklahoma City bombing and had come to New York City as a volunteer.

I noticed another relative traveling alone on the boat. He was accompanied by the priest and a Red Cross worker, both of whom looked worried about him. He appeared to be between 18 and 25 years old, but because he obviously had Down syndrome, it was difficult to tell his age. Paul told me that the boy's father had worked in Tower Two, and the boy had met his dad every day at 5:30 P.M. so the two of them could go home together. Every single day since 9/11, he had gone to meet his father, adamant that his dad was still alive. Even though his mother had told him repeatedly what had happened, he would not accept it. He went to the same spot every evening and waited there until 6:30. Everyone assumed he was in denial, but according to Paul, his simple explanation was, "My father is my best friend. He would never leave me." His words left a lump in my throat.

As we approached lower Manhattan, we couldn't see the site itself, as it was blocked by a row of the buildings across the waterfront. An entire section of one of them was gone; and on the rest of the building's facing, stray windows were blown out in no particular pattern.

The dock was completely shut off to the public. A New Jersey SWAT team, dressed in black, patrolled the grounds. Each of us was given a mask and a hard hat, and we walked slowly behind the police, staying to the right to let the trucks go by.

At the memorial just outside the site, we stopped and said a prayer. As we walked by, every construction worker, police officer, military personnel, or volunteer stopped what he or she was doing and put their helmets over their hearts. They stayed this way until we passed.

When we finally reached the site, none of us could take our eyes off it. We constantly needed to be reminded to watch our step, because no one was paying any attention to the ground. We stopped at a newly constructed viewing platform about 50 yards from where Tower One once stood. We were only allowed to stay there for five to ten minutes.

The sight was inexplicable. Five city blocks were destroyed, 16 acres total. Only a fraction of the rubble had been removed. Firefighters were on top of the pile that was Tower One, hosing it down. A giant crane slowly removed pieces of the building, one at a time. At one corner of the pile was a large cross, formed by steel girders sticking out of a pile of rubble. The workers never touched it, even though it was in their way.

We were escorted from the platform. I remained in shock from the carnage, as well as the knowledge that my mother was in there somewhere. As I turned to leave, the boy with Down syndrome was walking up the platform. He went to the railing, looked out over the carnage, checked his watch, and said, "Let's come back at five-thirty. We're early. He'll be here then. My dad is my best friend."

I cried for him a second time that day, and it would not be my last. The support staff was looking away and crying, too. The boy was oblivious to everything.

I knew a lot about kids like this. My mother had worked for ten years with people with Down syndrome. She trained them for everyday life tasks, to hold jobs, and to maintain their own apartments. That boy appeared to be on the same track. I wanted to think he was being positive about his father returning, that there was strength in his stubborn hopefulness. But I knew he'd eventually be crushed by the truth.

I made a promise to myself that day to reexamine my priorities. Up until then, I had been a good father to my own children, but what else was I doing? As I left Ground Zero, I told myself I'd try to be more like my mom, who had raised five children and spent her life helping the disadvantaged. I also promised myself that I would be more like that boy's father, who had obviously given his son so much time and love.

On the way back, we stopped at the ad hoc memorial. I wished I had known we could leave personal items there. I would have liked my boys to have made something special for their grandmother.

I left my flower there for Mom, and took away with me the image of that beautiful boy, still waiting for his best friend.

Paul Keating

That's What
Friends Are For

David Sanger

Drummer
Austin, Texas

After graduating from college, I took off on a 15-month backpack adventure around the globe. It was one of those head-clearing, no-regrets things you do when your future and your past reach out in a tenuous handshake. *Go now,* you think, *or you'll never forgive yourself.*

Halfway around the world I hooked up with a fellow traveler named Oscar, who at 50 was twice my age and four times as experienced. Oscar was a Hungarian-born, self-made American who had already retired from a career as a hospital administrator—this after surviving the bloodshed of the Soviet occupation of his native country, where he had been captured, beaten, and tortured for being part of the resistance. He had escaped to America where he told people he was from New Jersey, which was comical because he sounded just like Bela Lugosi.

While we were in Athens, Oscar used his Eastern European charms to fascinate a young woman we encountered, and she accepted his invitation to join us on our travels. Her name, impossible to forget all these years later, was Ankitsa, and she was from Yugoslavia. Ankitsa told us she'd recently been released from a Greek prison, where she had served six months for possessing a small amount of marijuana. As part of her release agreement, she said, she had to leave Greece. And so we had a companion.

Yugoslavia in 1982 was only slightly better than the Hungary Oscar had left behind, and Ankitsa felt the need to go home—this despite her doubts that things would change for the better for her. When I asked her what she would do, where would she live, how would she survive, she responded simply with, "My friends won't let me starve."

My friends won't let me starve.

What a thing to say. Ankitsa was putting her faith in the good will of her friends, absolutely convinced that they would keep her alive. Her logic was beautiful: She knew in her heart that she would always help her friends; so it only made sense that no friend would permit her to face undue hardship.

What she was saying was that she believed people are good.

Since the day Ankitsa spoke these words to me, I have lived by them. In fact, I converted a small room in the back of my home in Austin into a sort of halfway house, where friends could stay when they needed help. I used to refer to the room as my "home for wayward boys."

But women stayed in it, too. A friend once told me she was broke and living in an empty rental storage unit. When I found out, I brought her home.

"Come live in this room until you find a job," I told her. And she did. Not everyone can make ends meet all the time. Stuff happens in a life. Sometimes an act of generosity can change things for the better.

Then there was my friend Gary who had broken up with his girlfriend and needed a place to crash. Got you covered, Gary.

Judith, on the other hand, wasn't really a close friend, but she needed somewhere to live after getting out of jail. People make mistakes, so I figured I could lend a hand before she made another one. So I brought her home, too. I would not let her starve.

The shortest stay of any of my guests was three months; the longest, perhaps six. Meanwhile, there was also a couch in my living room, perfect for the quick overnight or two. Lots of folks took me up on this offer, as well.

I don't say any of this to brag. I just look at it all as a way of accumulating my karma points. "My friends won't let me starve" provided a kind of traction for me, a rule to live by.

As for Ankitsa, she was not allowed to travel through Greece to get back to Yugoslavia, so Oscar and I had to leave her at the Turkish border at 5 A.M. on a foggy morning. Very *Casablanca*. Oscar managed to get back in touch with her months later and reported that she was doing fine. She was staying with friends.

Grandma's Big Secret

Anne Shaw Heinrich

Public Relations
Dwight, Illinois

Yes, she modeled lingerie for Vandervoort's Department Store."

I've never been quite so delighted as I was the day I found out that my grandmother had once modeled undergarments. This small bit of information puts a smile on my face and a chuckle in my heart every time I think about it.

I learned about Gram's "racy" past from one of her sisters as I was struggling through the sad task of preparing a eulogy that would celebrate the life of this woman, one whose blood courses through me so deeply I swear I can hear it.

My grandmother died at the age of 93, just as I was returning from a ten-day trip to Australia with my husband. Before I'd left, I had visited with her, knowing she wasn't well.

"You had a good life, didn't you?" I asked her at one point.

"Yes," she said smiling.

"Are you afraid?" I asked.

"No," she said. "I don't think so."

I sat beside her for a while longer, holding her hand. Then I noticed the difficulty she had breathing.

"Oh, poor girl, poor girl," I heard myself say.

"Oh, I'm no girl," she replied. "I'm an old woman."

That was Grandma Shaw.

Naturally, hearing that Gram had died devastated me. Her passing opened up a huge hole in our family. So when it was determined that I would deliver the eulogy at her funeral, I asked her sister Margaret to tell me a little more about this woman whom I'd grown up adoring.

I wanted to get a bigger picture of my grandmother's life. I wanted to know and share something about the young Mary, the Mary before the gray hair and wrinkled skin, the Mary before me, the Mary before my father was born.

I'd known for some time that she was a model, and looking at pictures of her as a very young girl, I was not surprised. There's a snap to her spirit, a sparkle in those eyes, an amused look that challenges the looker to say something, do something, or get out of the way. To a hot-blooded young man of her day, that challenge quite likely packed an erotic jolt.

She was the oldest of six girls, none of whom finished high school. They came from a poor Irish-Catholic family in St. Louis; so at around the age of 20, my grandmother took up modeling as a way of supporting the family. That Gram would take on such a glamorous type of work wasn't surprising to hear. According to Margaret, her sister was extremely funny, sassy, and terribly independent. She'd tell you the truth—directly—whether you wanted to hear it or not.

When my grandmother and grandfather got married, they did it on their lunch break from work. They were working-class poor folks, so there was no big hoopla—just a quick civil ceremony, after which they went back to work and met up again later that night.

But it was the modeling that really intrigued me. Over the years I'd seen some charcoal and pencil sketches of Gram, and thinking it might be nice to talk about them in the eulogy, I asked Margaret about them.

"You mean the ones where she's wearing lingerie?" Margaret responded.

I was speechless. I had never seen those.

"Grandma modeled lingerie?" I managed to ask.

"Yes," Margaret replied matter-of-factly. "She modeled lingerie for Vandervoort's Department Store."

"You've got to be kidding!" I said.

"No, honey," said Margaret, now clearly tickled by my reaction. "It's the truth."

My first response to the news was pure delight. It genuinely made me happy. But once my laughter subsided, I began to wonder what made this information so special to me. Thinking of our parents as sexual beings is troublesome enough; imagining grandparents as their sensual selves was a place I'd never allowed myself to visit.

And yet once the cover was blown on Gram's lingerie career, it brought my understanding of who she was to a completely different level. I'm almost ashamed to admit it, but I'd never thought of her as a younger person with passions and struggles of her own.

Obviously Gram was comfortable with herself, proud of those curves and that face and that hair, all of which she knew would render someone— quite likely my grandfather—helpless. There's a picture of the two of them, impossibly young, sitting on the back of a pickup truck. They're dressed casually, enjoying the company of a few friends. They've got their arms around each other, her other arm resting lazily on his leg. And she's got that amused look on her face.

Although I can't be sure, my guess is that they probably didn't consider themselves parents that afternoon, the notion of one day having grandchildren seeming even more preposterous—something as far in the distance as the moon. No, in that shot they are just Patrick and Mary, two lovers on a hot Sunday afternoon, sharing a cool drink and the touch of skin on skin. I'd imagine they were also anticipating, even scheming, about a chance to be alone together, waiting for a moment to kiss, to trace a finger along the back of a neck, take passion for a spin—to talk love talk with their eyes.

That young girl in the photograph hadn't felt the kick and punch of a child from the inside. She didn't know the joys of motherhood, let alone those of being a grandparent.

And still I am confident that my grandmother was sure of a few things: that she could turn a head; that a cold vanilla Coke tasted good; and that there was something to be said for spending some time sitting with a young man on the back of a pickup truck.

Knowing that my grandmother modeled lingerie has changed my perception of time and deepened my understanding of her as a woman. It's prompted me to take stock of the years that have passed in my own life and the changes still to come.

There's something liberating about aging. It's made me more aware of how my children perceive me and the impact I'll one day have on people not even born yet. I'm imagining grandchildren and great-grandchildren and realizing all over what a blessing life really is.

We're given these miraculous bodies and a finite time on earth that promises moments of joy. Some of that joy we can feel and touch and hear and taste. The rest we can't even imagine.

My grandmother modeled lingerie! How do you like that?

Sassy

Patti Virella

Writer
Bronxville, New York

Some people have great memories of high school, but not me. I had no friends—no buddies, no confidants, no one I could really talk to.

I did, however, have Sassy, a beautiful, dark-haired golden retriever whose energy and loyalty were bottomless. She wasn't only my friend—she was my *best* friend.

Sassy and I shared everything together—ice cream, secrets, and tons of laughs. Whenever we went to my family's house in the Adirondacks, Sassy would spend hours running up and down the hill, diving into the river, then climbing out and sprinting back to me. She knew she wasn't supposed to go in the water, but both of us laughed each time she made her wet return from another rebellious swim.

Sassy and I also shared a secret language of looks and glances. One raised eyebrow from her meant, "Oh, boy!" (This usually preceded any task that looked like it would be fun for her, like my dad changing a light bulb.) Tongue out, eyes wide meant, "I'm happy!" And rolling over with her neck craned toward me meant, "Love me." I learned from a young age that sometimes unspoken words are words, too.

Among her many jobs, Sassy was my boyfriend-approver. When I was dating Brandon (a 17-year-old high school dropout who just *knew* he was going to be a famous DJ in a matter of months), Sassy looked at him, puckered her snout, and growled her disapproval. But when his best friend, David, came over, she smiled and begged to be petted. Uh-oh. Was I dating the wrong boy? Sassy must have thought so. So she was more than my best friend. She was also the protective big sister I never had.

By the time I was in my teenage years, I was, to put it mildly, a little difficult. My parents had divorced when I was small, and subsequent custody battles left me feeling very angry. I wanted a normal family. So at the age of 15, I was sent to live with my dad and stepmother ("Steppie"). They did their best with me, but I still felt discarded and desperately in need of being loved. I know I gave Dad and Steppie a run for their sanity. I am not proud of this. But every day I spent at school was more painful than the one before it. I couldn't break into a crowd—any crowd—because I felt so different from the rest. I spoke my mind; they spoke as a group. I read Charles Bukowski; they watched MTV. I wrote poetry; they gossiped.

So at some point I stopped trying to fit in. I sank deeper into myself and wrote poems about my life—good poems, I thought—that expressed my angst and what it felt like to be a square peg in a round hole. I shared these poems with my father and Steppie.

Throughout all of this, Sassy was there to help me try to keep it together. She instinctively knew how much I hurt. After all, she was the only one who would see me come home from school, crying from the hateful words shouted by the girls in the cafeteria who teased me about my hair, about liking Björk better than rap. About being *different* from them.

It's going to be okay, Sassy seemed to say with her big and hopeful eyes.

"What do you know—you're a *dog?*" I'd say back through my tears.

It's going to be okay, those eyes would repeat. Then she'd lick my tears and roll over for a belly rub, making us both feel better. On many occasions, she actually kept me from running away from home.

How could I leave her? I'd think to myself. *I just can't.*

By the end of the school year, things hadn't gotten much better, so Dad and Steppie informed me that I was going to spend a month at Bennington College in Vermont. The July Program at Bennington, they told me, was a summer camp that allowed students to pick their own classes and make their own schedule. All sorts of creative kids went there, Steppie added, many of whom probably liked writing as much as I did.

But I knew what "creative" really meant: *Weirdos.*

"It will be fun and you'll be able to express yourself," Steppie told me, standing in the doorway to my room. "And you do need a change, Patti."

My father nodded in agreement, making it clear to me that I was going, whether I wanted to or not.

I was not happy. I didn't want to leave New York and definitely didn't want to leave my dog. But Dad and Steppie called the shots, so I packed my bags and we piled into the car. As the skyline of New York gave way to the treetops of Vermont, I sat in the back, stony, not speaking with either of them and holding onto Sassy for dear life. I was scared again, but this time I knew I would be alone, without Sassy to lean on.

When we arrived at Bennington, Sassy leaped out of the car behind me and followed me to the registration desk where I picked up my room keys. Then she trailed me down the hall to my dorm room, staying with me while I unpacked. Was she checking out the place for me? I remember that she jumped on the bed to test it out.

Once everyone left, I sank into a funk. I began counting the days until I could be home again. Granted, home wasn't a very happy place for me; but it was better than being stuck out here in the sticks—where there was no cable; where crickets and bugs made strange noises in the night; and where I knew for a fact that I would never make friends. The kids here would think I was even stranger and uglier—both inside and out—than the kids back home did.

Then an amazing thing happened: Bennington turned out to be awesome. I got to try all sorts of things and decide for myself if I liked them (such as writing) or didn't (such as architecture, where my structures didn't have a brick to stand on). I learned that it wasn't a waste of time to try something and fail—you just move on. And, most important, I finally had friends, people I could talk to and laugh with and count on; people who didn't kick you when you were down. They *were* weirdos after all—*wonderfully weird* weirdos who did all different kinds of things. Like Teddy, whose architecture project was a model of an upside-down movie theater. We never quite understood the purpose of that.

But more than anything, these were kids who knew what it felt like to hurt inside, just for being different.

In those 30 days at Bennington, I also had an epiphany or two about the way I was living my life. I realized how much my reckless behavior was hurting my family and myself. I let go of a lot of the anger and pain I was harboring inside of me. I learned to be happy.

Throughout my time at Bennington, Steppie would send me cards "written" by Sassy, telling me all about her adventures back home.

"I missed you at Chapel Pond today," one of them began. "The water was so cold it made my paws ache. I hid under the bed on July 4th. I didn't like the fireworks." Those letters made me miss her even more.

On the morning Dad and Steppie came to pick me up, I was jumping out of my skin. I couldn't wait to see Sassy, and I kept anxiously circling the great lawn in front of the school, waiting for my dad's car to pull up.

Finally, it did. The back door swung open, and Sassy was the first one out, bounding through the air and tugging my father along behind her. At last, he let go of the leash and Sassy made a beeline for me.

I dropped to my knees and hugged her hard, and she gave many kisses in return. It was the best feeling in the world. Then I pulled back to look her in the eyes.

See, I told you it was going to be okay, those eyes said. And I finally believed her.

A Hitchhiker's Tale

Robert J. Simmons

College Consultant
Arlington Heights, Illinois

As a high school teacher and the father of five children, my dad was never at a loss for words when it came to imparting life's lessons. To make sure that his messages sank in, he would always attach a little story to each bromide. Dad was a great storyteller, an important talent for any educator.

I recall my father teaching me at a very young age about the value of making mistakes. "Very few of us live a mistake-free life," he would say, explaining that errors and misjudgments were a natural part of the learning process. Therefore, he'd say, it was my job to pay attention to—and learn from—as many mistakes as possible. If I did, I would surely grow.

The story that usually tailgated Dad's lecture on making mistakes went something like this: He once knew a good-hearted, six-year-old boy whose helpfulness was a joy to behold. No family chore was too small for him. One holiday gathering, as his mother was preparing for a big sit-down dinner, she asked him to go into the kitchen and retrieve a bowl of cherries she had placed on the countertop. Dutifully, he entered the kitchen and reached up above his head and grasped, by mistake, a bowl full of gravy. Before he could get a secure grip, it slipped out of his small hands and the contents proceeded to cascade down the side of the counter and spread onto the floor like an oil slick.

Trying to dodge the calamity, the little boy slipped, stumbled against the counter, and sent the elusive bowl of cherries sailing over the edge and onto the floor. Embarrassed and ashamed, he sheepishly returned to the dining room.

"Where are the cherries?" his mother asked.

"I spilled the cherries," was his response.

Rather than show disappointment, the mother smiled and wrapped her arms around her son.

"That's okay," she said consolingly, "it was an accident."

In the years that followed, this story became the standing family saying. Whenever someone made a mistake, all they had to do was openly admit that they "spilled the cherries" and all would be forgiven.

According to Dad, not taking full ownership of the mistake would have been the biggest mistake of all.

Basking in the warm glow of my father's wisdom was one of the benefits of being the son of an educator, but as I grew older it seemed to be more of a liability. Everyone in our small Western Pennsylvania town knew that my father taught biology and health education and coached several sports at the public high school. In other words, my life was an open book.

For example, one day during my freshman year I walked into my science class—which was taught by my father—only to find the announcement "It's a Girl!" written across the chalkboard. So my entire class knew that I had a baby sister without me having to say a word. There were some days when I just didn't feel like being "Mr. Simmons's kid."

My buddies used to tease me that I would never dare play hooky, having a father who was a teacher and all. Cutting school for a Ford City boy was typically an innocent adventure that involved hitchhiking to the local state park, then bragging to his friends about how easy it was to thumb a ride on Route 66. Springtime was the best time to go, when the restlessness of the school year was at its peak and the fragrant air hinted of warmer days to come.

Toward the end of my junior year, my friend, Chucky, finally convinced me to skip a math test and two more classes and spend the rest of the afternoon at Crooked Creek State Park. As we walked along Route 66 with our thumbs extended, the brisk April breeze felt liberating. With each new car that drove by, we attempted to make eye contact with the driver, hoping that one of them would feel compelled to take us at least part of the way to our final destination.

A white Cadillac zipped past us with its tailfins flashing in the sun.

A sputtering Chevrolet approached and passed us.

Undeterred, Chucky and I zipped up our jackets and forged ahead into the wind—until we heard the engine of a large vehicle at our backs. Turning around we began thumbing for a ride as a yellow school bus approached. It was too early in the afternoon for the buses to be returning children home.

"It must be a team bus," I told Chucky, with an air of authority that only the son of a high school coach would have.

The bus slowly passed us, and I found myself staring at the faces of the

Ford City High School baseball team. Sitting next to them was their coach—my father. His eyes widened, then narrowed, as he tried to focus on the two roadside figures that were rapidly receding in a cloud of dust.

I began coughing and trembling. Too embarrassed to admit that I'd just seen my father on the bus, I told Chucky that it was the exhaust from the tailpipe that had suddenly rendered me pale. But I was clearly distracted, and began to replay the incident in my mind.

Had my father even seen me? Maybe the bus was moving too fast for him to notice. Yes—that's it! Perhaps it could all be explained by some mathematical equation about a moving vehicle and a stationary object—and perhaps that question was on the test I failed to take that day.

Our hitchhiking adventure continued, but how we spent the rest of the afternoon is still a blur to me. All I could think about was what I was going to say to my father when I got home.

"We should do this again," Chucky remarked at the end of the day. But I knew that this was going to be the first, last, and only time I would ever play hooky.

Back home, my two-year-old sister trailed my mother in and out of the kitchen as Mom set the table and called for her four rambunctious sons to come to dinner. Freshly changed out of his coach's uniform, my father intercepted me in the hallway on the way to the dinner table.

"So, Bob, how was school today?" Dad asked. His tone was pleasant but there was a glint of suspicion in his eyes. I hardly had a chance to mumble a response before I heard his follow-up question.

"Didn't you have a test in math class?"

Before Dad could pepper me with any more questions, I looked him straight in the eyes and confessed.

"It looks like I spilled the cherries, Dad."

Suddenly, the stern demeanor on Dad's face softened into a smile, as he realized that I was willing to take accountability for my actions.

Years later, the story of "how Dad caught Bob playing hooky" was added to my father's repertoire. Told from his perspective—riding along Route 66 in the back of a yellow school bus—the tale became a family favorite. My own daughters would roar with laughter, envisioning the look on their grandfather's face as he watched his own son thumbing for a ride on Route 66. My hitchhiking adventure that day was not only the first and last time I ever played hooky, it was the last time I was ever embarrassed to be my father's son.

Robert Hammer

Just Enough of Today

Shara Pollie

Development, Urban Education
Bryn Mawr, Pennsylvania

In *The Lion King,* Mufasa, the father lion, explains to the cub Simba about the circle of life, and how we, as parents, pass the torch from one generation to the next. I remember observing my young son Ryan watching the movie and absorbing those lessons. I knew he would be on his own one day, and I wondered about what kind of person he'd grow up to be, and how he might approach new relationships.

When Ryan was 15 he wrote a song for a girl he really liked. That romance was his first introduction to real intimacy; but when the school year ended, she would be going away to college.

"I knew that you'd be gone," Ryan wrote shortly before she left. "I could never say too many good-byes."

The song was poignant and tender, but for me one lyric stood out above the rest. It was a simple expression of hope that the memories Ryan shared with his girlfriend would ease him through the hurt he felt after her departure—a plea, asking only for "just enough of today to ease all the pain of tomorrow."

I remember thinking at the time what a profound emotion that single line brought out in me. It seemed amazing to me that a teenager could strike such a chord in a grown-up. Ryan was using words in a way most adults never do, and I was deeply moved, as a mother and as a woman.

A year later my mother died, and each person in our immediate family was asked to participate in the memorial service. My assignment was to speak about my mother's relationship with her surviving husband, John, who was now 82 and very fragile. They'd only been married for 15 years, but they had experienced a lot together. When I spoke to John in the days before the service, he expressed a kind of regret, wishing that he'd had more time with my mother to fulfill all of the plans he'd had for the two of them. I had no idea how he would withstand her loss, or if his threshold of pain was high enough to survive.

What can I say to this man, this dear old man, I thought, *so lost and heartbroken?* Then I discovered Ryan's song again and knew right away that these were the perfect words to recite at my mother's service. And I did.

Ryan was floored that I used his lyrics for such an important event in our lives. Not only did this link him to my mother, but it also brought us back to that old idea of the circle of life: When we are young children, our parents take care of us. When we get older, our children respond in kind. Now, through me as the messenger, Ryan was taking care of John.

Just enough of today to ease all the pain of tomorrow.

When I spoke those words that day, I hoped they might help comfort John through the rest of his life and convince him that the time he'd had together with my mother was enough to hold on to. I was also struck by the perfect symmetry of it all: Ryan had been born just before John came in to our lives; John saw himself as Ryan's grandfather. Now here I was, taking the words of a 15-year-old heartsick boy, and using them to comfort an 82-year-old heartsick man.

One was just coming in to adulthood, the other gently leaving it—both of them experiencing a fleeting moment of innocence they would never see again.

Shana Pollie

The Greatest Gift

Stella Pulo

Writer, Performer, and Literacy Consultant
New York, New York

"Weirdo! Four-eyes! Clarence the Cross-eyed Lion!"

These were the names my schoolmates taunted me with when I was just five years old and the only kid in class who wore glasses. I had contracted rubella at the age of three, and as a result I was badly cross-eyed. When I was finally old enough to have the eight-hour surgery required to fix them, I started wearing glasses. The optician my mother took me to had only one frame design available, either in pink or blue. But it wouldn't have mattered if he'd had all the designs and colors in the world from which to choose. I felt funny and strange, and the teasing in class was worse than hell.

When my darling Nannu (Maltese for Grandpa) would pick my brother and me up from school, he would always know when I'd been crying because my glasses would be smeared. He'd reach across my lap and into

205

the glove box and pull out my favorite chocolate. Before he started up the car he would ask me what had happened at school that day that had made me sad.

"They called me weirdo!" I'd say miserably.

"Weirdo?" he'd respond. "*I'm* the weirdo. I've got hair on my toes and in my nose and in my ears—everywhere, except on my head!"

That's when I'd start to giggle.

"You're very special," he would say. "And like special people, there's something different about you. And different is good."

As a child, I really needed to hear that. Nannu gave me permission to like myself, to feel okay about not always fitting in.

My grandpa was different from all the other grandpas. He loved fishing and prayed in earnest to Saint Andrew, the saint of fishermen, that when he died it would be with a fishing rod in his hand. He could be wildly eccentric, too, in ways that often embarrassed us. He once came home from a trip to Kmart with two plastic, floral shower curtains and three yards of white tulle fabric.

"I'm going to make a fishing coat out of the curtains," he announced. "As for the tulle, I'm going to use it to keep the mosquitoes off of me at night! Don't tell your mother," he would add quickly. "She'll think I've gone cuckoo."

Cuckoo, maybe, but also the sweetest man in the world. In hot weather, he'd bring cold watermelon to school for my brother and me. And whenever we were punished by our parents for doing something wrong, he'd hide candy under our pillows so we'd fall asleep feeling happy.

It didn't matter how old I was, my Nannu always knew what was going on inside of me, just as he had in the front seat of his car when I was small.

And if he couldn't figure out what was bothering me, he'd simply tickle me around my rib cage until I told him.

As a teenager in a working-class suburb of Melbourne, Australia, I had career aspirations that weren't what my family or my teachers at school envisioned for me. I wanted to go to university, but that was something we saw people do on American TV shows, not in real life. My grandpa would set me straight, reminding me that I didn't have to be like everyone else—that I had the courage inside me to follow my own path.

"Do you know what 'Stella' means?" he'd ask. "It means 'Star'! And if you add an *r* to the end it becomes 'Stellar'—and that's as good as it gets, special, different, *and* stellar!"

Those words have always inspired me to follow my dreams, and when I moved to New York City I packed them up and brought them with me. I'll never forget how I felt when my Nannu told me I was special, as if this was the greatest gift he could ever give me. And it was.

Stella Pulo

Win-Win

Mauricio Heilbron, Jr., M.D.

Trauma and Vascular Surgeon
Long Beach, California

My wife and I always knew we wanted to be parents. There was never any question about it. We wanted to have a family, to *be* a family.

After a few years of trying to conceive, it became painfully obvious that nothing was happening along those lines. Undeterred, my wife and I decided to seek help, venturing into the world of "the infertile couple."

We underwent years of frustrating—and often humiliating—tests and procedures with nearly a dozen different doctors. The hormonal manipulations made my wife, shall we say, emotionally unpredictable. She bravely endured painful injections, surgeries, everything they tossed at her, and she did so with grace.

Still, time after time, while waiting hopefully for the results of yet another stupid blood test, we'd invariably be told, "Nope, sorry. Please try again." This was difficult for me, but unimaginably wrenching for my wife.

We tried keeping our efforts a secret, but when the bill for my semen analysis was accidentally sent to my father (!), the cat was out of the bag. From then on, our private failures became public and all the more painful.

After all this, we never received a useful diagnosis about our infertility, and all we had to show for our effort was a massive debt.

Deciding that enough was enough, we looked into adoption. At first, we were both ambivalent. For my wife the big question was: What's more important, experiencing pregnancy or having a family? She struggled with that for a while.

For me, it was little different. Both of my parents are from Colombia, South America, and like it or not, I was stuck in that whole Latino machismo thing. I often fantasized about what my wife and I could create from our own combined genetics. All of this kept me—and us—from moving forward.

One day, I was exchanging emails with my little brother, Max, who knew what my wife and I had been going through. We'd been writing back and forth about the adoption option, when Max wrote:

"Adoption is one of those rare things in life that is truly a win-win."

Looking at the words on the screen, I was struck by how insightful they were. Adoption *is* a win-win—a family wants a child, a child needs a family. The next day, my wife and I made a phone call to see an adoption lawyer.

The attorney and his staff put us at ease within minutes, explaining the entire process clearly and thoughtfully. Here was a lawyer who changed my opinion about lawyers. He was as passionate about his profession as I am about mine—to the point where it's less a profession than a calling. As a physician, I know the importance of making patients feel they are well taken care of. I felt we were in good hands.

We signed up to adopt right away. We were told the process would take nine months to a year, but only three days after delivering our paperwork, we received a phone call from our attorney: A baby had just been born, and the birth family wanted to meet us that night.

How could this be? We had expected to wait up to a year. We didn't have a diaper, a pacifier, even a bottle. But none of that mattered to us, as we raced off to meet our new baby.

The next morning we came home with our beautiful son, Benicio Andres. He was born on April 17th, ten days before his father's birthday, and eleven days before his Uncle Max's. He was the best birthday present any of us could have asked for.

Max was right—definitely a win-win.

Just Getting Started

Cynthia Harris

Church and High School Volunteer
Victoria, Minnesota

My husband, Dick, and I were inseparable through our 43 years of marriage. We were blessed with six sons in eight years.

Dick was a managing partner at a brokerage firm in Chicago. But the market crashed and the firm went bankrupt. Over the next ten years, Dick would hold 13 different jobs, delivering newspapers, working in a warehouse for Safeway, installing security systems, even selling clothes. As he went from one job to another, our family followed. We moved from Chicago to Boise to Denver.

No matter how difficult things got, Dick would always say, "Don't worry, honey, we're just getting started."

Our eldest son, Rich, was a competitive runner. In 1984, he went to the Olympic trials in Los Angeles. Dick was there, of course, cheering him on from the stands. He watched in shock as Rich caught a spike at the finish line and fell out of the race. Rich was devastated. He didn't make the team.

"You fell," Dick told him, "but you're just getting started." Dick was right: Rich went on to run the fastest mile recorded in the United States that year.

My husband didn't just say these words when times were tough. He also said them at moments of triumph. When one of our sons passed a test or won a game or landed a job, Dick would announce, "Hey, look at you! And you're just getting started!"

Dick was almost 67 years old when he went in for heart surgery. He never said he was scared or worried, though I did see him clench his jaw in pain once or twice. I remember watching the two orderlies wheel him down the hall to the operating room. All along the way, Dick was talking to them. "How are you? What's your name? Do you play football?" So like Dick. He was finding out about the lives of two strangers when his own life was in danger.

Just before they entered the OR, I walked up to the stretcher and said, "I love you, see you later."

"See you later," Dick responded. He never woke up from the operation.

Dick taught us all not to be quitters. He was one of those people who was born with the verve to live life as well as it could be lived. I can still picture him heading off to the brokerage firm, in his Brooks Brothers suits, shoes polished, perfectly groomed. He always looked immaculate, even when he was doing the paper route.

After my soul mate died, I felt lost. With a heavy heart, I tried to keep going. There were times I thought I'd never be able to go on without him. Then one day I heard Dick's voice in my head. *Come on, honey, you're just getting started.*

Dick is buried in Minnesota. I moved there to be closer to him and our children and grandchildren. He's been gone for five years, but his special words live on. The Celtic cross monument that marks his grave will always be there for all to see. It reads:

RICHARD M. HARRIS

JUNE 2, 1933

MAY 19, 2000

"WE'RE JUST GETTING STARTED"

Cynthia Harris

PART SEVEN

On the Job

*"My father's words had always been the right ones.
It just took me a while to figure that out on my own."*

Stacking the Logs

Frank Lunn

Business Owner, Entrepreneur
Bloomington, Illinois

Fathers and sons don't always see eye to eye, and my dad and I were no exception. Although we shared a name and a stubborn strength in our own convictions, we had different ideas about how to achieve success.

"Find a good company, an excellent boss and mentor, and keep stacking the logs until you retire," he'd say. My father came of age in a time in which the prevailing wisdom was: The older and more experienced you are, the more valuable you are to your company.

This philosophy clashed wildly with my own. In my early years of adulthood, I was constantly looking to get rich quick. Every time I'd start a new business, I'd swing for the fences and try to hit a home run, always inspired by visions of entrepreneurial glory and fame. I didn't recognize it at the time, but I was actually competing with my father, trying to prove to him that I could be an even better businessman than he was.

What I didn't realize was that my father wished for my success as much as I did. He cringed at the shortcuts I took, expressed disappointment at my rash decisions, and took every mistake I made personally. Each time one of my get-rich-quick schemes failed, he would repeat, "Keep stacking the logs!"

By 1990, the information age had dawned, and many people across the country found their job security threatened. In my father's case, his company was sold to its most bitter rival, and he suddenly found himself working for the other team. To add insult to injury, this proud, man-of-his-word salesman was shoved into new and unfamiliar territory, where worn-out shoe leather and a firm handshake no longer did the trick. He was also forced to learn about modern technology. Deep into his 50s, he was given his first new computer—or as he liked to call it, his "confuser"—which everyone told him would make his life easier. And like always, he adapted.

When I returned from serving in the first Gulf War, we became much more receptive to each other's point of view. I still wanted to run my own business and be my own boss; but now that I was married, with a child bearing my father's name, I began to hear what he was trying to tell me, and to understand the value of his experience.

I eventually came to see that, in business, there are no shortcuts or magic formulas—just steady progress toward your goals. Today I am the president of a marketing company, and I run my business according to my dad's simple but profound wisdom: that success is about a series of incremental achievements; and that, instead of banking on home runs, it's best to keep trying for singles, with the goal of getting on base. When you swing for the fences you often wind up striking out.

A few summers ago, with my wife and kids surrounding us, my father gave me a birthday card ending with his now signature phrase, "Keep on stacking those logs!" My wife had it framed, and today it occupies a special place in my office.

My father's words had always been the right ones. It just took me a while to figure that out on my own.

Passing the Test

Margery Hauser

Retired
New York, New York

Ever since I was a child I never wanted to be anything but a teacher. Even in seventh grade, when the class was assigned a "What I Want to Be When I Grow Up" essay, I wrote about teaching.

So when I graduated from Columbia Teachers College years later, I was thrilled that my lifelong dream was about to become a reality. However, when I first got my New York City teaching license, I was not immediately assigned a permanent position. Instead, I was sent to fill a vacancy—mid-semester—in a program that was being covered by a different substitute teacher every day.

Not the easiest way to start a teaching career.

Despite the fact that my teaching license was in French, I was in charge of a program that consisted of English, social studies, and remedial reading classes. On top of that my training hadn't provided any practical experience working with students in a classroom setting. And while the senior staff was friendly, they had no time to sit down and help me deal with the situations that all new teachers encounter.

Inside the classroom, things were even more daunting. Because the students had seen a different teacher every day, the first challenge I had was gaining their trust. Also, because of my almost purely academic training, I was having a tough time handling classroom discipline. In addition to all of this, I was struggling to make up the time I had missed at the beginning of the school year. I was definitely stressed.

When school break rolled around, I decided to go home to Massachusetts to visit my family. I looked forward to seeing my father, who had always been a wonderful influence on my life, particularly in the ways he encouraged me to broaden my mind. When I was younger, he liked to take me to a museum in the afternoon, and then once we got home, play classical music and ask me which pieces of music reminded me of which paintings. He was also someone I could always go to for advice.

So I told him how I felt.

"I'm exhausted and frustrated and worried," I said. "My dream is turning out to be a nightmare. I've wanted to be a teacher for as long as I can remember, and now I feel like a total failure."

My father looked at me with the same warmth and wisdom that I remember from my childhood, and then asked me one question:

"When do you feel the worst—in the morning when you get up to face a new day at school, or at the end of the day, when you get home?"

I thought for a moment and said, "At the end of the day. The mornings are okay."

"Then you'll be just fine," he said, with a big smile. "You're still learning the job and you're not doing as well as you'd like. Keep at it and you'll be ter-rific. But if you ever get to the place where the mornings are the bad part, that's when you know you're in the wrong line of work."

My father was absolutely right. As hard as it was for me during that first difficult year, I never woke up dreading the day ahead. This would remain true for that entire year—and 35 more. (And all at the same school!)

I passed my father's question on to many new teachers, whenever they came to me with the same frustrations I once felt. Almost without excep-tion, those who answered "morning" soon packed up their lesson plans and headed off to other careers. But those who answered "end of the day" turned out to be the teachers we all remember, the ones who came to school loaded up with bundles of props and supplies—and a healthy dose of magic.

These are the teachers who can't get into the classroom fast enough each morning. It's safe to say their students probably feel the same way.

Margery Hauser

Coulda-Woulda-Shoulda

Linda Roth Conte

President, Public Relations Firm
Washington, D.C.

Right now I'm looking at a note that tells me someone I work with is living in Coulda-Woulda-Shoulda Land.

As I sit down to write this, I notice that the graphic artist I normally use has left me a message saying she won't be able to do the necessary artwork for a major project of mine. She says it's because we're too close to deadline and there's a holiday coming up. She says there's no time to finish the work.

"We *could have* gotten it done," she says, "if you *would have* gotten it to us sooner."

Coulda. Woulda.

I will call her up and convince her otherwise. She has to do it.

If you've never been to Coulda-Woulda-Shoulda Land, you definitely don't want to visit. Trust me—nothing ever gets done there. There's never time to do your work. And things are always too hard. Or too complicated. Or too late, too risky, too hot, too cold, too everything.

And, oh yeah—everyone always seems to figure out what you should have done after the fact. That's where the shoulda comes in.

I first heard the expression in the early 1980s, when I was a young publicist working on computer exhibitions. Everything was done at a frenetic pace, and our shows' producer, Gerry, did not tolerate excuses. He found it impossible to accept reasons for why things couldn't happen, no matter how sensible those reasons may have sounded. Whenever I had to tell him that some task he'd assigned simply wasn't going to get done, his reply was always the same:

"Don't live in Coulda-Woulda-Shoulda Land. There's nobody else there."

The first time Gerry said that to me, it made perfect sense; and to watch him work was to see those words in action. Gerry could multitask long before the phrase was coined, and he was a gold-medal screamer, to boot— usually because something wasn't getting done.

But he never accepted failure, never let himself down, and inspired others to do the same.

Over the years, I've come to understand that Gerry was saying more than just, "Get the job done." In a deeper sense, he was telling me to live in the here and now, in the present. As a result, to this day I don't accept roadblocks—and if one does pop up, I just work around it. I think of Gerry's words and I go for it. I find a way to make things happen.

This is not a boast—it's a lesson in survival. When you own your own business you're not only responsible for making that business attractive, but you're also convincing people to stay with you—from your customers to your employees. To do that, you can't listen to the couldas and the wouldas and the shouldas. The front door is blocked? Find the back door. And if there isn't a back door, you need to break down a wall and make one.

An example. One December I was actively pitching a major account—the Krispy Kreme doughnut chain—to hire us to handle its publicity. It was a big assignment, and five other firms were being interviewed for it. I knew that my company had only one chance to make an impression, and our interview was just a few days away. To complicate matters, it was eight days before Christmas, so everyone was already in holiday mode.

Not surprisingly, the coulda-woulda-shouldas were out in full force. But I pressed ahead, creating a red-and-green doughnut Christmas tree, complete with Winnie the Pooh ornaments. Then, on a whim, one of my employees took the wrapping from a Krispy Kreme sugar packet, made a tiny paper hat out of it, and put it on Pooh's head—with the logo in plain view. It sounds goofy, I know, but my gut told me it was the thing to do.

When it came time for the interview, our entire staff—decked out in Krispy Kreme T-shirts—made a festive event of the executives' arrival.

We got the job. They say the little paper hat sealed the deal.

There are always a million reasons why you coulda done it better, how you woulda done it sooner, and how you shoulda seen it coming. But for me, it's always been far more satisfying figuring out how to make something happen than accepting any excuse for it not happening.

Which reminds me: There's this graphic artist I need to call. . . .

Sandra Roth Conte

Wanted

Gor Yaswen

Education and Training
Sebastopol, California

There they were, staring at me, three words I could have put together myself long ago, but hadn't. Could those words be talking about me, I wondered, right there in the want ads of a newspaper?

In 1975, after quitting my latest substitute teaching post in disgust, I was scraping together a living as a street mechanic, picking up jobs from small classified ads in the *San Francisco Chronicle*. Besides being a lonely way to spend the day, it was haphazard and degrading; and spending more time with machines than people only deepened my isolation. It was frustrating to realize that the only things I could be hired for professionally granted me no satisfaction personally.

But that night, perusing the want ads, I accidentally stumbled upon how

I might combine two unsuccessful pieces of my life to make a happier future:

WANTED: AUTO MECHANICS TEACHER

Now here were two things I had done—only not together. I'd been hired to teach varied subjects and grades in public and private schools but had never really gotten to *teach*, instead becoming embroiled in eternal discipline disasters (meriting, I thought, combat pay). I then turned to mechanics, but became tired, as one friend put it, of "hiding my light beneath Volkswagens." I was literally at the lowest and least creative vocational position I could attain, and anxious for a change.

According to the woman who placed the ad, the San Francisco YWCA Adult Education Program was seeking someone to teach urban professional women how to deal with the cons of unscrupulous mechanics, and in the process, hopefully make them savvier about their cars. While the Y might have been an unlikely place to find a middle-aged Jewish man, I was delighted with the opportunity.

The job was just two evening hours a week in a downtown classroom, and from the moment I began it felt effortless. I loved the job and my presence was roundly appreciated. Here were grown-up, intelligent women who actually wanted to learn something I knew. It was a whole different dimension from what I'd experienced in classrooms before. At last, I was really teaching.

My students were delighted to meet a personable mechanic who could communicate technical concepts plainly and simply. I taught from my experience, threw in funny stories, and sketched flicker-fast illustrations, leaving the women in my classroom audience breathless and the blackboards dense with chalk. I think the ladies were actually surprised to discover that an auto mechanic could know his stuff *and* be charming, too.

Soon, I added a hands-on, Saturday session to the class, meeting outdoors in the wide drive of an office building, with 15 students' cars parked alongside each other's, and my tools doled out for everyone's use. We spent pleasant afternoons there; and by learning to perform certain procedures on their own vehicles, the women all became less fearful of—and more intrigued with—their cars.

The classes became the most popular in the program and eventually expanded to another branch. But most important, I had become successful at something I enjoyed, I was being paid fairly for it, and people respected me. When this led to other, more substantial jobs, I knew that I had at last found that elusive and viable vocation. And while two wrongs do not usually make a right, my twin vocational failures, when put together, had become a success.

With little thanks to my own intelligence or initiative, I had been led to the right place at the right time and found a new career. And all because someone had placed an ad for something she wasn't sure existed, to find a man who had not yet known what he was.

What You Tolerate

Gerry Oguss

Business Owner
Northbrook, Illinois

I grew up in a *Leave it to Beaver* world. During high school, I helped my dad with his parking garage business as a cashier and bookkeeper. After graduating in 1971, I parked cars in many of the luxury hotels and residential buildings we served in Chicago. It was the only business I ever knew.

Then in 1984, at the age of 36, I took over the family business—despite my father's doubts that I could pull it off. For the next 12 years, I watched it grow into a respectable, midsized company.

On the surface, things appeared to be sailing right along; but somewhere in my gut I knew I'd been asleep at the switch for quite some time. Our department heads were being territorial; our clients were complaining; and the triangle of management, employee, and customer was not in sync—and I had confronted none of it. What's worse, there was no one I could talk to about this because I didn't know who I could trust. The Beave had lost his innocence.

So in 1997, I joined TEC (The Executive Committee), an organization of CEOs devoted to helping business heads sort out their problems. I attended a two-day leadership course conducted by a very astute man named Pat Murray, who within minutes of his first presentation hit the nail right on the head.

"You stand for what you tolerate," he said.

He kept on talking, but I didn't hear another word. *You stand for what you tolerate.* It was like he was talking to me. I *had* been tolerating too much, and in the process, my company no longer stood for what I believed in.

I returned home from the conference energized by my determination to rethink the basic values of our company—values that meant something to me. I shared Pat Murray's words with my wife, Barbara, who had recently rejoined our staff, and together, we came up with a blueprint for how the company should run: Whether business was up or down, our priorities would be fair treatment, honesty, respect, and integrity—a philosophy that, we believe, is the cornerstone of any excellent business.

Back at work, I was eager to share this new strategy with my CFO. I read her the list Barbara and I had drawn up.

"You know I share those values, don't you?" she said to me when I finished reading.

"No, I don't know," I responded. "Do you think fairness, honesty, and respect should be the guiding principles of our company?"

"Of course I do," she replied, "unless it's not in the best interest of the company."

Unless it's not in the best interest of our company? I knew then that my chief financial officer and I didn't have the same company in mind.

You stand for what you tolerate, Pat Murray's voice said in my head. Soon after that, I let my CFO go.

Over time I made additional adjustments to our management and staff. Barbara became the head of human resources, where she acted as the company's official gatekeeper, hiring only those individuals who shared our values. As business improved, Barbara and I turned our attention to our personal life, applying the same stand-for-what-you-tolerate philosophy. Together, we spent countless hours talking about what really mattered to us, not only as a couple, but as parents, as well. We had been married 25 years, but until that point, I don't believe we ever shared such meaningful thoughts. What had always been a good marriage became a much deeper one.

Relationships are never easy, whether they are family, business, or friends. But that simple idea, "You stand for what you tolerate," has positively affected my relationship with my wife, my business, and my children and grandchildren.

Not bad for just six words.

Truck No.15

Bert Goolsby

Legal
Columbia, South Carolina

They tell us that love comes in various forms. One of those forms is tough love—and when you're on the receiving end of it, you never forget it.

Take the case of my younger brother, Tommy. He was a happy-go-lucky guy, the kind of fellow people immediately took a liking to the moment they met him.

After graduating from Dothan High School, Tommy headed off for the University of Alabama. He played in the Million Dollar Band, played the field with the girls, played the fool with his fraternity brothers, and played at studying—little realizing that all along he was playing with fire.

A day of reckoning came in the form of final examinations. After taking his last exam and attending his last Christmas party—where he had a really good time—he took the Greyhound bus home to spend the holiday season with our parents and as many former high school buddies as he could round up. He had hoped to get home before his grades got there.

He didn't quite make it. They had arrived that very morning.

When Tommy knocked on the front door of our house, Mother was already standing there, holding his grade report in her hand. She promptly told Tommy that our father wanted to see him right away, down at the Pepsi-Cola Bottling Plant where Dad worked as superintendent.

When Tommy got there, Dad, who had only a fifth-grade education, took him outside to the parking lot and pointed to Truck No. 15, the company's oldest delivery vehicle still in use. Unlike the newer models, Truck No. 15 had racks rather than compartments to hold its cases of Pepsi and other soft drinks. It could be loaded and unloaded only by hand.

"Truck Number Fifteen," Dad said to Tommy. "See it?"

Tommy nodded, not quite grasping the meaning of Dad's question. During the summer, when we were high schoolers, we had always worked *inside* the plant, not outside doing deliveries. That was a hot, demanding job and Tommy had no concept of what it took.

"Yes, sir," Tommy said, never taking his eyes off Truck No. 15. "What about it?"

"What *about* it?" Dad asked. "I'll tell you what about it—and I suggest you listen real good. If you don't get them grades of yours up, you gonna be driving that truck. That one right there. Truck Number Fifteen. Got me?"

Tommy mumbled something and made a face. He probably figured our father was kidding, because driving that particular old truck was about the lowest thing anyone could do, especially on a hot summertime route.

"Okay," Dad said, "I done warned you."

Tommy returned to the university for the spring semester. His grades showed some improvement, but not much. Obviously, he didn't take Dad's warning very seriously, figuring that our father would never follow through. When he came home for the summer, Dad took him to the plant and handed him off to the sales manager, who escorted Tommy outside. Tommy was stunned.

"There you go, Tommy," the sales manager said with a laugh, gesturing to Truck No. 15. "She's all yours."

Tommy took a long look at the truck, and then back again at the sales manager. "What about my helper?" he asked. "Where's he?"

The sales manager laughed again. "That truck ain't got no helper. We only use it in the summertime for routes like you gonna be running."

And run he did. All summer long Tommy sat in the hot, grimy cab of Truck No. 15, driving down dusty country roads and blistering asphalt highways, carrying soft drinks to stores and other retail dealers, then gathering up their empty bottles and crates. He labored long hours in the scorching South Alabama heat, which is about 20 degrees hotter than *hotter 'n hell*.

Tommy worked his route from six o'clock in the morning to ten or eleven at night. When he finished, he'd have to unload the empties from Truck No. 15 and then reload it with full cases of drinks. And he would have to do it all by himself. Finally, before he could go home to rest for the evening—or what was left of it—he had to account for all the drinks he had sold that day and the money he'd taken in. By the time he got home, he was often too tired to eat or sleep—6 A.M. always, always came early, no matter what time he got to bed.

In the fall, when it was time to return to Tuscaloosa, Dad told Tommy he was proud of the work he had done at the plant that summer but now he had an opportunity to get the education he'd never had the chance to get for himself. That school year Tommy earned A's and B's. With all that he got from his studies that term, I think he also realized that there was something he learned from our father, as well.

Tommy graduated from the University of Alabama and enjoyed a successful career in business, designing and manufacturing carpets and accent rugs. In 1990, he became president of the University of Alabama National Alumni Association.

To what does Tommy attribute his success? The words first spoken to him by our father that winter day in 1956:

"Truck Number Fifteen."

Burt Brooksby

Love at Work

Ruth B. Spiro

Writer and Homemaker
Deerfield, Illinois

graduated from college in the mid-1980s, just in time for the economy to take a tumble. With no real job prospects on the horizon, I took a position as a secretary at a large advertising agency, hoping to get my foot in the door. Most of my co-workers there were young and single, and we often socialized during our lunch breaks or after work. Many of them were settled into their jobs and satisfied to stay put. Not me. I believed my job was only a stepping stone to a better one. And I worked very hard to prove myself.

To my delight, within a year I was promoted to a new position. The problem was, now I was supervising the secretaries who had previously been my peers. Some were resentful, and worse, others expected that the friendship and camaraderie we had enjoyed would now exempt them from being held accountable for their work. I quickly grew frustrated, trying to work both sides of the fence.

All of this made me uncomfortable with my new authority, and I became ineffective in my job. I was quickly losing my friends and angry with myself for not being able to manage it well enough. How could I do the job without them hating me? How could I earn their respect and not their resentment? I was clearly in a no-win situation and failing on all fronts.

To help me get a handle on my new responsibilities, the department manager enrolled me in a professional development course to improve my supervisory skills. Sitting in the stuffy, windowless classroom, I had difficulty concentrating. The class was dull, and most of the participants were middle-aged men in jobs vastly different from mine. They couldn't possibly relate to my situation, I thought. Meanwhile, I was anxious about being out of the office during a busy time and worrying about what might be happening in my absence.

On the second day of the class, I received a message to call my office immediately. To my surprise, I learned that my immediate supervisor had been laid off, and that when I returned to the office, I would assume her responsibilities in addition to my own. I couldn't believe this was happening. Here I was trying to get a handle on the changing dynamics I already had in my job, and with this news, my situation had turned from bad to worse.

When I walked back into the classroom, I slumped into a chair at the back of the room, next to a gray-haired gentleman who was in sales. Noticing the look of distress on my face, he asked what was troubling me, and I told him the story about how my relationships with my co-workers had deteriorated with my promotion, and how I had no idea how to change things.

The man listened attentively as the words—and tears—flowed out of me. When I finished, he offered a piece of advice that would change the course of my career.

"Find something to love about each person," he began. "It might be difficult to discover—and it might be something very small—but I promise you this: If you look hard enough, you can find one thing to love in everyone. And once you do, you'll be able to figure out the best way to work with each of them."

The comment threw me for a loop. First of all, the man looked like he should be sitting in a boardroom discussing pension plans, not talking about loving people. More important, when I thought about what he said, I realized I'd been doing the exact opposite. I had been looking at each person in my department not as someone to love, but as a problem to be solved, an obstacle to overcome. If nothing else, the man's words gave me an assignment that I could immediately put to the test.

When I returned to my office, I did exactly what he proposed, searching for something to love in each of the people I'd considered so difficult.

The strategy worked like a charm. For example, one of our secretaries was particularly unproductive. But the more I thought about her, the more I realized that she was actually sad about having to leave her new baby at home with a sitter while she came to work. So instead of letting her inefficiency bother me, I chose to love her emotional attachment to her child. Pretty soon I discovered that if I showed interest in the new photos she displayed on her desk (almost daily!), she became much more pleasant and cooperative—not to mention productive.

Then I turned my attention to another colleague, an overly demanding account executive whose severity made him unpleasant to work with. But I had always been impressed with his commitment to his job. So I decided to love the passion he had for his job, and once I did, I came up with the idea of reassigning him a secretary with a similar work ethic. This improved our relationship, he worked better, and it made everyone around him a lot happier.

The most challenging task was finding something to love about the department manager. This was the woman who had been responsible for firing my immediate supervisor (a single mother with a young son to support), so there wasn't a lot there to love, if you know what I mean. Still, I eventually learned that she had a fascination with Barry Manilow! And because I enjoyed his music, too, I decided to make this the thing to love about her. Although I never quite trusted her entirely, whenever I felt uneasy in her presence, I simply imagined her dancing to "Copacabana," which, if nothing else, helped me to relax.

What I learned from all of this (not only at work, but in my personal life, too) is that no one is a 100 percent difficult person. If we take a moment to look for the better part of someone's nature, everybody benefits. We not only help ourselves, but also possibly help someone else become the best they can be.

I never learned the name of the man who gave me the advice that day in the windowless classroom and never had the opportunity to thank him for his invaluable words. But it's easy for me to remember what I love about him.

Ruth B. Spiro

Shirkaholic

John Donohue

Electrical Engineer
Southbury, Connecticut

My dad was a man's man, a World War II vet who had fought at Okinawa. He liked to go out with the guys and have a good time, then come home and relax, maybe do his hobbies. He enjoyed building things, like electronics projects and the big train set we had up in the attic. He was good with his hands.

When we were growing up, Dad worked as an engineer for a radio station that played big band music. That was his era. As a father, he was sometimes stern, sometimes good-natured, and he liked to play catch with my brother and me in the backyard. Unfortunately, I wasn't very athletic, and the ball spent less time in my glove than it did hitting me in the mouth.

My mother was more of a taskmaster, and would often get on Dad's case to do things around the house. She believed in that old work ethic: If dinner was over and it was still light outside, there was more work to be done. She came from a Pennsylvania Dutch family and had grown up on a farm, so her specialty was the garden—planting and watering and weeding. My father, a Brooklyn boy, was far less involved with growing things and limited his yard work to mowing the lawn and trimming the hedges.

One day when I was nine years old, my mother told my father to trim the hedges after dinner. Not exactly thrilled about the assignment, he roped me into lending a hand. As usual, he'd do the actual trimming, leaving it to me to pick up the cut branches and put them in the trashcan.

On this particular day, though, the hedge was a hawthorn bush with little red berries. It had the longest, sharpest, nastiest thorns in our yard, and even when I wore my mother's best nubby garden gloves, it was still nearly impossible to pick up a branch without getting stabbed.

I immediately began strategizing a way to get out of the job, carefully weighing the words in my head. I was precocious for my age and had a pretty good vocabulary. I read constantly—everything I could get my hands on. So while my dad trimmed the hedge, I took a deep breath and started describing to him the many reasons I wouldn't be available to help him today. I already had too many demands on my young life, I said—school, church, Sunday school, church choir, Cub Scouts, piano lessons, and of course, all of Mom's chores. Surely this new task—collecting those evil hawthorn branches—was one chore too many.

As my little speech wound down, I rummaged through my vocabulary for a final comment: "I believe I have too many responsibilities," I concluded.

Looking back, I genuinely expected my father to be impressed with my command of the language at such an early age. I was certain he'd tell me to stop working immediately, take off the gloves, and go on to enjoy a carefree life.

Not quite. "Shut up and get to work," he grumbled. He didn't even look at me when he said it.

I recall being sort of stunned, staring at the back of his head as he continued trimming the bushes. This whole little edifice that I had created for myself suddenly came tumbling down. Not only hadn't my father been remotely convinced by the logic of my argument, he completely ignored it.

I remember this story whenever I'm feeling sorry for myself, like the time we had a new baby in the house, my wife's mother was sick, and a lot was going on in my life. I was feeling overwhelmed and was tempted to complain. But Dad's words came echoing back and stopped me in my tracks.

Expressing yourself is a good thing. Talking about your feelings is important, too. But sometimes you just have to shut up and get to work.

John Donvan

PART EIGHT

Love & Romance

*"I remember thinking that my mother's
advice was somewhat negative.
Then I got married, and began to understand."*

Falling for Charlie

Janet Guillet

Advertising Copywriter
New York, New York

It was the spring of 1996. I was 36 years old, divorced, and in a relationship I knew was never going to lead to anything. But I was too comfortable and too lazy to jump back into the icy waters of the dating pool. I had just heard about something called AOL that allowed you to chat with people all over the country from your own living room. This sounded like a very good thing for me, and it was sure to take the sting out of dating.

So I installed AOL on my new Mac Classic. It was the early days of chat rooms, so at that time, when you first logged on you'd be dumped in the "Lobby." This was where you'd find other people who didn't know they could get into specialized rooms with like-minded folks (i.e., "Married but Flirting Manhattanites," etc.).

It was in the Lobby that I spotted a fellow chatter who went by the screen name of GEliteman (which, as I would later learn, stood for GE, as in

General Electric, as in the company he worked for). I don't know why I picked his name—just a hunch I guess—so I clicked on it to see if his profile sounded promising. The way I figured it, if the guy was into stuff that was *skeevy* to me—like cars or World Wide Wrestling—I wasn't interested. But maybe GEliteman had something else to offer.

Turns out he did. According to the data he supplied, his name was Charlie, he was 34, divorced with a seven-year-old son, and lived in South Florida. Hobbies? "Working out and wine."

That was enough to spark my curiosity. The idea of a single father was appealing to me (I'd always been a sucker for *The Courtship of Eddie's Father*); and as for the wine reference, I was definitely intrigued, having just finished a Windows on the World wine course. So I decided to IM him.

"Hey Charlie," I wrote, "what kind of wine do you like?" That was all it took: We began chatting. And chatting. We chatted every day for two weeks.

I like this guy, I thought. *I wonder if he's normal.* After all, in New York a single, straight, *normal* man in his 30s is a very, very rare breed. (This was also in the days before anyone scanned in pictures, so we still had no idea what each other looked like.)

One day in mid-chat, I asked him a question that had been nagging at me:

janny104: You sound so great. Why aren't you attached?
GEliteman: Because no one wants to play with a Charlie-in-the-Box.

I couldn't believe it. Charlie had written words that immediately touched my heart. They were words straight from my childhood, spoken by Charlie, the unhappy jack-in-the-box from the Island of Misfit Toys in my favorite Christmas TV special, *Rudolph the Red-Nosed Reindeer.*

Words that had always made me sad when I was little, long before I knew what the feeling of love was all about.

Words I myself have used whenever I need to describe my own feelings of being out of sync with everyone around me.

Not only was I impressed that Charlie knew that line, but that he wrote it back to me without explanation, just assuming I would know what he was talking about. That immediately put me at ease, because if *he* had no problem confessing that he was a Misfit Toy, I knew I could feel comfortable being myself, too.

With that one line, "No one wants to play with a Charlie-in-the-Box," I knew that Charlie *got* me. And he knew I got *him.*

Finding love the second time around requires a different set of skills from the first go-round. In my case, I discovered that I was less interested in sorting through the angst and ambiguities of dating (does he like me? will he call me?) than I was in exploring the mysteries of love itself. Informed by my lackluster first marriage, my eye became sharper as I looked for a man who would satisfy not only my desire for a lover and partner, but also for a friend. My ear became more attuned to those little things that told me we were on the same page, that we didn't have to spend time drawing roadmaps to romance, but could just naturally find our way to each other.

My hunch about my Charlie began proving itself to be accurate every time we booted up our computers to talk. Charlie was from a different pond from the guys I'd been seeing in New York and not at all interested in the game playing that goes along with dating. And even though he was a businessman and not in the same creative industry as me (and thank God for that—I'd been down that road before), he was still funny and charming and always knew what to say (write). There were a lot of little signals that he could be someone worth pursuing.

Yes, he was floating out there in the ether with thousands of other strangers; but the warmth I felt from him made me feel like he could just as easily be right around the corner, like a neighbor or a friend.

Some online romances stay online, but Charlie and I needed to take the next step—meeting face-to-face. I was going to be in California for a three-week commercial shoot, and I asked him if he'd like to fly out to meet me. But before I let him answer, I had one big stipulation.

"We have to have an alternate plan if we don't hit it off," I said. "As nice as you sound online, you could still be a nut. And besides, we have to accept the possibility that maybe this thing just won't work out."

The fact that Charlie immediately agreed to my ground rules—booking himself a flight to L.A., renting a car, and reserving a room at a Holiday Inn down the street from where I'd be staying—made me that much more attracted to him. Here was *a man with a plan,* someone who knew what he wanted and had no problem going after it.

My girlfriends told me I was crazy.

"Hey," I said to them with some assurance, "this either turns out to be a fairy tale come true, or a story we can laugh about over drinks one day."

But when Charlie walked into that hotel bar in California a few weeks later, I knew right away that it had all been worth it. *Of course,* I thought as I spotted him spotting me, *you're the guy I've been looking for.*

Charlie never stayed at the Holiday Inn, after all; and once I returned to New York, he began making regular trips up from Florida to see me. On his third visit—just three months after our first IMs to each other on AOL—he brought an engagement ring, And I accepted it.

Nine years of marriage and one child later, it looks like I wound up with the fairy tale. And you know what? After all this time, I *still* want to play with a Charlie-in-the-Box. Even though his name is really Jeff.

Janet Guillet

Love Song

Laura Neumeyer

Academic Counselor
Austin, Texas

I first met my husband, David, when we were in college. I was studying music education and he was a piano major. David was considered the golden boy of the department. He won all the competitions and performed regularly around the college and the state. It was generally agreed that he was the best pianist at our school.

David not only played beautifully and musically, he also had nerves of steel. I used to marvel at how he could instantly shut everything out, walk onstage, and deliver a flawless performance. His concentration and focus on the music was incredible. I used to tease him by saying that he could be waiting in the wings to go on, someone could throw a bucket of cold water on him, and he would still be able to sit down at the piano and not miss a note.

David and I were dating by the time he was a senior. His recital that year included Six Bagatelles op. 126, by Beethoven. Some of the Bagatelles in this opus are not flashy, but delicate and subdued. They require great musicality and a controlled, gentle touch that can bring out the subtleties of the music. One day as he was practicing for his recital, I commented to him that a very quiet passage in the third Bagatelle—a soft, long trill in the right hand over the tender melody in the left—was one of my favorite moments in the piece.

As this time in our relationship, things were not perfect. When we'd first met, David was involved with another girl. I had fallen hard for him, and in the early months, he was seeing both of us—that was difficult for me. Even though it had been a while since they had broken up, the memories of that triangle lingered in the background, and I still felt a small current of insecurity about us.

And then there was everything that David was. He seemed to have it all: honors, awards, admission to a prestigious graduate school on a full fellowship. I was in awe of David, and I wasn't sure how I measured up in his eyes.

Whenever David performed he always drew a good audience, and the evening of his senior recital was no exception. The hall was packed. I leaned back in my seat and let the beauty of the Bagatelles wash over me. But when he came to the passage I found so moving, he stumbled over a few notes. The moment was fleeting, but the audience definitely heard the fumble. You could hear a collective gasp. This just never happened with David—missing notes. He quickly recovered and went on to play the rest of the recital superbly.

Later that evening as we talked about his performance, I told him how surprised I was that he'd made the small mistake. He turned to me and looked into my eyes.

"I was thinking of you," he said.

I knew then how much David loved me. Suddenly my insecurity about his previous relationship vanished forever. I felt that he valued me in a way that rose above even his music or his scholarly pursuits. To know that I could penetrate his fierce concentration—his total immersion in the music—left little doubt how much I meant to him. It was one of the most romantic moments in my life.

We have been married for 33 years, and the romance and tenderness remain to this day. I still listen to the Six Bagatelles every now and then. They never fail to take me back to that special moment.

Laura Neumeyer

Jane Austen Meets the New York Giants

Geralyn Ruane

Tutor
North Hollywood, California

It is a truth universally acknowledged that a woman should never come between her man and his Sunday football.

But what can I say? I couldn't resist. It was Sunday—a time of exhaustion after a six-day workweek—and I needed my fix of *Pride and Prejudice*. I wanted to escape into a good strong dose of Jane Austen and her Napoleonic waistlines, rakish secrets, and parlor-room discussions about screens embroidered with I know not what.

"Jesus, Ger, I was in the middle of the game!" Ron was not happy.

"You weren't here," I said, never peeling my eyes from the screen. I mean, seriously, how could I? It was my favorite part: the end of tape three, when Darcy proposes to Lizzy at Rosings. "Anyway," I added, "halftime lasts half an hour."

As it turns out, halftime does *not* last half an hour—plus, the game had only cut to a commercial. Ron had simply quit the couch for a minute to use the bathroom. He didn't boot me out, though, or wrestle the remote from me. He tried to reason with me instead.

"Ger, you watch this almost every day. You have it memorized. *I* practically have it memorized just from osmosis. The Giants play only sixteen games all year. You're just being rude."

At that point, I tossed him the remote—not because he'd shamed me, but because Darcy had just taken his dignified leave of Lizzy, and tape three was over.

I got up from the stolen spot on the couch and left Ron to his tackles and whistles. I took a turn around the room, snagging *Nancy Drew and the Mystery at the Ski Jump* on my way past the bookcase. I'd seen the beat-up classic in the used bookstore by the gas station, and I hadn't been able to resist. What girl doesn't love Nancy Drew?

As I shuffled into the bedroom with my dusty treasure, I closed both the hall door and bedroom door behind me. The crowds faded away.

I stretched across the bed, ready to get lost in adventure with the amateur sleuth. But before I could get comfy, I had to fix the pillows. Ron *never* put the pillows right when he made the bed. They were supposed to be tipped up, leaning back against the wall where a headboard would be (if we had one), not just lying flat on the comforter. Finally settling into the adjusted shams and ruffles, I opened my book and eased into the simpler time of 1950s Nancy Drew.

But I couldn't stop thinking about the 1980s me. I was the girl who'd day-dreamed about finding true love one day. Now I was the woman who'd woken up to real life. I tried to push the thought out of my head, but a surge of NFL music blasted through the closed bedroom door, and I threw the book aside. Nancy Drew—with her titian hair and teal blue convertible—just wasn't doing it for me today. Oh, hell, Ron wasn't in love with me anymore, I was sure of it. How could he be? How could something like romance survive life after 30? How could passion ever triumph in its battle with *routine*?

I curled onto my side in single spoon position and spotted the card my friend Rebecca had made me for my birthday last year. It was tacked into the crumbling plaster. Rebecca had printed out a picture of the smitten Mr. Darcy, and written a caption that smashed together some bits of Darcy dialogue, as if he had eyes only for me.

"My dearest, loveliest Geralyn," it read. "It is your birthday, and *that* is the material point."

Rebecca and I were both hardcore *P&P* fans, and we slipped lines of Jane's dialogue into our lives wherever we could.

I suppose I wanted to live the romantic classic because the best part of my own story had already been written. I had fallen in love six years ago, then committed myself to the guy four years later. Now there was no room left to dream. No great beyond. I crushed my face into the pillow. *What am I supposed to dream of? What did I want?* I heard a referee's whistle and put the pillow over my head.

Three hours later, I woke up to an unfamiliar cooking smell. I climbed off the bed and shuffled to the kitchen where I found Ron in the midst of a Project. Whatever he was concocting, it needed two pans, all three pots, and every spice in the cupboard. He was making shrimp fried rice.

"I thought you were allergic to shrimp," I said to him, leaning against the kitchen door frame.

"Well, *you* like them," he said. "Anyway, it's clams that get me sick, not shrimp."

"But you *never* eat shrimp."

"Thought I'd try it," he said with a shrug. "And even if I don't like it, at least it won't put me in the hospital. And *that* is the material point."

He cracked an egg.

I looked at Ron, his last words still ringing through my head. *That is the material point?* Had Ron just quoted Mr. Darcy like it was no big deal? Had he actually slipped a line from *Pride and Prejudice* into ordinary conversation? That meant he knew the story and understood how much I loved it.

That is the material point.

50–50

Brenda Degner

Teacher
Muscatine, Iowa

Y ou've heard it a million times: The odds of maintaining a marriage these days aren't very good. Not surprisingly, with the divorce rate climbing, there isn't any foolproof advice that can be offered to newlyweds anymore.

That's why I'm so grateful to my mother for offering those special words to me before I married, more than 30 years ago.

I was 23 when I got married, having met my husband in college. We were both working on the spring musical, *Little Mary Sunshine.* Curt was in the chorus, I was doing the choreography. When one of the girls in the play got hurt, I took over her role. She sang the songs from the orchestra pit and I danced to them. At the cast parties, Curt and I were the only two who didn't drink, so we just gravitated toward each other.

We began dating and over the summer decided we wanted to be married. Around Christmas that year, Curt's choral group was caroling at the mall, and I joined him. On a whim, we strolled into a mom-and-pop jewelry store to look at wedding rings. The owner showed us a ring with a yellow diamond in a white-gold setting.

"If you had one with a blue stone in yellow gold," Curt said, "we'd probably take it." The owner disappeared for a moment and then came back with a ring exactly matching that description! Curt choked a little, and in a slightly stunned voice said, "We'll take it!"

The local newspaper announced our engagement with the headline YOU'VE GOT TO HAND IT TO LITTLE MARY SUNSHINE, which was a famous line from the play in which we'd met.

Spring arrived, and with the wedding nearly upon us, the ladies of our local church circle threw a shower for me, which I attended with my mother. I knew all of these wonderful women, but most were quite elderly, from another generation. At one point, we played a game in which each guest wrote down her best matrimonial tip on a recipe card. When everyone handed in their cards, it was my job to read them aloud. Being young, I just assumed I knew everything I needed to know about how to make a marriage work, but I went along with the game. Most of the hints were pretty predictable.

"Try to keep meals on time," one woman wrote, "because husbands hate to wait."

Another suggested, "Never hang slips and pants in the bathroom to dry. Men don't like that."

And one very wise lady warned, "Be patient with your husband and never say anything in haste, for you will be sorry."

While all of the tips were kind of old-fashioned, they did make some sense. If people thought more carefully before they spoke, lots of misunderstandings would be avoided.

But then I got to the recipe card that my intelligent, beautiful, and very clever mother had written. Instead of jotting down some day-to-day reminder or practical household tip, Mom simply wrote:

"Remember, marriage isn't always a 50–50 proposition. Sometimes it's 60–40, and sometimes even 90–10—and *not* always in your favor!" I remember at the time thinking that my mother's advice was somewhat negative—certainly not how I'd pictured the perfect marriage.

Then I got married and began to understand. During our life together, my husband and I have faced many challenges and fought about all the usual things that couples fight about. He wasn't that great with money, so we had to compromise on who did the buying and how much we spent. As a teacher, I had my summers free, so I did pretty much everything around the house and yard, while he worked. Curt, on the other hand, called the shots on things he knew a lot more about than I did, like home renovations. Housework was another big battleground for us. He thought he could sit on the couch and watch TV while I ran around with the laundry basket. We never did settle that issue. When it came to giving each other space, he did his own thing, but he was great at making sure I had the time to pursue the things I loved, too—especially my karate classes!

Throughout all of this I couldn't help but notice how true my mother's words were. Over the course of 30 years, Curt and I have given what we could, when we could. Sometimes one of us provided 90 percent while the other drifted into the negative zone. Other times, like magic, the numbers would reverse themselves, and the one who'd previously carried the heavier load would fall back as the other gave for the both of us.

Never was this more apparent than when our children were younger. Our son had a serious, lengthy illness as a teenager; and a year later, our daughter fell off a bike, requiring extended emergency care. My husband—as wonderful as he can be—has an amazing capacity to block things out, so he didn't participate much in our children's recuperation. This was very difficult for me, but it was his own way of dealing with it all. He just assumed I'd handle it—and I did.

Hardly was this a 50–50 proposition; but as my mother said, it rarely is.

For 28 years, I taught a family living class at my high school, and often shared my mother's advice with my students, hoping it would have the same kind of impact on them as it had on me. Most of the time, the words do command the attention of the class, because, without fail, every time I recite them, tears fill my eyes. (Yes, I cry in front of the kids!) I don't know if my mother's words ever went on to impact my students the way they impacted me, but if they were helpful to even *one* student, it was worth the time it took to share them.

My mom and dad have been married for nearly 58 years, and I know that they continue to work those percentages each and every day. In the end, life isn't always even—it's sometimes lopsided. But my mother's point was, if you give of yourself, you'll be taken care of, too.

I know my story probably won't be the most important one in this book, but what it says means a lot to me, and I thought it might be meaningful to other newlyweds, too. Whether or not my marriage lasts forever, my mom's advice certainly will. And as for that card she wrote to me, it's still in the front of my recipe box—and always will be.

Brenda Klyn

Grab Him and Kiss Him

Kaye Whillock *

Copy Editor
New York, New York

I had this mad, obsessive crush on a guy named Patrick at work, and all I was getting from him were mixed signals. Every time we ran into each other, he'd talk about us going out, but then he'd never call. Once we went kayaking, and another time he gave me a Rollerblading lesson, but those were the only two times he followed through. We had great conversations when we were together and he seemed genuinely interested in me, but weeks would pass and nothing moved forward. I was fixated on him for about six months.

One day I told my sister-in-law about all this and asked her advice. I had no idea what to do with this guy, I said, and yet I couldn't get him out of my system.

"Grab him and kiss him and see what happens," she said.

*The writer has chosen not to use her real name.

New Year's Eve 1999 was the night. We were both working the late shift at a publication whose offices were right off Times Square. *This is fate!* I thought. I dressed up in a sleeveless Chinese shirt and a very short skirt and wore makeup I don't usually wear to work.

Five minutes before midnight, everyone in our office walked outside to watch the famous ball drop. My hopes about Patrick were incredibly high. Standing in Times Square, directly beneath the falling ball, we listened to the crowd count down.

10, 9, 8, 7 . . .

I looked over at Patrick. He was watching the ball.

6, 5, 4 . . .

I moved a little closer to him.

3, 2, 1 . . . Happy New Year!

Fireworks began blasting into the sky. I grabbed Patrick and kissed him full on the mouth. Inside my head, I had enough excitement for five people, so I couldn't really tell if there were any sparks coming back. So I grabbed him and kissed him again, this time making sure he knew that it wasn't just an ordinary New Year's kiss.

His kiss back wasn't so hot.

Had I followed my sister-in-law's advice, that would have been that: I'd grabbed him and kissed him and saw what happened—nothing. But when we all went back inside, I forged ahead, continuing to keep an eye on Patrick, even as he returned to his desk without saying a word. Just then, a guy in the office came around and invited us all to an after-party.

Still hoping against hope, I called out to Patrick, "Hey, come with us!" He said no without explanation. If our sparkless kiss hadn't convinced me that he wasn't interested, now I knew for sure.

It's not easy being rejected, and it took me a while to get over it. But my sister-in-law's advice had pushed me to accept the fact that a relationship with Patrick was never going to happen. It not only cured me of an obsession, but it also taught me to pay attention to *the moment.*

Exactly one year later, New Year's Eve, I was invited to a party at a friend's apartment. Just after midnight, I began talking to a nice guy named David. This time, instead of being blinded by the outcome I wished for, I paid attention to the actual signals. That was four years ago, and we've been going together ever since. It's the best relationship I've ever had, or expect to have. This is my guy.

And, just in case you're interested, the first time David and I kissed, I knew it right away. Despite what the song says, sometimes a kiss is *not* just a kiss.

The Anniversary Card

Elizabeth Morrissey

Homemaker
Newtown, Connecticut

I was 12 years old, and my grandparents were about to celebrate their 40th wedding anniversary. My grandfather took me along with him as he shopped for a gift for my grandmother. I can't recall what he bought, but I do remember that when we returned home, my grandfather let me sign the card for him. My grandmother's name is Anna, but he did not have me address the card with her given name or any of the usual affectionate terms one spouse might use for another. There was no "Dear Sweetheart," "My Dear Wife," or "To My Beloved." Instead, he asked me to write on the envelope: "To My Pal." Being 12, I did as I was told and thought nothing more about it.

I have been married for 15 years, and have four beautiful children. Throughout it all, my grandfather's words have come back to me on more than one occasion. That simple phrase, "To My Pal," has become more meaningful to me, as it continues to shape the foundation of my family life. I have come to depend upon the friendship that my husband and I have built together. Not every day is easy, but when you are married to your pal, you quickly learn that bumps in the road are just that—bumps and nothing more.

My sister was married last June, and I was the matron of honor. I was terrified that I had to make a toast at her bridal shower. I felt a tremendous responsibility to say something wise that she would always remember. So I spoke about the ever-changing nature of marriage. I talked about the excitement of the engagement, and that initial rush of good wishes, celebrations, and nicely wrapped gifts. I reminded her that, inevitably, when the honeymoon is over, hard work and challenges lie ahead—but how a good and enduring friendship with her husband would see her through the rough times.

And I concluded my toast by remembering our grandfather, whose 50-year marriage to our grandmother was a beautiful testament to that memorable phrase of his, "To My Pal"—three simple words that are not so simple at all.

Elizabeth Morrissey

You Just Know

Lisa Mercurio

Entertainment Executive
New York, New York

The mere idea that I would one day be a divorcée seemed positively surreal to me. Some things in life are impossible to understand until you find yourself there. And for me, divorce was certainly one of those things.

First of all, it left me feeling unable to trust myself. *How could I have made this mistake?* I kept thinking. I also couldn't stop asking myself how I could be a failure at *knowing* love? I had always envisioned myself happily married. My childhood and upbringing had supported that notion; and as I grew up and ventured out on my own, I continued to imagine myself finding the right man and getting married—preferably sooner than later.

After college, I was living in New York City. By day, I worked at a major record company, and by night, I practiced piano in pursuit of my dream of becoming a concert pianist. Invariably, all of the concerto competitions I entered seemed to be won by someone named Gyorgi or Ming-Mao. Despite a healthy dose of denial, it slowly became apparent to me that my career plans weren't exactly meshing with my reality. So I began dating a bit more.

Among the men I went out with was an old high school friend, not because I was particularly attracted to him, but because it was convenient. He was also wealthy, so I fell into the rhythm of enjoying a more privileged life. Trips to the Caribbean, lavish gifts, and luxurious dining clouded my vision. I thought I loved him, and so we married.

Nine years later—it was a Monday morning, I remember—he sat me down on the edge of our bed.

"I'm having an affair," he said.

I was shocked by his confession, of course, but I soon learned that this was just the tip of the iceberg. As it turned out, he kept company with a *lot* of girlfriends. My shock turned to anger. Having become increasingly immersed in my job as a high-level executive and mother to our newborn twins, I realized that the idea of infidelity hadn't ever occurred to me. To be honest, I guess I never imagined that anyone else might want him. (Note to self: Where there's money, there's *always* someone else.)

The more I thought about my predicament, the less I could avoid the inescapable truth: I had married a raging narcissist; and if ever I was going to respect myself again, I knew I would have to pull the plug and ask him to leave.

And I did.

In the weeks and months following our breakup, what was most difficult for me wasn't losing him, or the adjustment to single parenting. Instead, it was the feeling that I'd lost my compass. I knew I wanted to be able to trust myself again, so that I would never, ever make the same mistake. I wanted to know love with absolute certainty.

During that newly free and healing period of exploration, I asked a happily married friend a simple question.

"How do you know when you really love someone?"

She paused for a moment and said, "You just *know*."

It seemed like one of those non-answer answers that friends sometimes share, but coming from *this* friend, I believed it. I began to trust the idea that love would one day make itself obvious. About a year later, it did.

I was in Chicago on business when I met him. I was terrifically attracted to him—smitten, even. He was warm and handsome and also a composer-conductor, which made me feel like fate had delivered me back to my roots. Our time together in Chicago lasted only a few hours. We walked around the city, taking in the sites, talking about music, and enjoying each other's company. He was kind and gentle and soft-spoken—and funny, too. It felt good and easy to be with him.

At one point, I asked him how he would proceed with a recently divorced mother of twins. He gave a one-word response: "*Slowly.*"

The answer was so simple, so true. He wasn't trying to be clever or glib; he was telling me how he felt—and it was just what I needed to hear. After a year of doubting my own instincts, I began to wonder if I'd just met my soul mate.

For now, though, I needed to get back to New York. My children were waiting, and so we said good-bye. I remember that he didn't even try to kiss me.

On the flight home, my mind and my heart were racing. And yet, I wasn't afraid. I wasn't wondering if this feeling was one-sided, or distorted, or artificial. I felt calm and excited at the same time.

You just know.

When I walked in the front door, my children were happy to see me and even happier to see me happy. I must have been wearing my feelings on my face, because when I told my twins' nanny about my date in Chicago, she beamed.

"Oh, darling," she said. "We could use a conductor in our lives!"

Just then the phone rang. I picked it up and said hello. It was him.

"Could you possibly give me the number of your fax machine?" he said, his voice new but already so familiar. "And could you go stand by it and wait for a second?"

He didn't say what he was faxing or why, but moments later, the fax machine rang and then began churning out a sheet of paper. On it was a single, elegant line of handwritten music, with a lyric underneath.

"Lucky was the day I met Li-sa," it read.

In that one moment, reading those seven words, I knew I *could* know love again. And more important, that I could trust my instincts.

A pretty lucky day for Lisa, too.

Australian Love Story

Diana Harley

Wife and Mother of Six
New South Wales, Australia

I was sitting up in bed as best I could, curly hair in a total frizz, my old pink chenille dressing gown wrapped around me. A beautiful new bundle, my fourth child, was sleeping soundly in the hospital crib next to me. At first, I was elated—then relieved—that the birth was over. Soon enough, though, I was feeling a bit sore and sorry for myself.

It was lovely just to have my husband of 15 years all to myself, if only for a short while. Our three other children were with their grandparents, and with the new baby asleep, I knew we could enjoy this time together.

We'd met when I was 16 and he was 15. Both of us worked at Woolworths in a busy Sydney suburb. I remember the first time I saw him. He was standing outside the staff room reading the notice board. He'd just started that day, and I suppose he was pretty nervous. He didn't know anyone else there. I recall thinking to myself that he looked interesting, and I hoped that he might pack bags at my checkout station at some point.

In fact, he did. Eventually, he *always* seemed to be packing for me. We got on really well and a lovely friendship developed. After a few months, he got promoted to parcel pickup, but we always managed to catch each other's eye.

Our first date was to his prefect's ball, and we both had a great time—so much so that I couldn't understand why he didn't ask me out again. It wasn't until a year later that he asked me out on a second date, this time to his eldest brother's engagement party. I didn't want to be used as a mere escort for the evening, so before I accepted the invitation, I asked him a question.

"Why didn't you ask me out again after our first date?" I said.

"I wanted to," he confessed, "but I was too shy."

That was a fine enough answer for me, and we became inseparable after that. Over the next four years we both finished our studies, obtained our university degrees, and then married.

We started out pretty poor. I had more money than he did because I'd been working longer and was a good saver. So we began putting away as much as we could. We rented a unit and lived frugally, and after six months we were finally able to buy our first home—a two-bedroom weatherboard out in the burbs. Times passed, jobs and houses changed, and after six years of marriage we had our first child. Two more followed.

Job dissatisfaction led us out of the city and to the country. It was a huge wrench leaving family and friends and a life that I really enjoyed. Still, we packed up our home, our children, and the cat and followed the moving van on the seven-hour drive south to another life.

Snippets of those 15 years with my husband flashed through my mind as I sat quietly on the hospital bed with him. Life together hadn't always been so wonderful. We'd had our ups and downs. At one point, the fights and misunderstandings had made parting a real possibility. Living in virtual isolation without a support network of family and friends hadn't helped, and we struggled through that time as best we could. Both of us made our fair share of mistakes.

I was lost in these thoughts when my husband produced from his pocket a tiny box wrapped in gold paper, tied with a silver bow.

"For you," he said solemnly, watching me carefully as I unwrapped the delicate cube. "It's that eternity ring you've had your heart set on. You've never asked me for it, but I've noticed the way you always stop to look at it in the jeweler's window whenever we go into town. You know the one."

"I know," I whispered, the tears now welling in my eyes. I gingerly opened the box.

"Thank you," I said. "It's perfect."

My husband took a breath. "I know I'm not the most romantic person in the world," he began. "Far from it. Haven't been in the past and not likely to be in the future—you know, a leopard doesn't change its spots and all that. But I love you. Always have and always will. I know things haven't been easy and there's no saying that the future's going to be any different." Then he leaned in and said, "But I do know that things aren't right when we're not together, and I don't ever not want to be together with you."

It was those seven words—"things aren't right when we're not together"—that made the tears start to trickle down my cheeks. Simple, perhaps even silly words, but they were the deepest truth and why I was still married to this man after 15 years and four children. True, neither of us was perfect, nor was our life, but I knew then that I didn't ever not want to be together with him, either.

"Things aren't right when we're not together" became indelibly etched in my mind from that day forward. My husband and I now call them *our* words, and they remain to me the most precious expression of love.

Diana M. Harley

PART NINE

Keeping the Faith

*"Those words immediately took the pressure off me.
I could be as mad and hurt as I wanted to be,
and that was okay."*

Yelling at God

Carol Kodish-Butt

Social Services
Edmonton, Alberta, Canada

My young husband had just died of cancer, and there I was, a frightened widow and mother of an 11-year-old son. My husband, Gary, had been my love, my confidant, and my protector. Now I was alone.

Although my religious belief was shaky at best, I still felt driven to cry out my pain, to spew my anger at the God who had taken Gary from me. I took out the Yellow Pages, searched for a synagogue—there are only three in Edmonton—and called the first rabbi on the list. I told him I needed to have a discussion with God—probably a loud one—and that I needed to be alone in the synagogue to do this. I promised I would speak to him afterward. He agreed.

Walking into the sanctuary, I shook uncontrollably.

"How could you do this to me?" I screamed at the God I wasn't sure even existed. "To *him*? To our *son*? How could you do this?"

My fight with God lasted for more than an hour, my pain pouring out of me every step of the way. I cried out my fear, my hatred for what lay ahead. I judged God harshly as the cruel thief of all that had kept me whole. It was the hardest battle I had ever waged, the most violent words I'd ever spoken.

At the end of the hour, I was overcome with guilt. How could I allow myself to feel this kind of anger and hatred toward a God I had been taught was my ultimate protector? What kind of person was I?

I quietly climbed the stairs to the rabbi's office.

"I'm Carol, Rabbi," I began. "My husband just died and I have spent the last hour screaming at God. I'm sorry, I feel so guilty."

The rabbi shrugged his shoulders, smiled gently, and spoke with a New York inflection—an odd accent to hear in this western Canadian setting.

"At least it's a relationship," he said.

I didn't know whether to laugh or cry. Let's face it, the line was funny—especially with the accent. But more important, those words immediately took the pressure off me. I didn't have to stop the way I was feeling. I didn't have to make it all better. I could be as mad and hurt as I wanted to be, and that was okay.

That day in the synagogue, I learned not only about grief, but about my relationship with God, as well. I learned that I did not need to sit in judgment of my chaotic feelings. I learned to accept and honor my sadness, wherever it took me. I learned about true connection—to God, to those around me, to my beloved husband, whose memory I will always carry in my heart.

I learned about the preciousness of having a *relationship* with grief.

In the days ahead, I found others who would guide me. For example, after having a vivid dream about my husband, I spoke with a doctor about the nature of reality. The comfort I'd felt in seeing my love again was overwhelming, I told him, yet it was eclipsed by my pressing need to know: Was it real?

The doctor smiled and warmly explained that I didn't really need an answer. We grab onto these moments of connection as they come along, he said, and hold them to us.

"Was it real?" he repeated. "Does it matter?"

Frequently, fear would take hold of me, and I began to question the worthiness of caring for anyone, when we could lose our deepest anchors at any moment.

"Hope is not about everything turning out okay," a friend told me. "It is about being okay no matter how things turn out."

I had many teachers during this most challenging time of my life. But I will never forget the kindness of the rabbi who set me on the path to coping with my anguish. As the director of a grief support program, I now reach out to others who are traveling through their own painful journeys. Twenty-one years later, I continue to teach what I learned back in those terrible days after I'd lost my precious husband: that grief must be honored and expressed; that we need to put aside our self-judgment and allow ourselves our feelings, whatever they may be—even if it means yelling at God.

At least it's a relationship.

Carol Kodish-Butt

An Unexpected Prayer

Steve Martinez

Police Officer
Omaha, Nebraska

I was off duty when the phone rang at home. The voice on the other end of the line said the words every policeman hates to hear:

"Cop's shot, University Hospital."

When one of us goes down we have a system in place that spreads the word like a forest fire. I threw on my shoes and bolted out the door, already making calls on my cell phone. Not knowing the identity of the officer was almost too much to bear. Way too many cops in town had been shot lately; in the past two years, one had been killed in a crossfire, another paralyzed in a pursuit accident. Both of them were friends of mine.

At the hospital, several of my fellow officers and I shared what little we knew about the shooting. One friend had been hit in the foot, and the other was in surgery with abdominal wounds.

The suspect was African-American. He had been shot and killed by a police officer who was, more than likely, white. A large crowd was already gathering at the crime scene, and according to reports, they were becoming unruly. With race relations at the time not being the best, the situation was sure to get heated, on both ends.

As two of my colleagues and I went for a soda in the vending area, we passed a group of people watching news of the shooting on the hospital television. They looked edgy. One of them, an African-American woman, spotted us and asked if we were police officers. Immediately, I feared the worst, picturing her shouting in anguish about racist officers shooting minorities.

"Yes, ma'am, we're officers," said one of my colleagues. I cringed, expecting the shouting to begin.

Instead, the woman quickly grabbed two of us by the hands and said something I *never* expected to hear.

"Let's pray together."

Tears immediately rolled down my face. Then, as she requested, all of us stood in the hallway and prayed.

Her words and her humanity filled me with hope when I needed it most. An incident like the one that had nearly taken the lives of my two friends can make a person bitter. And even though she had every reason to be bitter herself, she instead had the wisdom to cross the divide.

Together, she had said—and she was right. We were all in this together.

Good Enough for Now

Rebecca Marie Barkin

Music Publicist and Writer
Los Angeles, California

At 19 years old, my faith began to unravel. I was attending a university that had built its reputation on diversity, formidable science IQs, and one-upping the status quo. I was also dating a brilliant and wonderfully kind young man of Hindu faith, whom I found to be enlightening, interesting, and challenging. It was a particularly curious time in my life, as I found my Catholic ideals quickly shrinking away. With each passing day, they seemed to me to be increasingly rigid and downright impractical.

During a visit with my great aunt, Sister Ann Patricia of Saint Luke's Convent, whom I affectionately called "Sister" for the whole of my life, I began to feel disturbed by the uncompromising standard of Catholicism—a standard I'd been letting down in just about every way imaginable.

Once that kind of skepticism has been triggered, doubt can tap you on the shoulder pretty frequently. Slowly, everything about Catholicism seemed not to make sense to me. The world was offering too many alternatives to flatly deny, and soon enough, I found myself in the trenches of a principled war with my priests, my catechism teacher, with sermons and confessionals and Catholic middle management. Under their jurisdiction, and simply for celebrating a belief system other than ours, God was prepared to send herds of wonderful people straight to hell when the horns blew—my Hindu boyfriend included. So, as one might imagine, I was feeling like an outlaw.

Admittedly, over the years and through numerous ill-conceived prayer sessions I had asked God for inappropriate things: an undeserved good grade, a date with a hot basketball player, even heart-attack prevention as I continued to ingest ephedrine for the sake of a good run.

But those are a child's mistakes, and with each passing year I was learning to scale back my requests and simply ask for a general brand of forgiveness, good health, and the absence of catastrophe. Life was teaching me about humility, unavoidable pain, and happiness by way of karma. Prayer was becoming less about penitence and more centered on cosmic questions and positive thought.

During my visit with Sister, my discomfort pressed on me, urging me to seek solitude. So I slipped into the convent's cozy, yellow chapel and looked upon the altar for answers, as I had once found them there. The altar was modest and inviting and laced in gold. The pews creaked as I settled in. I'd spent a lot of time there as a smaller person with smaller concerns, running up and down the long corridors, gazing upon the towering statues of biblical heroes with ease and acceptance. Now their moral magnitude made me squirm.

But this old building had its own long story and it understood the necessity of passing time, so it listened and tolerated my dissidence.

I must have been there for ten minutes before Sister came in and sat beside me. After a few moments of silence, I gave in to my troubles.

"I've been questioning my faith a lot lately," I mumbled, my chin sagging to my chest.

She was silent, motionless, looking to the altar.

"I just don't know that I believe in God anymore," I continued, the words pushing out from a deep breath, a stab at bravery.

My gaze drifted over the walls. Porcelain depictions of the Stations of the Cross, chipped and wood-splintered, hung evenly between the stained glass windows I'd cleaned with a toothbrush as a young student.

"Do you believe in people?" she asked softly.

"What do you mean?"

"Do you believe that people are born with good intentions—that they're compassionate by nature?"

"Yes, I think so."

"Well, I think that if you believe in the innate goodness of people, you believe in God. That's good enough for now."

The simplicity of the statement struck me as both beautiful and liberating, and how brilliant of her to give me a truth I'd witnessed firsthand in her kindness. Sister's words provided me with a valuable daily dose of faith, as I hastily headed toward the most tumultuous period in my young life.

There is a significant learning curve between 18 and 25; suddenly each brick in the foundation on which you've built moral decisions seems alarmingly brittle. But in questioning that foundation, you also begin to build anew; and throughout my struggle, I had a new, simple mantra to hold on to: Humans are driven toward compassion, babies are born in lightness, and people are soulful.

I have never found anything in science that explains the compulsion to do good, to help strangers, and to foster loving relationships. I have, however, always felt the pull of a higher power; I had only lost his shape. So, stumbling forward, warmed by the idea that someone might see a little light in me, or even rediscover faith in a friend's kind gesture, I set about finding God in regular people.

Sister, I give back to the world the beautiful truth that you once gave me.

Rebecca Marie Bardin

Circles in the Dirt

Jon B. Fish

Church Property Manager
Orangevale, California

When I was a child growing up in a small desert town in Utah, my dearest friend was a boy named Jimmy. We did everything together—built pushcarts, played Cowboys and Indians, chased blue-bellied lizards in Ash Creek, and sat together in church. I loved him like a brother.

One day when we were about seven, we had a bad disagreement. I can't remember what the fight was about, but I do recall we fought it out at our fort. Sparks flew, names were called, and off we stomped—separately—to mourn the loss of our friendship. I was sure we'd never speak again.

When I got home, my mother comforted me.

"These things happen in life," she said. I nodded glumly, but her words didn't satisfy my demands for justice. My problem with Jimmy was something that only another *man* could understand. So I sought out my father, who was working up the road in a small corral we owned. Normally, I would have ridden my stick-horse or chased around one of our pigs, but that day I had bigger fish to fry.

After listening closely to my story—hearing how upset and angry I was with my *former* friend, and that I never, *ever* wanted to see him again—my father thought for a moment.

"I know you're angry with Jimmy," he said, "but he's your friend. You should forgive him." And with that he took a long stick in his hand that he'd been using to clean the chicken coop. He drew three large circles in the dirt. In the right circle he wrote the name "God." In the left circle he wrote my name. In the center circle he wrote "Jimmy." Then he looked at me.

"When you don't forgive someone," he said, "you let that person get between you and God."

At first I was hurt that my dad put Jimmy closer to God than me. But his point was made, and it was right there, written in the dirt for me to see.

My father and I talked for a while longer—about apologies and friendship and forgiveness. He reminded me that we all hit bumps in the road, even with our closest friends, but not to let that spoil the ride.

By the next morning, Jimmy and I were best pals again—chasing the lizards, running the pushcarts, and searching for John Wayne on the nearby mountainside.

My father's lesson has served me well through 38 years of marriage to my high school sweetheart. We have five children and 18 grandchildren. For such good blessings, I have my father to thank. His words to an angry little boy a half a century ago taught me everything I ever needed to know about selflessness and generosity. And I feel all the closer to God for it.

Coming to America

Herbert Launer

Retired
Great Neck, New York

I f the plural of tooth is teeth, why isn't the plural of booth *beeth*? If the teacher taught, why hadn't the preacher *praught*? And for goodness sake, why on earth is it one goose but two geese? Nothing made sense.

It was May of 1939. I was a 14-year-old boy in the seventh grade in Cleveland, Ohio, where I had arrived, alone, from Austria a few days earlier. My English vocabulary consisted of only a few words and phrases, including "Hello," "Good-bye," "How are you," and "My name is . . ." Had I known the story of *The King and I,* I would have concluded, in the King's words, that the English language is truly "a puzzlement."

I was born in Vienna in 1925, the only child of struggling middle-class parents. I was attending an elite high school when Nazi Germany annexed Austria in 1938. As a Jewish student I had to sit in the far corner of the classroom wearing a badge emblazoned with the word "JEW."

Then came November 9, 1938—or *Kristallnacht* ("night of the broken glass")—and the beginning of the terror period for Jews. That evening I was nearly kicked to death by my closest non-Jewish friend, and my parents and I were beaten by four hoodlums who had invaded our apartment, smashed the furniture, and dragged my father out to the street to scrub the sidewalk.

Due to the immigration laws of that time, we could not come to America as a family, so my parents sent me off alone at age 14 with only the ten dollars I was allowed to take. I left Vienna on April 30, 1939, then traveled through Switzerland and on to France, where I boarded the *Queen Mary* for New York. I still have my passport marked with the red "J."

When I arrived in Cleveland, I moved in with relatives. It was here that I had that first puzzling encounter with the English language. Imagine how amazed I was to learn that there was no ham in hamburger, no egg in egg-plant, nor any apple *or* pine in a pineapple!

Almost immediately after starting school I met ten other kids who were also recent immigrants. One of them, a Romanian, proposed we form a "Refugee Club." We decided to band together as a way of sharing our insecurities.

But there was a catch: In order to hold meetings in the school, we were required to get the permission of our principal. Gentle and soft spoken, Mr. Goodwyn was the kind of man who could make a point without being dog-matic. He was a wonderful educator, and the person who started me on the road to becoming an American.

"If you really want to start this club," he began," "I will give you my permission. I only ask that you hear me out first before making any decision."

Mr. Goodwyn offered us an alternative. Instead of forming a group based on our common bond as outsiders, he suggested that we concentrate instead on learning American customs, American colloquialisms, and American sports.

"Don't forget your heritage," he counseled, "but try not to maintain an Old World ghetto mentality. Make it your business to study ten to 20 new English words a day, and I will help you with pronunciation and the correct usage."

Despite Mr. Goodwyn's sincere advice, the group decided to form the Refugee Club anyway. I was hesitant to join at first, but one of the girls in the group was beautiful and she let me kiss her—so I immediately became a member. But our principal's words ultimately proved more powerful than those kisses. The more I thought about what Mr. Goodwyn had said, the more I understood that a great lesson lay within our principal's words. I decided to drop out of the group, choosing to make my own way in my new country.

It wasn't easy at first, becoming a regular American guy. Not long after I arrived in Cleveland, the local pool opened for the summer. Like any kid, I was eager to go swimming. Having no idea about current American fashions, I put on the customary one-piece tank suit I'd brought from Vienna. As soon as I stepped outside the changing room I realized I was the only boy who looked like he was stuck in a Roaring Twenties newsreel. I tried tucking the shoulder straps into the bottom part of my suit but that didn't work; and holding the top half down with one hand while swimming with the other was impossible. Too poor to buy an American-style bathing suit and too embarrassed by my appearance, I never returned to the pool.

But America continued to dazzle me. I was constantly amazed by the abundance of food in the grocery stores. I marveled at the radio shows of Jack Benny and Fred Allen. I saw my first professional baseball game in

Cleveland; and when I moved east to be with relatives in New York, I learned to play stickball on the streets of Brooklyn.

At the age of 16, I went to Washington, D.C., seeking information about my parents' whereabouts—if they were, in fact, still alive. On September 1, 1939—the day Hitler invaded Poland—I discovered they were safe in London. I tried everything I could to get them visas to enter America. At my wits' end, I was referred to a minister in Brooklyn who offered to help my parents if I would convert to Christianity.

This wasn't assimilation, this was blackmail! Even though I wasn't an observant Jew and wanted to fit into this new culture, I wasn't about to erase my own identity. (I'm sure my parents wouldn't have been thrilled about me converting, either.)

In 1943, after being inducted into the United States Army at Camp Upton in Long Island, I asked to serve in the Army Air Corps. I wanted to be trained as a pilot. But I was told that because I wasn't an American citizen, I could not enter the Corps. The officer who informed me of this policy said that I would be assigned to Fort Bragg, North Carolina, for artillery training.

"I don't understand," I said. "You mean I can get killed for my country on the ground, but not in the air?"

Assimilation can be awkward and funny and ironic and sad. It is about holding fast to our history and customs, even as we embrace our new land. Most important, it is a choice we are all free to make.

Today, I am a volunteer guide for student groups at the Museum of Jewish Heritage in New York. After showing a short film about Jewish life throughout the world, I ask them what heritage means to them. Usually, there's not much of a response.

"Who are you named after?" I prompt them. "A grandfather? An uncle?

Who?" When I remind them that they probably have photographs of their ancestors on a shelf somewhere in their home, they realize that their heritage is right there in front of them, even as they take their place in the modern world.

Not long ago, I was invited to speak at a synagogue on Long Island on the anniversary of *Kristallnacht*. Afterward, a couple approached me.

"Oh, you're from Vienna," said the man in a thick accent. "And you're Austrian. I am, too!"

"No, I'm not." I responded. "I'm a Jew who was fortunate to get out of Austria. I'm an American."

The gentleman looked confused.

"America is my home," I explained, "and my heritage is right here." With that, I pointed to my heart and my head.

I heard Mr. Goodwyn's voice inside of me that night. In my personal hall of fame, he still occupies the highest pedestal.

Eventually, I would be reunited with my parents. Once in America, they enrolled in an English class for the foreign born, and I gave them private lessons. To further their education, we conversed in English nearly all the time, and the language never seemed to be "a puzzlement" to them.

This was never more obvious to me than during their 40th wedding anniversary party at an Israeli nightclub in Manhattan. Upon returning to our table from the dance floor, my mother commented, "Your father has two left feet!" Obviously, she found nothing odd about her husband having *feet* as opposed to *foots*—and two left ones, at that!

Hubert Launer

Being Carried

Denise Horbaly

Health Care
Charlottesville, Virginia

My mother gave me a copy of the poem when I was a little girl and sent it to me again a few years ago. It now hangs on my refrigerator door, alongside my children's artwork and report cards. You may have heard of it. It's called "Footprints," and its most profound line is its last:

> *During your times of trial and suffering,*
> *when you saw only one set of footprints,*
> *it was then that I carried you.*

My life stumbled in the autumn of 2003. I hesitate to say it stopped, because what fell on my family required a rapid, constant momentum with no opportunity for rest. In August of that year, my husband, who is an orthodontist, was diagnosed with carcinoma of the tongue. Cancer in this location is usually associated with individuals who use tobacco products. My husband had never been a smoker. Imagine how the air was sucked out of the room when the surgeon read us the pathology report. You could have knocked us over with a feather.

From that moment on, our lives became consumed by a torrent of questions and decisions. How many opinions should we get? Should my husband receive chemotherapy as well as radiation? Would he be able to continue working? Who would bring the children home from school on those six-hour treatment days? And how would we keep all of this to ourselves until we were ready to share the burden?

When a family lives with a life-threatening disease, the unknowns are endless; and despite my husband's and my medical backgrounds and our ability to make well-informed decisions based on the information handed us, we still felt like we were on the fast track to a dark and ominous place. At the end of each draining day, we would ask ourselves if we had indeed made the right choices.

Second-guessing became second nature. After much deliberation and consultation with our team (which by now had designated my husband as its star player), a course of action was reached: His treatment would consist of four months of intense chemotherapy, eight weeks of radiation, and then surgery to remove the lymph nodes on the right side of his neck.

Once the treatment regimen began, we quickly fell into a pattern, but the chemotherapy was taking its toll. One night, my husband could handle dinner; the next he couldn't even come to the table. Some nights he was unable to enter our house because even the smell of the cooking launched an assault on his senses, broadsiding him with a dizzying wave of nausea.

Before we knew it, we were entering the radiation phase of his treatment, which was even more taxing on his body and his will to persevere. I watched my husband rise early each morning, five days a week for eight weeks straight, and go off to the hospital to receive a cure that was truly far worse than the disease that had invaded his body.

Toward the end of his radiation, I would meet my husband at his office after the treatments. He needed me to apply dressings to his throat and neck, allowing him to get through a full day of patients. Even the sensation of air on his newly burned skin was too much to bear; yet the dressings were a cool and soothing gift—and all I had to offer him.

Like the chemotherapy before it, the radiation phase ended just when my husband felt he could take no more. That last drive to the hospital for his final treatment was a moment for celebration. We quietly counted our blessings for a challenge conquered. Four weeks later, he had his scheduled surgery and the results were nothing short of a blessing: His neck was clear of any disease.

Throughout the ordeal, I had faced each new hurdle with prayer. I prayed and prayed and prayed some more—in the shower, at the gym, while cooking dinner, even during homework time with my children. But then a day came when I realized I couldn't pray anymore. Even during the recovery phase, solitude just wouldn't come, and the more I tried to feel a sense of peace, the more I failed.

That is when I heard the words that would see me through the rest of this trying time. My family and I were at church the second Sunday after my husband's surgery. Following the service, one of my husband's patients, Mrs. Barbara Mincer, approached me and asked how we all were faring. She specifically inquired about me.

By this time, I had become somewhat frank when asked questions of this sort. So instead of responding with the expected, "Oh, I'm doing pretty well, thanks for asking," I told her how tired I was and that I could no longer pray.

"I feel like I have forgotten how," I said.

"That's okay," Mrs. Mincer responded. "For now, you're being carried."

The moment Mrs. Mincer spoke those words to me, my head began to spin. Someone in the outside world was reminding me about a poem that, until then, had been a private and personal touchstone in my life.

Someone had made the connection for me! This was the salvation I had been looking for but could never find. I needed a reason to justify my vacant heart, and Mrs. Mincer had provided it for me. How huge her small words seemed! A new sense of calm entered the room—and my life.

I've always been someone who believes that whatever happens will happen, whether we kick it or succumb to it. And yet the thoughts expressed in "Footprints" told me I wasn't alone. I was being helped. It was okay that I'd reached my limits and temporarily shut down. It was okay that I could no longer feel strength in my soul, or firm ground beneath my feet. I wasn't supposed to. I was being carried.

After that, my life came full circle, and I let go of the troubling thoughts that had consumed me. I shed the anxiety that fueled the daily grind. It was like losing weight. I felt lighter, happier, and could concentrate on the future. And the answer had been on my refrigerator door all along.

Denise Horbaly

Repairing My World

Tom Yulsman

Professor
Niwot, Colorado

My mother was a very private woman. I debated whether I should share this personal story beyond my circle of family and friends. But as I thought about it, I realized that there comes a time in all of our lives when we are called on to find—and share—the right words. Most often, this is a sacred responsibility, which can make it an incredibly frightening one.

My mother wrote such words to me at some point during a spring weekend in 1982 when she decided to commit suicide.

I had spoken with her by phone on Saturday, checking in to see how she was coping with the chronic back pain that had been plaguing her for more than a year—and, more important, with the depression she'd endured for most of her adult life. She seemed in good spirits, unusually so. I had been hoping that she would gain some relief after many months of suffering, and in fact she had. But not for the reason I had imagined.

Evidently, her fateful decision had helped lift the intolerable burden enough for her to put some cheer in her voice. I believe that by helping me to feel relieved, she also wanted to hide from me what she intended to do. Even in retrospect, I am unable to think of anything she said that I could have interpreted as a cry for help—to stop her before she took her life.

I called her two days later, on Monday morning, but got no answer. There was no reason for her to be out of the house. Because of her back, it was difficult for her to get around, and I often helped with shopping and other errands. So I waited a bit and called again. No answer. At some point, I began to suspect what had happened.

I dashed out of work and hailed a taxi, telling the driver that it was extremely urgent. We raced the mile or so to my mom's apartment house near the Hudson River, but time seemed to slow down. Along the way, I tried to convince myself that I was wrong. When I finally opened her door, I learned that I was not. She had taken an overdose of painkillers and antidepressants.

After calling 911, I found the note on her desk.

I don't know exactly when my mother wrote the words that would help me overcome a trauma so severe it could have caused permanent psychological harm. But fortunately, she chose words that would absolve me of the guilt loved ones often feel in situations like this and helped propel me toward the future without paralyzing self-doubt. And because of those words, I was able to attain more happiness than I thought possible.

Twenty-one years later, when it was time to offer my son, Sam, a Bar Mitzvah blessing, I wanted to offer my own right words, but I also felt compelled to include ones my parents had passed on to me, so that I could send him forth into adulthood as a compassionate young man who would engage in *tikun olam*, the Jewish tradition of doing things to "repair the world."

I told him about how my dad had inspired in me an intense curiosity about nature and a sense of wonderment. And I spoke about a photo of Sam taken in Utah's Canyonlands National Park.

"You are gazing upward, with the sun lighting up just your face," I said, "and you have a look of awe and wonder. It struck me that this had been passed along, from Grandpa to me and then to you. I hope you will always be capable of feeling the joy etched on your face in that picture."

Then I began to tell Sam about my mother.

"It is one of my everlasting regrets that you never got to meet your Grandma, because she was a remarkable lady," I said. "But in a way, you have met her—through the incredible works of art that surround us in our home, artwork that she lovingly collected and which reflects something else about her: her ability to take sheer joy in beautiful things, which you do in the piano music that you play so wonderfully."

I went on to tell Sam of his grandmother's incredible determination, which enabled her, as a single mother, to raise me, run a household, go to work every day, and earn a degree in art history, all at the same time.

"So here is a blessing from Grandma Rita through me," I continued. "Life can be a bit of a roller coaster; it can provoke sadness and anxiety, but also thrills and joy. May you continue to approach your life with that same uncanny combination of focus and serenity that are already such a remarkable part of your personality."

I couldn't complete my blessing without sharing the words my mom wrote to me shortly before she died. "They have been a great comfort to me when I began to have self doubts," I said to Sam, "and I think she would want to say them to you if she were here."

I unfolded the paper I'd kept with me for 21 years and read aloud the last thoughts my mother ever expressed:

"I love you beyond all words. Be strong. You are already a beautiful, tender, talented, and accomplished young man—an asset to your friends, family, the world you live in. Oh, how proud I am of you!"

Even at the greatest depths of her despair, my mother had found the room in her heart to rise above her pain and leave me with the precious gift of love. Her words were, and remain, a powerful blessing to me, and I was honored to pass them on to my son.

I decided to share this story to encourage others to meet a similar moment in their lives head on—to overcome fear simply by opening the heart and giving freely. The impact can be profound beyond all reckoning.

PART TEN

Essentials

*"My mother had expressions for everything—she must
have had hundreds of them—but I latched on to
one in particular, and I've kept it close to me all my life."*

Covering All the Bases

Jay Ratliff

Airline General Manager, Retired
Dayton, Ohio

Know what you are going to do with the ball before you get it."

As a kid playing baseball in Carlisle, Ohio, I had heard my father repeat that phrase so many times I actually thought he invented it. So like any good teenaged son, I ignored him and his stupid advice.

One night, late in a championship play-off game, our junior high school team was locked in a scoreless tie against a great opponent. The crowd went into a frenzy when their speedy leadoff batter ripped a triple in the bottom of the ninth inning. I paced nervously around my position at first base.

As our pitcher tried to regain his composure, I happened to glance at my father in the stands. The minute our eyes connected, he began pointing at the side of his head.

What? Is he crazy? Now? I'm supposed to stop and think about every possible thing that could happen on the next play—*now?* There are ten different ways a runner can score from third with less than two outs, but why consider them now? Any ground ball hit my way goes to first base for the out, right?

No, wait. Then the runner would score. How 'bout I scoop up the ball and hold the track star at third, protecting the run? No. That won't work either. We desperately needed that first out.

I was killing a billion brain cells trying to figure out the best option. I finally decided that if a ground ball was hit to me, I could prevent the run from scoring by sprinting down the first base line toward home, tag the oncoming runner, and keep Roadrunner at third.

I'll never forget the feeling I had when all of this raced through my mind as our pitcher went into his windup. What a total waste of time expending so much energy on something that had virtually no chance of happening.

It took exactly one pitch for my father to become a genius.

Big swing. Slow roller. Right toward me. Crowd screaming.

I reacted without thinking. I sprinted down the line toward home, tagged out the oncoming batter, and watched The Flash scurry back to third.

Perfection.

As I flipped the ball back to our pitcher, I glanced again at my dad in the stands. His huge grin told me that he knew his message had been received loud and clear.

A few years later, I began working in customer relations for a commuter airline. I was only 18 and worried if I was good enough for my job. But eventually I figured out how I could apply what my father had taught me on the baseball field to what I was doing at the airport. It's all about anticipation. Cancelled flights, rerouting passengers, medical emergencies, security problems—all of this requires a certain *what-if* mentality. So just as I had done that night on the baseball diamond, I approached my new job by covering all the bases.

My attention to detail didn't go unnoticed and I was quickly promoted into management, nearly a decade before it usually happens. I eventually took an early retirement. For that, I can thank my dad.

Whenever I speak at professional training seminars, I enjoy retelling the play-by-play of my favorite baseball story, and how my father's "stupid" words made all the difference in my life. If they could help my team win the championship (and, yes, we held the other guys scoreless and racked up 13 runs the next inning!), then they can help others, too.

Jay Catliff

Every Person I Meet

Kathleen Nash

Family Therapist
Montgomery County, Pennsylvania

In spite of having only a sixth-grade education, my father was one of the smartest people I've ever known. Most of us equate intelligence with academic degrees, prestigious awards, or an Ivy League degree. But what Pop possessed didn't come from books. Life was his teacher.

Pop's father had deserted him, his mother, and his four siblings during the Depression. My father quit school and tried to find as many ways as he could to support his family. As a poor black kid growing up in urban Connecticut, Pop faced many hardships.

I was in high school when I learned about this family history. It came as a shock to me. Surely, my father must have had some extensive, formal schooling, I thought, especially considering how knowledgeable a man he had been all my life, so full of wisdom and advice.

The most important topic in our home had always been education, followed closely by showing respect for ourselves and others. Pop wanted all of his children to go to college. He and Mom instilled a love of learning in me, which inspired me to choose education as my academic major.

One day, I asked Pop how *he'd* managed to obtain so much knowledge without going to college.

"You need to learn something from every person you meet," he said.

"That's it?" I asked. "That's how come you know so much?"

"Yes," he said. "Everyone you meet has something to teach you—and you have something to teach them."

I thought about this for a while. "But what if I don't like the person?" I asked. "Or what if the person is just terrible?"

"Everyone is equal in God's eyes," Pop replied. "You are no better than someone who lives on the street or the big-shot businessman. We all deserve respect. And everyone has something to teach you."

What Pop said jogged a memory. I remember being five years old and visiting my neighbor's Sunday school class. I felt out of place because I didn't know most of the kids. Then I noticed another little girl sitting at a table all alone, with her back to the rest of us. I asked the teacher about her.

"Don't talk to her!" the teacher whispered fearfully. "There's something wrong with her." Nobody in the class went near the girl because of the teacher's reaction.

All that year I had a recurring nightmare. I was sitting in the classroom, coloring, when suddenly I looked over at this girl. She slowly turned around to reveal the face of a monster. She had big teeth and piercing eyes. In my dream, I would scream, and then I would wake up.

Years later, my friends talked me into participating in a Special Olympics Day being held at our high school. I spent the day helping a little girl with

Down syndrome and had a great time. I'd never met anyone who enjoyed life more than she did. She rejoiced in just *being*.

When I got home that evening, I was overcome by a sad revelation. All those years ago back in that classroom, I *had* actually seen the face of that little girl, sitting by herself at her table. Now I realized she had Down syndrome, too.

The Sunday school teacher's behavior taught me a lesson about what fear and ignorance can do. The little girl at the Special Olympics taught me a lesson about what acceptance and understanding can do. My father was right: We do learn something from everyone we meet.

Today, I am an advocate for children with disabilities. I hold master's degrees in education and family therapy and work in community outreach. I meet some very special people in my job; and just as my father had promised me, I continue to learn from each and every one of them.

Not too long ago, I was working with a five-year-old child, asking him if he understood why his brother, who is autistic, behaves the way he does. The child looked at me as if I'd asked the most absurd question he had ever heard.

"Because that's how God made him," he said.

At only five, he'd already learned my father's lesson.

Kathleen Nash

Help!

Jacqueline Sia

High School Student
New York, New York

I went to a strict Catholic school in Chinatown, New York City, where my teachers concentrated heavily on academics. But my eighth-grade teacher was different—he was kind of eccentric. Rather than spend all of his time on things like English and math, he told our class that he preferred teaching *life* lessons, such as the value of friendship, or the value of one's culture, or the importance of creating one's own identity.

I resented this. *How can talking about life—and how to deal with it—help me progress with my academic subjects?* I wondered. I found no value in these life lessons, and besides, I felt we were falling behind in how much we should know, especially since we'd be starting high school the next year.

But one day, Mr. Matthews made an announcement.

"Instead of beginning with our normal English studies," he said, "today we're going to play a game." This piqued our interest, as we rarely played games in class. Mr. Matthews began handing out random slips of paper, each one bearing the name of a different piece of fruit.

"When I say, 'Go!'" he instructed, "everyone has to yell out the name of his or her fruit. When you find another person with the same fruit, form a group. And by the way," he cautioned, "you are only allowed to say the name of the fruit, and nothing else."

But there was a twist. Mr. Matthews pulled me aside and quietly told me that my slip of paper would not have the name of a fruit on it, but instead the word "Help."

"And I want you to keep yelling the word at the top of your lungs," he added, "no matter what happens."

My first reaction was to laugh. I thought this was a ridiculous and embarrassing idea, and I didn't want to make a fool of myself by acting different from everyone else. I didn't understand why I had to do this, and I asked Mr. Matthews if he was serious. He was—so I agreed reluctantly to follow his instructions.

As soon as all the slips of paper were handed out, Mr. Matthews yelled, "Go!" and everyone scrambled to their feet, yelling out the name of their fruit. Cries of "Apple!" and "Orange!" and "Banana!" filled the air. I took a deep breath and began yelling, "Help!" Mr. Matthews watched all of us very carefully.

At first my calls of "Help!" weren't loud enough, and my classmates didn't understand me. One tried to figure out what I was saying, thinking I hadn't understood the instructions. Another just looked at me oddly. Before long, my classmates were staring at me. Obviously I wasn't part of their group, and they were wondering what on earth I was doing. Why was I crying, "Help"?

Finally, Mr. Matthews shouted for us all to stop and sit on the floor. I looked around the room. Everyone except for me had found his or her fruit group.

"So, tell me what happened," Mr. Matthews asked the class.

"We yelled out the name of our fruit, and got into groups," one classmate answered.

"What about Jackie?" Mr. Matthews asked. "What was she doing?"

"I think she was calling for help," someone said.

"Then why didn't you help her?"

No one said anything for a moment. Then one of my classmates spoke up.

"I didn't know why she was screaming for help. I didn't know what to do."

Mr. Matthews gave a satisfied smile.

"And that is exactly what it will be like in high school."

All of us were fascinated and listened carefully as Mr. Matthews explained.

"Next year in high school, you are going to be in a new environment," he began, "and just like Jackie here, you may be the ones crying out 'Help!' with no one responding. Which is why you all need to watch out for one another. To pay attention and to listen."

To my surprise, Mr. Matthews's crazy game opened up my world, teaching me about the importance of looking out for others. It also taught me that when people form their own little cliques—as they often do in school—someone is always left out. That's the "help" person.

Any one of us can be the "help" person at one point or another. So whenever I see someone silently calling for help, I think of Mr. Matthews's fruit game. And that's my sign to "Go!"

Jacqueline Sia

One Does What One Can

Kathy Faught

Masseuse
New Haven, Connecticut

My mother found a story in *Reader's Digest* that stuck with her. Here's how it goes:

A man is walking down the road and happens upon a robin lying on its back, with its feet sticking up in the air.

"Cock Robin, why are you lying on your back in the middle of the road?" the man asks.

"The sky is falling, the sky is falling!" Cock Robin replies.

"But why are your feet sticking up in the air?" the man presses.

"Because," says the little bird, "one does what one can."

I was a little girl when I first heard this story. I thought it was funny. But for my mother, it was an entirely different story. Her whole life had been dedicated to doing what she could to hold up her piece of the sky. During World War II she taught herself Braille transcription, then translated novels from French to English to Braille for the many soldiers returning home blind. She also worked with polio patients, all the time believing that in order to improve the world, one must do what one can.

I was 16 years old when the robin story first took on meaning for me. I had learned that various organizations were trying to raise money for famine relief in Bangladesh, so my friends and I rode the train from Stamford, Connecticut, to New York every day, asking wealthy passengers for money. Sometimes our plan didn't work; other times, we'd get four guys sitting together, all of them trying to one-up each other with how much they'd give. We did this for a couple of weeks, at one point raising over $200 in one day. We sent the money off to the famine relief organizations, knowing we couldn't save Bangladesh all by ourselves, but trying to do our part.

As an adult, I began volunteering for Recording for the Blind and Dyslexic, a service for people with print disabilities. One day the staff was told that the organization had suffered a fiscal crisis and would have to close if we didn't raise $40,000 by the end of summer. It was already May. If ever the sky was falling, this was the time!

More than 100 volunteers banded together to organize bake sales, auctions, musical fundraisers, and card parties. No one thought we had a prayer in reaching our goal, but by the end of the summer we had collected close to $50,000. In our own way, we'd caught the sky before it was too late.

Some people are born proactive and others aren't. But I never cease to marvel at how the story my mother told me continues to guide me more than 30 years later.

Sometimes, this can be dangerous. I have been known to be the kind of person who not only confronts litterbugs, but I also climb out of my car when I see someone toss garbage out of his window at a stop light, and then

I throw it back into his car. (When it's a full cup of coffee, I drive off as fast as I can!) I have also told drug dealers face-to-face to get off my block. Maybe this is foolish—even reckless—but like that little robin, I truly believe that one does what one can.

I recently went to a women's march in Washington and looked at all the people who had gathered together for the event. I thought about whether my presence was really doing anything to change things. In the end, I took comfort in the fact that maybe it was. After all, my little birdie feet are still sticking up in the air, and the sky hasn't fallen yet.

The Chemistry Test

Eric Dodson Greenberg

Lawyer
Silver Spring, Maryland

It was one of those moments when disaster looms so large, when things have gotten so ridiculously bad, that the absurdity of the situation almost catapults you out of your body. You're actually watching yourself with a strange combination of incredulity and horror, and asking, "How did I get myself into this?" And, of course, the answer is always so obvious: "You screwed up, bub."

I *had* screwed up. I was in my senior year of high school, and had just learned that I was on the verge of failing chemistry for the entire year. By then, I'd already been accepted to a reasonably prestigious liberal arts college; and I'd just represented my state at the national debate-and-speech championships in two events.

Okay, so I didn't need to win some prestigious award like the Westinghouse Science Prize to prove anything to anybody, but failing chemistry wasn't exactly the way to go, either.

Science was not my strong suit and never had been. So I employed a strategy that I thought would hedge against my academic weaknesses. Because chemistry was a requirement for graduation, I'd decided I'd put it off until my senior year, when colleges I applied to would only see my grades for the first two academic quarters.

Good plan. I aced the first quarter and, although my grades dropped the second quarter, they were still respectable. Unfortunately, then I shut my mind off like a Bunsen burner—stopped studying, failed quizzes and tests, stopped thinking about ions for what seemed like an eon. And now as the school year was coming to a close, I wasn't sure if I could mathematically muster a passing average for the year. (I wasn't that hot in math, either, by the way. But that's another story.)

After our last chemistry class, my teacher, Mr. Topper, stopped me on my way out of the classroom. Mr. Topper was one of those classically frightening teachers whose genius is lost on the young. To us, he was special only because of his uncanny resemblance to Yoda from *Star Wars*. For real. He was also very serious about academics. Beneath the clock on his wall he'd posted a sign that read, "Time passes. Will you?" Not very likely in my case.

Pulling me aside that day, Mr. Topper offered to make me a deal. If I passed the New York State Regents Exam for chemistry—a mandatory, statewide final test—he would give me a passing grade for the year.

"And Mr. Greenberg," he added for dramatic and pedagogic effect, "do you know why I'm willing to make you that offer? Because I know that you won't pass!"

Of course, for all his great skills, Mr. Topper had somewhat underestimated me this time. I could see right through his ploy: He was using basic reverse psychology to trick me into passing. But just because I knew what

Mr. Topper was up to didn't mean I was off the hook. I needed to pass that test.

And I wasn't off the hook at home, either. Despite my desperate lobbying, my father laid down the law:

"You can't drop chemistry," he announced.

So there I was, trying to teach myself chemistry in a span of only a few days. The words were so foreign to me—actually, they weren't even words: AU, FE, ZN. I didn't know my protons from my neutrons. But I read and read and read. And I started to learn chemistry.

In the movie version of this story, there's a moment when it all comes together and I start to sing a song about radioisotopes in Spain falling mainly on the plain. But it wasn't like that. I just toughed it out—and in the end, I scored a 76 out of 100 on the exam. No Golden Beaker Award to be sure, but a respectable and, more important, distinctly passing grade.

Mr. Topper kept his word, and I passed chemistry for the year with a C. It would be great to tell you that, inspired by my C in chemistry, I went on to win the Nobel Prize for my discovery of a new element. On the contrary, I can't tell you anything about chemistry. Within days of the exam, I promptly began to forget everything I'd taught myself. And the truth is, hardly a day goes by when I'm not able to get along just fine without having any knowledge of chemistry.

But here's the point: Chemistry didn't change me—*passing* chemistry did. In that singular experience, I learned that if I tried, I could do things that were difficult for me. I learned not to fall back on, "This is hard for me, therefore I won't do it." In fact, when I hit my first academic challenge in college, I thought, *Hell, if I could pass chemistry* . . . How ironic that such an important life lesson came from a class I'd tried to dodge.

Even now—more than 20 years later—whenever I'm in one of those ridiculous, horrible, "How did I get into this?" predicaments, I'm back in Mr. Topper's classroom. By daring me to pass that test, Mr. Topper inspired me to push my limits. And by not letting me quit, my father forced me to dig deeper. Passing that chemistry exam, I found something that has stayed with me—something that drives me to pass all those other tests that life hands out every day.

The Credit Hammer

Archie Harper

Fisheries Biologist
Helena, Montana

A few years into our marriage, my wife and I were struggling with our household budget. We had a child on the way, expenses were mounting, and we were going through our money way too fast. We knew we were relying too much on credit.

One afternoon, my father-in-law, Lloyd, paid a visit. An accountant from Bozeman, Montana, Lloyd Raffety was well liked by everyone in his community. He loved nature, enjoyed philosophical discussions, and seemed to have friends everywhere—from the cattlemen on the range to the guy behind the counter at the drugstore.

He was also one of the most active listeners I've ever known. He'd look you square in the eye, squint hard when you spoke, and never interrupt. Then he'd communicate to you exactly what he thought, always with sincerity, and never talking down to you.

So I invited Lloyd out onto the porch for a chat. Some people might be uncomfortable discussing problems in their lives—especially money problems—but I always felt at ease with Lloyd, so I asked his advice about borrowing on credit in order to finance the future.

"Credit is like a hammer," he said. "It's a great tool for building what you want if you know how to handle it. But be very careful with it, or else you can hit yourself in the thumb."

I made what I can only call an on-the-spot attitude adjustment. Before, I had thought about money mainly in terms of making more of it so I could buy more things—a house, cars, appliances. But now I began to think about postponing purchases, getting into the savings habit, and closely monitoring what money came in versus how much went out. Believe me, it's not an easy adjustment.

Shortly after Lloyd's and my talk, my wife and I thought it all through. We put together a budget, calculating our expenses, from major purchases down to the smallest grocery bill. We carefully tracked our banking habits month by month and got a sense of our cash flow. This has helped us emotionally, too. It's made us feel more relaxed about our money situation and given us a sense that we have some control over it.

We also made new rules. We now buy our vehicles in cash and never buy new. We put away 10 percent of every paycheck for unknown contingencies. And to reduce health care costs, we exercise daily (actually that's been fun to do together) and watch our diets (that's been harder!).

Over time, my wife and I have tried to pass on Lloyd's philosophy to our children: Make your money before you spend it. Avoid credit. Live beneath your means. It's an ongoing exercise in the game of life, and thankfully our kids are doing quite well with their money.

I'll always be grateful for my father-in-law's words. "The hammer effect" has truly helped my wife and me, and we haven't yet ended up with any bruised thumbs.

Archie Harper

The Pride Inside

Stephanie Castillo

High School Student
Queens, New York

The saying, "sticks and stones may break my bones but names will never hurt me" is not always true. Certain words *do* hurt, especially when they come from people you never thought would say something hurtful to you.

But nobody ever talks about how words that people *don't* say can hurt you, too.

My mother shows her love to everyone. She is always telling my two younger brothers and me how proud she is of all of us. I never get tired of hearing those words come out of her mouth. Whenever she says them I feel good about myself, and that makes me want to do even better.

My father is very different. He doesn't express his feelings a lot. He's a math teacher and he goes to school at night, so I don't see him much. But when we're together, he never says things that make me feel special, or make me feel like he's proud of me. If I show him something I feel good about, he says, "That's nice, but do better next time." Not exactly what I'm hoping for.

But the day I finished my first semester of ninth grade and showed him my report card with a 90 average (the first time I'd ever hit that!), he actually looked at me and said, "Nena [my family nickname], I am very proud of you!"

I was in shock. It was the *first* time I'd ever heard my father actually say that. I just stood there staring at him, wondering if he had a high fever or something. Maybe he was delirious. Anyway, when I heard my father say those words, my self-esteem went flying through the roof. I gave him a big hug and he kissed my forehead. I promised to continue doing good work and make him proud of me again and again.

What I figured out from this is that not everybody shows their feelings. And even if they don't tell you they're proud of you, that doesn't mean they're not.

Besides, what *really* matters is that you're proud of yourself.

Stephanie Castillo

Nana After Hours

Lloyd Lederkramer

Health Care
New York, New York

My Nana would go anywhere, anytime, to play gin rummy. She had come to live with us in the Bronx just after my 17th birthday. One Saturday night, while she was out playing cards with one of her friends, I was up writing, completing a paper for my sociology class.

I glanced at the clock as I finished typing. It was 2:15 A.M. I went into the living room to check for Nana, and saw that the sleep sofa she used remained closed. I became worried.

I paced the floor, even though I knew pacing was not a normal grandson activity. I watched television. I tried to write. As time passed, I became more and more anxious, unable to figure out what to do. I didn't want to wake up my parents, but couldn't help wondering, *Isn't it supposed to be the other way around? Aren't adults supposed to stay up late, fretting until their children came home?*

Then again, I'd learned long ago not to second-guess Nana. She had always been her own person. Arriving in America in 1900 at age 16, she lived a simple life in New York. Her peasant upbringing never left her, though, even after many years in the city. She didn't own lots of clothes, but she always managed to appear well dressed. That's because she was so enterprising. If one of her dresses got stained, she'd embroider a flower over it. (We could always tell the size of the stain by the size of the flower.) She could speak five languages, bake the best Hungarian pastries, and adored her daily dose of *The Edge of Night*.

But now it was the edge of morning and I was starting to panic. Finally, at 3:25, I heard the key slip into the lock. Nana strolled in, looking just as she always looked—calm, reserved, and nonchalant.

"Nana!" I barked. "Where have you been? Do you know what time it is?"

She replied casually, in her heavy Hungarian accent.

"Playink cods. Vut choo tink?"

As she hung up her coat, Nana seemed annoyed that I had confronted her and went off to the bathroom. She returned a few minutes later wearing her robe. She sat down next to me on the sofa and lit up a Tarrytown, her current cigarette of choice.

"Nana," I said, "I was so worried. It's late. Don't you need your sleep?"

She turned to me and slowly removed the Tarrytown from her mouth.

"Luydee," she said, *"You slip a-lunk time in da grownt."*

"Nana, what are you talking about?" I responded, trying to decipher her accent. "Are you saying, 'You'll sleep a long time in the ground?'"

"Yes, Luydee, you slip a-lunk time in da grownt." And then she smiled.

Maybe the sight of that smile is still so vivid because Nana didn't smile very often. Or maybe it's because she knew I needed to lighten up. I *was* acting a bit too serious for my age.

Even now at 53, I always remind myself that life speeds by too fast to take for granted. I left New York for a job that took me to the Midwest for a few years because Nana's words pushed me to take the opportunity. "I can come back and sleep later," I told myself. I've stayed awake on planes so I could catch a glimpse of foreign countries. I've danced at nightclubs into the wee hours of the morning, then eaten dinner in Chinatown at 4 A.M. I've stayed up an entire night to be with a sick friend. I wouldn't trade any of those times, and I thank my Nana for that.

My grandmother eventually moved across the Grand Concourse to live with my widowed aunt and help her raise her child. Even though she had enjoyed her time with us, she went where she felt she was needed. Nana knew she would eventually sleep a long time in the ground.

The Accidental Accordionist

Kay Hickman

Systems Analyst . . . and Street Musician
Leander, Texas

I have always loved music, especially European folk music. So when I got the chance to volunteer at the famed Irish Festival in Dallas, I was thrilled. All I'd have to do is count money for six hours, and I would get free admission, free parking, a free T-shirt, and a weekend of wonderful music. I couldn't wait.

After a long drive, I checked in and discovered that my job wouldn't be as enjoyable as I'd imagined. We money counters were placed in a back room, far away from the music, with a security guard at the door to make sure we didn't steal any of the cash we were counting. I spent my three-hour shift on Saturday thinking about how stupid I'd been to volunteer for this because I was missing out on all the music. I dreaded returning there on Sunday. I would rather have been home, cleaning house.

While I was thumbing through a particularly fat stack of bills, a man sat down beside me. He appeared to be about 80 years old. He'd come to count money, too, he told me—but unlike me, he was smiling broadly and seemed genuinely happy to be there. He pulled a Walkman out of his bag, put on his headphones, and got to work.

"You must have done this before," I said to him after a few moments.

He took off his headphones and leaned over to me. "Oh, yes," he said. "I do this every year."

"Don't you miss hearing the music while you're stuck in here?" I asked.

"I'm eighty years old," he replied, "and I've learned something just recently that I wish I'd learned a long time ago: Life is so short that we need to make every minute count. The problem is, not every minute is great. So if I have to do something that's not pleasant, I find a way to make it pleasant."

With that, he put his headphones on and got back to work.

I resumed counting money, but couldn't get the man's words out of my head. In fact, I continued thinking about them for several days after the festival, considering all the ways I could apply them to my life.

The first thing I did was take a cue from the man himself. Because I love music so much, I began using my Walkman whenever I was by myself, whether I was shopping or waiting at the doctor's office. This was a great start, in that it gave me real enjoyment throughout my day.

Next, I decided that my daily habits left me no time for taking care of myself. For years, I'd been going to work, looking after my three children, watching TV, and reading the newspaper. There had to be some other *pleasant* pleasures available.

I'd always loved accordion music, so I bought a button accordion and started learning how to play it. Having no one to teach me, I used the internet, finding the music I liked from other accordion players around the world.

To make more time for practice, I quit watching TV (well, the shows I didn't like, anyway) and stopped reading newspapers. The latter wasn't very hard to do: The papers never seemed to have much happiness to report.

It took me a while to learn to play the accordion well, but I practiced every night when I got home from work. Finally, I got the hang of it. I now moonlight as a street musician—a busker—which was always a secret goal of mine. I perform for the simple joy of it. What makes it so special is the energy I share with the public—I don't get that kind of connection in my day job. The extra cash comes in handy, but my favorite part is when people stop and dance. *That's* the magic.

I still think about that old man I met ten years ago at the Irish Festival, and how he taught me to enjoy this short life of ours. If it hadn't been for him and that unpleasant job I was stuck in, I wouldn't be having such a pleasant time now.

Kay Hickman

A Bird on Your Head

Wanda Thomas

Retired Technical Consultant
Wright City, Missouri

The most important thing my mother taught me was independence. As a child, I took after my father, who was mild and somewhat meek. My mother didn't want me to end up the same way. So if I got a test grade that I didn't think was fair, she made me walk down to the school and confront the teacher myself, just to find out what was going on. Little things like this taught me to be more assertive and stand up for myself.

My mother also had expressions for everything—she must have had hundreds of them—but I latched onto one in particular, and I've kept it close to me all my life.

The first time I heard her say it I was quite small. We were living in Kortes, Wyoming, at the time, a place so rural and remote—it really rose out of nowhere—that the closest convenience store was 30 miles away. Only 10 or 12 families lived in Kortes, and the town mothers took turns each week teaching Sunday school to the kids.

One Sunday it was my mother's turn. Only four or five children had shown up in class that day, and I remember that on the felt board my mother had arranged flannel characters who were depicting a story about temptation.

"You can't stop temptation from coming along," my mother said, "but you do have a choice to do something about it." When my classmates and I looked at my mother puzzled, she paused and rephrased her comment this way:

"You can't stop a bird from landing on your head, but you can keep it from building a nest there."

That comic image has stuck with me for life. It's made me the person I am. Whenever I feel blue, or I'm having a bad day, I think, "That's quite a bird up there, isn't it?" But instead of letting those feelings overwhelm me, or having a pity party for myself, I take action and shoo that bird away.

This has saved me more than once in my life, especially during my first marriage. I suffered a lot of mental abuse from my husband—things that I'd never imagined when we first got married. But just as I began to start believing that everything was my fault—which is what abusers want you to think—I remembered my mother's words. A bird had landed on my head for sure, but I was going to keep it from building a nest.

It wasn't easy ending my first marriage, but I did it because I knew I needed to. Finding strength in my mother's words, I remarried a few years later to the love of my life. I've never been happier.

My mother was not a perfect person. She was an alcoholic, which was difficult for me growing up. Our mother-daughter relationship was not the best. But I'll always be grateful that, despite the problems she had in her own life, she still cared enough to prepare me for mine.

Wanda Thomas

PART ELEVEN

Letting Go

*"I stood outside the church, trying to prepare myself
to give the hardest speech of my life. Normally,
words come easy to me—but not this time."*

Growth in the Valley

Richard Cook

Computer Technology
Charlotte, North Carolina

This is a bittersweet story of love and faith.

In the fall of 2000, my dear, younger brother Gary was in a hospital in Ft. Lauderdale receiving chemotherapy for lung cancer. Six years before, he'd supposedly been "cured," when a portion of his left lung was removed. When the cancer reappeared, however, it did so with a vengeance. Gary was in bad shape.

His hospital room was filled with young people from his church, all of us singing songs of praise and trying to lift his spirits. The laughter got so loud that more than once we were asked by the nursing staff to please quiet down.

At one point Gary's doctor entered the room to check on him. When he left, he pulled me into the hallway to talk privately.

"It's too far progressed for us to do anything," he said soberly, showing me on the X-rays how the spots on his lungs had spread. "I'm so sorry," he said.

"How long does he have?" I asked.

"Maybe a month or two," the doctor replied.

I was crushed. I couldn't tell Gary that night, so instead I returned to the room and lamely rejoined the singing, not wanting to spoil this gathering of well-wishers. But it was impossibly difficult to watch the joy now that I knew the sad truth.

A few days later, Gary was discharged. He was sent home to rest and advised to come back if the pain became too great. He still didn't know about his true condition. It was up to me to tell him.

It was the hardest thing I've ever had to do. Up until now, Gary thought he was going to make it. This would be the first time that he was told just how dire his situation was. I took my sister with me when I went to see him. As I gave him the awful news, I felt like I was hitting him in the head with a baseball bat. To my surprise, he was entirely calm.

"It will be okay," he assured me.

I felt completely hollow and began to break down. Here someone I loved was being given the worst news possible, yet he was comforting me.

After that, there wasn't a whole lot more left to say. So Gary, our sister, and I just sat together for a while. I returned home to North Carolina shortly afterward.

Over the next several weeks, Gary did the best he could. Amazingly, he went back to work at the church, where he was involved in youth programs. But then he grew too weak to continue.

Soon after, I got a call from a friend of Gary's, telling me that I'd better hurry back to Florida to see my brother. The end was close.

When I first walked into Gary's room, I was absolutely stunned. In the eight weeks since I'd last seen him, the cancer had completely decimated his body. He'd once been a robust six-foot-two and 200 pounds. In fact, a year earlier he'd even made jokes about getting pudgy. Now, he was totally emaciated, like a skeleton in a wheelchair.

I asked him how he was, then immediately regretted my words. What a stupid, horrible question. He was in pain and dying, that's how he was.

But instead of responding negatively, Gary asked me to come closer, as his voice was incredibly weak at this time. Looking directly into my eyes, my brother smiled.

"Richard," he whispered.

I waited.

"Everyone wants to be on the mountaintop all the time," he said to me, his voice calm and reassuring. "It's a beautiful sight when you get there. But nothing grows on the highest peaks. The growth is in the valleys.

"I'm just growing," he said finally.

He wasn't sad. He had no regrets. He had resolved himself, and was in a very spiritual place. How could he do that? I still can't get over it.

On Thanksgiving Day, I drove a few hours north to join my wife and her family for the holiday meal. Just as we were sitting down, I got a phone call from Gary's friend, who gave me the sad news. My brother had passed away.

He was 41 when he died, and close to God. And that is where my strength now comes from.

Gary's words continue to inspire me. They've taught me about the strength within all of us, not just when dealing with illness, but whenever we hit bottom. Like my little brother, I'm just trying to grow.

Richard Cook

My Father's Daughter

Karri Watson

Writer
Knoxville, Tennessee

It is my favorite scene from the movie *Elizabeth*. King Henry VIII has just died, leaving his throne to his teenaged daughter, Elizabeth, who is played by Cate Blanchett. During a council meeting with her father's advisers, Elizabeth is reduced to tears by their bullying and runs from the chamber. As she stands crying in a darkened room, she studies a life-sized portrait of her father that hangs on the wall, illuminated only by a shaft of sunlight. Suddenly, she stops crying and slowly straightens her shoulders, pulling herself up to her full height. The transformation is inspiring: Just seconds before she had appeared powerless and weak. Now she is proud and confident.

Fully composed, Elizabeth returns to the council chamber and lays claim to the throne, informing the men that, from now on, she alone will make all final decisions. Sensing their worry, she proclaims: "I am my father's daughter. I am not afraid."

In that defining moment, Elizabeth's self-assurance and steely determination leave no doubt that she is truly the queen of England.

I thought about this scene as I stood outside the church where my father's funeral was about to begin, trying to prepare myself to give the hardest speech of my life—his eulogy. Normally, words come easy to me—but not this time. I felt as small and helpless as Elizabeth must have felt when her father died.

My father was a remarkably strong man. He'd suffered from kidney disease for more than 20 years, endured two transplants, and nearly died twice from peritonitis. In spite of all that, and against his doctor's advice to retire, he continued to work every day.

But for most of my life, Dad and I had a very turbulent relationship. When he drank, he could be abusive. But in an odd way, he and I were also alike: Neither of us would back down from a fight, no matter what. During the last years of his life, we managed to overcome our past and build a wonderful friendship. Time does that in families.

So when my father died, I was determined to write and deliver his eulogy, even though everyone in my family tried to talk me out of it. They thought it would be much too hard for me, mainly because they couldn't imagine doing it themselves.

I felt a mixture of grief and fear as I sat down to write, but I wrote anyway, believing that I was the only person who knew him well enough. After all we had been through together, I felt this final tribute was the least I owed him. I knew the best way to honor my father was to fight the good fight, as he had done for so many years. He never gave up. How could I?

The words just flowed, and I finished the eulogy in 30 minutes. I committed it to memory, but kept a copy of it with me just in case I faltered.

When it was my turn to speak during the service, I froze. My mind went blank, and it suddenly seemed impossible for me to walk up to that pulpit. I remembered Elizabeth, I straightened my shoulders, stood a bit taller, and walked proudly to the lectern.

I am my father's daughter. I am not afraid.

I delivered the eulogy completely by heart, never once referring to the copy I held in my hand. Elizabeth's words gave me the strength—and my father's memory gave me the will—to honor him with a loving good-bye.

It Went Unspoken

Mark Drought

Professor, Writer, and Editor
Stamford, Connecticut

He was never a big man. And in his hospital bed, wired to a wall stacked with medical apparatus, he looked even smaller.

Lying there with enough cables coming out of him to pick up ESPN, the man I'd always looked up to barely made a ripple in the sheets. My father had suffered a massive heart attack and he looked so frail. Without thinking, I gently squeezed his hand. He gave me a quizzical look—we weren't the sort of family in which men touched each other. I never doubted that my father loved me, but in the 22 years I'd known him, he'd never once actually said so.

There in the hospital—looking up at a son who's never had a good poker face—reality seemed to tap him on the shoulder.

"I'm not getting out of here, am I?" he asked with a sigh. He'd always given me straight answers, so I felt a need to do the same.

"No, you're not," I told him.

My father nodded, as if my answer simply confirmed what he already knew. Then he rolled slightly toward the wall, his movement restricted by all the tubes. I think he needed some time to get used to the idea.

I wanted to tell him so many things at that moment. I should have thanked him for giving me a pleasant childhood; I should have told him how I'd always thought my happy home life was normal, and that it had taken me years to realize how few men make good fathers. I should have said, "Thanks, Dad, for not being the distant sort of father that so many of my friends had grown up with. Thanks for taking us to the pond to play hockey on days you probably would have rather stayed home."

Instead, I just said, "I'll be back tomorrow morning," then left him alone with the last few minutes of the six o'clock news glowing faintly on the wall-mounted TV.

I once saw a documentary about lions on *Wild Kingdom*. The male lion takes almost no part in raising the cubs. He doesn't hunt or play with his offspring. In fact, about all he contributes to the pride is his seed. Nature hasn't bequeathed the males of most species with the instincts to be good parents. I'd been lucky.

My father and I were very different. A blue-collar guy, always dressed in khaki work clothes, Dad's life was all about tools, wood, and nails. I had dreams of becoming an academic. While Dad liked Perry Mason mysteries, movies with John Wayne on a horse, and books about armies and explorers, I surrounded myself with literary criticism, abstruse poetry, and Russian novels. And while I'd been happy to avoid the draft and stay as far from Vietnam as possible, Dad had enlisted in the Navy as soon as he graduated from high school, then ended up dodging Nazi U-boats in a convoy crossing the North Atlantic.

He was on watch late one night when the ship ahead of him, a gasoline tanker, took a torpedo. The night sky was lit up by the fireball, and Dad's ship swerved hard to avoid the flaming wreckage. When his watch was over, Dad lay in his bunk wide-awake. Surrounded by millions of gallons of gasoline, he'd been afraid to doze off, terrified by the real possibility he might die in his sleep, without ever seeing his 20th birthday. He got no sleep that night, but the next time he hit his bunk, he slept like a baby.

"I was just too damn tired to worry about dying," he once told me. "And it's funny. I've never really thought much about it since."

And now, here he was in the hospital, dying for real, and it was I who was unable to sleep. I thought about Dad quite a bit that night. There were hardly any bad memories and plenty of good ones—funny little stories and small kindnesses I'd enjoy telling for years to come. I thought about the standard he'd set, how high the bar had been placed.

For example, for most of his life my father worked at a yacht club in Greenwich, Connecticut. One spring, he needed a big, strong guy to help maintain the club's clay tennis courts. Someone recommended a local high school football player, who turned out to be friendly, polite, hardworking, and black. Dad hired him on the spot. The young man had been working on the courts for several weeks before someone on the club's board let my father know that this wouldn't do. Yacht club members had very specific ideas about the sorts of people they want to see from the decks of their boats, and Dad was told to correct his "mistake."

My father was in no position to argue. He worked at a place owned and frequented by the rich and powerful, and every last one of them was his boss. Besides, he was a small man, with a wife, kids, and a mortgage—a man who needed his low-paying job. But right and wrong had never been gray areas for Dad, so he refused to do anything about his hire. Sometimes, the only thing necessary for the triumph of good is for good men to do nothing. Strangely, there were no repercussions. The black kid went right on working on the crew, Dad wasn't fired, and the club survived desegregation.

I remembered this story as I was driving to the hospital the next morning. When I arrived, I was surprised to find Dad out of the intensive care unit, sitting up in bed with his tubes and wires removed, in the pajamas he'd been wearing when he was first admitted. Relaxed and comfortable, he actually looked better than he had in years. They say people ready to end their lives often appear happy because they've come to a decision. I think when Dad asked to be taken out of intensive care, he'd made up his mind.

We talked for a while about nothing in particular. My mother had wondered if he wanted to see a minister.

"I never had much use for ministers," Dad admitted. "And I can't see what use I'd have for one now."

At that moment, he asked me to look in *TV Guide* to see what was on later in the day.

"Here you go," I said, glancing at the page. "Four-thirty. *Wild Kingdom,* It's about cheetahs—you love that stuff."

"Four-thirty?" he said. "I'll be dead by four-thirty. I meant earlier in the day."

His words hit me like a thunderbolt. I already knew he'd be gone by four-thirty, but the way he said it, so casually, was almost as if he'd reached over and squeezed my hand.

At that moment I wanted to hug my father, but I didn't. Looking back, I wish I had. I needed the hug more than he did. Here in these final moments, he was once again setting an example. He wasn't begging Jesus to save him.

He wasn't cursing God for taking him at just 48 years of age. He was simply showing me that it was possible for a small man to die bravely.

In the years since that day, I've marveled at how easily my father had said those words to me. I've always hoped that when my time comes, I'll be that accepting of my fate. Because, really, how we die is the last real choice any of us can make.

There were a lot of things I wanted to say to him that morning. But I didn't say any of them.

Dad died a few hours later, just after *Wild Kingdom*.

Mark Dwight

A Matter
of Forgiveness

J.*

Stockbroker
Gaithersburg, Maryland

I'm named for my brother. Same initials, same number of letters. They were expecting me to be just like him, but I wasn't.

John was the prince. I didn't matter.

When my mother died in 1996, I didn't mourn her passing, not the way you'd expect a daughter to grieve. I mourned the loss of a relationship that never was. We were total strangers, my mother and I. We connected emotionally once, and that incident pretty much summed up our relationship: She was in the hospital, afraid again that she was going to die. Sobbing, she apologized for all those times she had hit me. Indeed, when I was young my mother frequently used a thin stick to discipline me, and it hurt.

But that day I put my arm around her and told her it was okay. Later, alone in the car, I burst into tears and thought, *No, it was not okay.*

*The writer has chosen not to use her full name.

When I was born, I believe my mother went through a severe postpartum depression. Very severe. How else to explain her disregard for me? But my mother was totally devoted to my brother, who was 17 months older than me. Growing up, my brother and I were totally alienated. I couldn't understand it, but as far as my family was concerned, there was no value to being female, and the prince deserved preferential treatment. Then the prince turned out to be gay. This totally devastated the family.

You have no control over the people you are born to. You don't get to choose your family. You simply have to deal with it and try to work through all of the issues.

But how? I had struggled with this through my adult life, unsuccessfully, despite restless, ceaseless ventures into all manner of personal improvement regimens, journeys into just about every religion under the sun, and enough therapy to make me dizzy. I discovered many things about myself, but I was clinging to anger, hurt, and betrayal, and it was eating me alive. I was awful to be around. I bored everyone to tears with endless stories about my horrible family.

One evening, I was sitting at home reading a personal-growth book about creative visualization. It was a paperback—I remember it so clearly. And there it was, in the middle of the page, on the left-hand side:

"All that has offended me, I forgive. Whatever has made me bitter, resentful, unhappy, I forgive. Within me and without, I forgive. Things past, things present, things future, I forgive."

The words are from *The Tao,* which I was no stranger to, though I'd never read it for enlightenment about forgiveness. But here I was, feeling like I'd hit a dead end, and the answer was right before me.

How all-encompassing the words were! They left out nothing. But I also remember thinking that, in order for such an idea to work, you have to *believe* in forgiveness.

So I accepted the idea. I photocopied the passage and taped it places where I would see it often. I memorized it. I used it to soothe me.

One of the things that forgiveness allows you to do is let go. So I stopped searching for the reason that my mother and brother treated me so badly. That began to help. I also sought to change my relationship with my father. We spent a great deal of time together during the last four years of his life, and I came to love him dearly. I even had "Love, Dad" tattooed onto my ankle in his handwriting. I'd gotten it off a birthday card he'd sent me. I miss him dreadfully.

I learned through the healing of my father's and my relationship that it's impossible to love if you can't forgive.

Curiously, if you Google the word "forgiveness" on the internet, you come up with thousands of entries, and they're mostly about religion. But in the end, forgiveness is a personal matter. It's something you do for yourself, not for anyone else.

I think of my past life and family relationships as boxes in the attic. If I want to bring them down and sift through the contents, it's my choice. Moving beyond such a place of hurt has been a great relief for me.

What's funny is that, on a number of occasions, I've looked for that book with the quote in it but have never been able to find it. I know it's somewhere in this house, among the hundreds of other books I own. I just don't know where it is.

But I'll forgive myself if I don't find it.

J.

A Hero's Return

Susan Luzader

Publishing
Tucson, Arizona

think I'm ready."

With those four words, my father-in-law, Zeke, finally agreed to talk about his World War II experiences in Europe.

Ever since I've known my husband and started our family 31 years ago, I've witnessed his and our sons' enduring interest in Zeke's war memorabilia, which includes, among other things, a Nazi sword. But Zeke, himself, would rarely talk about it. His wife wouldn't either.

Until five years ago. I was speaking with Zeke one day about my own father's experiences in the war. He was on a ship in the Pacific theater, when suddenly he spotted a Japanese kamikaze pilot aiming directly at him. He recounted to me the feeling of standing there, frozen, knowing there was nothing he or his shipmates could do. But at the last minute, the pilot changed his course and hit another, bigger ship that was sailing nearby.

Something in the retelling of my own dad's story must have given Zeke permission to tell his own. It was as if he couldn't hold it in any longer, and needed to share it with those closest to him. I guess he also finally felt that it was safe for us to hear it and no longer necessary to protect the women and children. After all, his own grandson had enrolled in the ROTC, claiming it was Zeke's history that made him want to serve. Zeke was very happy about that, giving my son a hug, which is a big show of affection for him.

So when I heard Zeke announce that he was ready to talk, I immediately got out my tape recorder. For the next three hours, Zeke recounted many stories, notably his participation in the D-day invasion of 1944. My mother-in-law kept interrupting us to remind Zeke that his beloved Arizona State University football team was playing on TV. But Zeke kept talking.

The next day, I transcribed our conversation and passed it among our family. My husband, Randy, asked Zeke if he would someday show us where all of this took place. Coincidentally, Zeke was traveling to Europe the next summer and agreed to let us accompany him on what would be a very special visit. We were all bowled over.

Suddenly we found ourselves planning a family trip to Normandy, so that we could walk along the French beachhead with Zeke and see firsthand where it all happened. My sons, who were 16 and 22 at the time, and who only knew Zeke as an old man, would get to see their grandfather as the hero and warrior he once was.

We began retracing Zeke's steps in Garmisch, Germany, where Zeke had been a tank commander in the Tenth Armored Division under the command of General Patton. We proceeded to Heidelberg, where he'd captured a large Nazi headquarters. The only places Zeke refused to go were the concentration camps he had helped liberate. He'd sworn to himself that he'd never return there.

We worked our way to the northern shore of France and to the legendary Omaha Beach in Normandy.

Walking down the asphalt path from the visitors' center, my knees nearly buckled as the white crosses and Stars of David suddenly began to rise up before me, all of them facing west toward America. I had seen the site in the movies, so I thought I was prepared for it. But nothing can really prepare you for the daunting sea of 9,387 American graves. It is one of those things that you can't really understand until you've been there.

Zeke Prust waded ashore on D-day, June 6, 1944, just below this cemetery, then journeyed across the European continent in the belly of a tank. He captured German castles, freed camp victims, and almost froze to death in the Battle of the Bulge.

But there were no tanks at Omaha Beach—just gunfire and scrambling for cover.

"All we could think about was getting to the top," Zeke told us, pointing up at the sandy bluffs. After that, he said, he didn't remember much, just fighting and dodging. When he finally reached the top of the bluff, the smell of dead horses and soldiers and the acrid odor of gun powder almost sent him back down the cliff.

Inside the Battle of the Bulge Museum was a group of Belgian schoolchildren. Zeke was wearing his old Army hat, and the kids' teacher must have noticed that, because she approached us and asked Zeke if he had served in the war. When all of the children learned that he had, they surrounded him and began applauding. They asked if they could take photographs with him, and when he agreed, they all said "Thank you" in their best English.

Zeke's grandchildren were amazed by all of this. Seeing children younger than themselves thanking their granddad made a terrific impact. For Zeke, the attention came as a welcome surprise. As a minister's son, he'd always been taught to be humble and not show his pride. But now he just beamed, thrilled and grateful at the notion that, 50 or 60 years later, he'd somehow made a difference in the lives of these kids.

Back outside in the warm weather, we looked around us and saw children flying kites against the clear blue sky, and a lone dune buggy digging circles in the sand. In honor of our family visit, the tide had backed out farther than Zeke had ever seen it, exposing the few remaining scars from 1944. The rusted remains of what was probably a landing craft poked above the waves, but was still too far out for us to touch. As his grandsons explored the beach, Zeke remained at the base of the cliff, safe near the grasses and bushes that have regenerated since the shelling.

"I have never seen the weather this nice here," Zeke told me. His wife, Mary Ann, had made the journey before and preferred to stay above the landing sight, quietly watching her family from a bench. She cried off and on during our visit.

Words and symbols also adorned the landscape. At the base of the stairs, someone had taken advantage of the low tide and smooth stones to write messages to the veterans and visitors. "Thank You USA," one says.

Someone else had created an American flag, carefully gathering bluish and white stones for the field of stars and red and white ones for the stripes.

Still another spelled out, "Thanks, Gramps." I looked at Zeke, who turned away.

Later on, we returned to the visitors' center, where I asked about an uncle, Joe Eck, who my mother told me was buried at Normandy. A young Frenchman immediately found Uncle Joe's name and grave location on a list. He loaded us into a golf cart and whisked us off to plot G, row 18, grave 14, which was just behind the chapel. Approaching the grave of an uncle I never knew, my heart began beating faster. Uncle Joe's plane was shot down on April 28, 1944, ten years before I was born, and yet I began to cry.

"Thank you, Uncle Joe," I whispered to his grave, flanked by my husband and sons. The Frenchman pushed a button on a remote control box and "Taps" began playing from the chapel. I thought of Aunt Tillie and how her eyes would light up whenever she talked about her first love.

That evening, the eight of us filed into the hotel dining room, which overlooked a golf course. The sinking June sun projected shadows of trees across the greens. My husband raised his glass and we all did the same.

"To heroes," he said.

"To heroes," we echoed.

"To Grandpa," one of the grandsons said.

"To Grandpa, the hero," the other one added.

The meal arrived and we drank wine, relaxing into the long summer evening. As the waiter cleared the dishes, Zeke spoke quietly.

"It was good to see that today. You know, I remembered more things about the landing . . ."

Conversation around the table stopped, as we all awaited his next words. Then Zeke just shrugged.

"But I guess you don't want to remember those things," he said.

Zeke stood to say his good nights, then he and Mary Ann walked arm-in-arm to their room.

For Zeke, I suppose, the whole trip had been an affirmation of something he'd known all along: that he had done the right thing. The love and support of his family and the adoration and respect of the Belgian children only confirmed it.

"I wish he had said more about what he remembered," my husband mused as we walked by the pool, our heads tipped to the stars.

Then again, sometimes saying nothing says it all.

Susan Luzader

Celebrating Jonathan

Amy Jaffe Barzach

Advocate for Children of All Abilities
West Hartford, Connecticut

I'd given up on all the usual words, now I was searching for the magic ones—words that would make the pain go away. It was just after New Year's when I lost Jonathan, my baby son, to spinal muscular atrophy. And I was stuck. Everything I read in books and magazines made sense, but nothing took the pain away.

Just before Jonathan died, I had sat with him in the hospital, his little hand clasped in mine, his three-year-old brother, Daniel, entertaining us with songs on his guitar. A copy of *Parade* magazine was on the table. On the cover were the words, DEAL WITH LOSS BY CELEBRATING LIFE. The meaning struck a chord in me, but its full impact was yet to come.

Jonathan died three days later. The despair that followed was unbearable; the days were difficult, the nights were worse. Searching for comfort, I came across a passage in *The Prophet* by Khalil Gibran that talked about celebrating life as a way of dealing with loss. I looked up from my book and saw the little memorial card my husband had made for me, which included a picture of Jonathan and the words from the *Parade* cover, laminated together.

This time, the words took a grip on me and wouldn't let go. I began to cry uncontrollably; but the tears felt different, like a new beginning. It was as if the darkness that had surrounded me for the past few months had lifted.

Deal with loss by celebrating life.

I remembered a sunny day shortly before Jonathan had become ill. I had taken him and Daniel to a playground, and while Daniel frolicked, I rocked Jonathan in his carriage. Suddenly, I noticed a little girl sitting in a wheelchair on the sidewalk, sadly watching the other children. Her fingers tightly gripped the spokes of her wheelchair; her little chin quivered as she tried to hold back her tears. She longed to be joining the other children at play, but with no accessible path to the equipment, she couldn't get close. And even if she could, there was nothing for her to do. Not one part of the playground was available to a child in a wheelchair.

The image of that little girl sitting on the sidelines continued to haunt me while Jonathan was struggling for life in the hospital. Now here I was at my desk, thinking about how to celebrate Jonathan's life. I had my answer.

What if I built a playground where *all* children could play? Wouldn't that be a true celebration of life?

The idea stayed with me through the next few months, as I struggled to find the strength and courage to begin the work. I started slowly, enlisting the help of my family; I recruited volunteers—more than one thousand of them. My husband made little memorial cards, just like the one he'd made for me, for our entire family. We carried them with us everywhere, and to this day, I still find them unexpectedly in the pockets of something I am wearing.

But as April 1st of that year approached—what would have been Jonathan's first birthday—I was once again plunged into despair. I'd see other babies who looked about a year old and my heart would break all over again. I longed for Jonathan.

Rather than run from the date, my husband Peter and I decided to have a party on Jonathan's birthday at the local hospital. We arranged for a story-teller and a singer to entertain the children. We spent the day crying tears of joy and tears of sadness.

We celebrated the day. And we survived the day.

Eighteen months from the day I'd first read those insightful words, we opened our special playground. We called it *Jonathan's Dream*. The moment I saw children in wheelchairs rolling up the ramp to the equipment, I was overwhelmed with tears of happiness.

Here were kids of all abilities, playing and learning together.

They were celebrating life. And I was celebrating Jonathan.

The Unthinkable

Terry Naylor

Solar Heating Contractor and Business Owner
Las Vegas, Nevada

My father, who had cancer, wanted to accomplish one thing in his short time left on earth, and that was to see the birth of his third child and only son. He got his wish, but just barely. My father passed away when I was only two months old, leaving my mother alone to raise two daughters and a newborn son. But we were a close-knit and loving family, and despite her struggles, my mom raised us to be good kids.

One night, when I was eight years old, the unthinkable happened. While coming home from work, our mother was killed by a semi–tractor trailer that had jumped the median and hit her car head on. We were devastated. The loss of our father had been terrible, but now we faced an uncertain future. It just wasn't fair.

Luckily, our aunt and uncle stepped in to care for the three of us. We were a strong family, but it wasn't an easy situation, considering my aunt and uncle already had eight kids of their own (and would later have two more). Overnight, my sisters and I went from being in a small, stable family of four to living in the bustle of a household of 15. I was suddenly getting no attention at all. I remember being left alone at church on more than one occasion. It was hard to keep track of who had gotten in the car and who hadn't.

As I approached my teenage years, I became withdrawn and resentful. I harbored angry, hateful thoughts about the man who had taken my mother's life. His one act had changed everything, and I wanted him to pay for my suffering. I wanted his life to go as badly as mine.

The more I kept these feelings inside of me, the more miserable I became. Then one day when I was about 14, my uncle sat me down for a talk. We had an odd relationship, my uncle and me. He wasn't a terribly loving man, but I wanted to have a dad so badly that I grabbed onto any attention he gave me. One of his favorite TV programs was *The Lawrence Welk Show,* and when I realized no one else wanted to watch it with him, I jumped at the chance. That one hour each week was the only real closeness we ever had.

So when he began talking to me about my mother's death, I paid close attention. He told me that he understood my pain and heartache and wanted to ease it if he could. He told me how the tragedy had not only changed my life forever, but also the life of the young man who was driving the truck that had killed my mother. He was only 19 or 20 at the time, my uncle said, and what he did was truly an accident. Now he was also going to have to live with it for the rest of his life.

My uncle told me something else I'd never heard before—that this same young man had stood on crutches outside the church where my mother's funeral was taking place, refusing to come in because of the guilt he felt in his heart. He stood sobbing as the mourners passed by, asking for their forgiveness. This was a sorrowful man whose pain could not be taken away.

My uncle finished the story with a statement I will never forget. He told me that forgiveness would turn my life around; that holding a grudge against this man would not ease my pain—or his—but would only tear me down. He said I needed to look to the future and think about all of the blessings that I'd been given in my life. He reminded me that my parents would want me to go on loving life and wouldn't want me to be unhappy.

I will not say my life changed that very day, but it began to. Little by little I was able to let go of my hate, and now 25 years later, I can say that forgiving this man *did* help me turn my life around. I never thought I could get to a place where every day I live is a day that I love.

Terry Naryl

My Sister's Letter

Paul E. Mulryan

Prisoner
Glennville, Georgia

I was doing what I usually do when I can't get to sleep: leaning against my window, watching the night tiptoe by. The tall searchlights swayed like windblown trees, casting shadows through the rise and fall of the prison landscape. My eyes followed their abstract shapes up to the edge of a fence line, draped in razor wire. My thoughts waltzed through a wave of nostalgia, arriving as they always do at the threshold of home.

The 26 years I had been behind bars on an armed robbery conviction—coupled with an errant past that ran the gamut from chronic drug addiction to chronic theft—had virtually severed my ties to my family.

A collection of childhood scenes rolled through my head: camping and fishing; stealing watermelon with buddies; a Cub Scout uniform, all dark blue and yellow; school and skipping school; my mom and dad, my brother and sisters, and a sister I had shut out of my life nearly three decades ago. A storm of sadness, joy, and remorse. What a roller-coaster ride solitude can be.

My eyes traveled to the free-world side of the fence and climbed the tall loblolly pines there, scaling limb after limb until there was no more tree to climb, just sky. A sky dark and forever, with one small point of light flickering in space. That lone star seemed to have been hung purposely outside my window. I watched it, remembering another star that visited me in Japan more than 40 years before.

Japan, 1963.

It was a perfect evening for a wish, the time of day when clocks tick slow and lazy, when shadows merge long and loose into shady landscapes. The Yokota sky was deeply mottled, marbling into streaks of magenta, amber, and cobalt blue.

My best friend Timmy and I lay back against the slope of a small hill, hands clasped behind our heads, grass cool and clean on the bottoms of our feet. We hunkered down into the indentations made by our nightly visits and began our vigil.

Behind quiet whispers, we watched that sky with unblinking stillness, waiting for the first evening star to sputter to life, ready to pounce. My wish trembled on my tongue.

Timmy and I were seasoned players in this game. Our "Starlight Star Bright" stanzas were fast, and we were ready.

Yeah, baby, we came to play. Nobody was as fast at this game as Timmy and me, especially, the Japanese. After all, their good mornings have twice the syllables ours do.

My father was a flight navigator, stationed at Yokota Air

Base. One third of my life had been spent on this tiny island, and I wanted to go home. I missed our small, white cracker box of a house. I missed our pecan trees and thick, ancient oaks, crowding quiet dirt roads in the middle of nowhere. I missed watching my mom spread cake batter in cake pans, my sisters and me dancing around her like a maypole, arguing over who gets the beaters, who gets the spatula, and who gets the bowl.

I missed it all terribly and wanted to go home. Tonight, that would be my wish.

Suddenly, I saw a glimmer of light.

"There it is!" I screamed.

Timmy sprang up beside me, rising up on his toes, adding two more inches to his 48-inch height.

"Where is it? Show me! Show me! Hurry up!"

I pointed out the faint light.

"Starlight, star bright, first star I see tonight. I wish I may, I wish I might, I wish upon this star tonight."

"I wanna go home! I wanna go home in three days!" I hollered, repeating it over and over. Timmy was screaming from his tiptoes.

"We wanna go home! We wanna go back home! Let us go, we don't wanna be here no more, *pleeeeease* let us go!"

Then silence.

We stood there as quiet as those dirt roads back home. Our wish, still sweet upon our lips, sped its way up through leafy silhouettes and fireflies. No other celestial body could be found, just our star. It hung in the sky, twinkling down, as if to say it heard us.

My mom's voice brought me back to earth.

"Pauleee!" she called, standing by the open front door, flicking the porch light on and off.

Flick, flick.

"Time to come home, hon."

Flick, flick.

"Coming, Mom!" I yelled, barreling home, jumping small shrubbery in single bounds like Clark Kent on his way to a phone booth.

Mom was waiting for me, her white and yellow striped dishtowel in her hand.

"Guess who's on his way home?" she asked, smiling, clearly about to reveal something special.

"Umm, I dunno. Who, Godzilla?"

"No, silly, your daddy. Guess why."

"Tell me!" I said, hoping for pizza *and* a movie.

"Your daddy's been reassigned. We're going back to the States Saturday."

"Saturday?" I mumbled, counting the days on my fingers. "Saturday is three days away! Mom, I wished it! Me and Timmy wished it on a star!" My hands flew in the direction of the sky, the hill, Timmy's house, and again, the sky.

"C'mere, I'll show you!" I grabbed her hand and tugged her and her dish towel to our small spot on the hillside.

"This is where we wished it, Mom, as soon as we saw the

star we made a wish to go home and it worked! We're really going home!"

As I relived the experience that night in my cell, I was so deeply moved that I decided then and there that I needed only one thing in my life: to go back home to my family. So with pen and paper, I sat on my bunk and did just that.

My first letter, along with my heart, went out to the sister I hadn't seen in 27 years. Then I wrote to the others. I expressed gratitude and offered apologies. I asked for forgiveness. I wrote all night.

That December evening I was reminded of who I used to be before I made so many wrong turns. I was reminded of all the love and happiness conferred upon me as a child. I missed it. I missed my family and my home. I missed life.

Those letters took me back home—and in return, they brought home back to me. Because when their responses began arriving in the prison mail, I knew that I was once again with a family that loved and wanted me.

As for the sister I hadn't seen in 27 years, her letter arrived late one evening, by itself. I carried it to my bunk and sat down, staring at it, afraid of what it might hold. It felt thin, light. Maybe it was just a short note telling me to stay out of her life and never to write again.

I unfolded the two slips of paper and began reading.

"I got your letter, and cried the minute I saw your handwriting. . . ."

I read and reread her letter, each time quietly breaking down behind the steel door of my cell. Finally, a settling of the storm.

The nine-year-old boy on the hillside in Japan is still very much alive. He stands with me some nights, and together we watch the sky and pine for the magic that is granted only through the grace of the evening's first star.

Dedicated to my sister,
Gloria Jean Eaton,
who died March 2005.
I love you and miss you, Glo . . . forever.

Paul E Mulryan

PART TWELVE

The Bottom Line

*"The maddening thing is,
the more he said it, the more I wondered
if there was anything to it."*

Nothin' But a Thing

Dorsey Prince Leonard

Health Care
Church Hill, Maryland

It ain't nothin' but a thing," said my husband, Rick, when I told him that a vandal had bashed in our friend's mailbox.

"That's the stupidest thing I've ever heard," I said to him, laughing. "You're an idiot."

The maddening thing is, Rick always said this, no matter what catastrophe befell us. But the more he said it, the more I wondered if there was anything to it.

I started paying close attention to when Rick said it, and I noticed that he never spoke the words with a smile or as a tease. If anything, he was dead serious, as if he was offering up deep and sage wisdom about life's unfortunate moments. He said it when his brother accidentally split a beautiful piece of hardwood flooring; after a tree limb gouged the side of our boat; when a long-hidden stash of money suddenly became lost forever; and when a deer jumped in front of his van, demolishing it.

Still not convinced that Rick's words held some greater meaning, I challenged him.

"How about the foreclosure on Daddy's movie theater?" I asked. "Losing the Chester devastated our family. How can that be 'nothin' but a thing'?"

"Your family survived," Rick pointed out. "Nobody got hurt, right?"

I glared at Rick, resenting his answer. I thought back to the day my father lost his theater.

It was one of the hardest things I'd ever had to do. Standing beneath the marquee of Dad's old, single-screen movie theater, I watched in silence as it was sold at auction. Bidders and curiosity seekers had gathered for the event, and watching it all, my memories replayed in fast motion. I recalled the kids' paradise of my childhood, with unlimited free movies and endless buckets of popcorn. I saw my mom in the box office, selling tickets, while Dad chased after sneak-ins. I saw my brothers and sister and me playing hide-and-seek in the darkened aisles. I remembered my romance with a handsome projectionist named Rick—and years later, the excitement in the face of my own small son, as he headed off to "Grandpa's movies" for the first time.

"Do I hear an opening bid?" the auctioneer asked.

The words had shocked me back into the moment. *This can't be happening!* I thought. *It's like having sidewalk surgery while people watch.*

"Sold!" the auctioneer announced, and a piece of me disappeared forever.

Rick saw the pain on my face.

"The movie house was bricks and cement," he said softly. "That's all it was—just a thing. And things don't really belong to anyone. Things come from the earth and get taken back by the earth."

I tried to let his words sink in. I remembered how nature had begun to beat down the Chester. How vines and weeds had taken it in their grasp, their long, gripping tendrils clutching to the sides of Daddy's old dinosaur, tugging at the old bricks. It was as if the building was being drawn back to the earth, turned to dust, and consumed.

"Okay," I said to Rick, "if a 'thing' is nothin', then what is somethin'?"

"Damned if I know," he answered.

But my mom knew. She said it often throughout her lifetime, but I never quite connected with it until I watched our family history get auctioned away.

"The only things in life that matter," she'd say to me when I was a little girl, "are the people you love and the people who love you."

"Oh, Mommy," I would respond, "that's so corny. Where's my doll?"

When you're small, things are important, people are not. At fifty, it's the other way around. You discover that dolls and boats and hardwood floors aren't what really matter. That goes for movie theaters, too.

Mom and Rick had said the same thing in different ways. Both were right, and there was nothing corny about it.

I used to enjoy my things. Things were important to me. My attic proved it. Nothing was ever thrown away, and if something dear to me got destroyed, I'd mourn for days.

But now I don't care. If something breaks, cracks, burns, sinks, splits, disappears, ruptures, shatters, explodes, splinters, snaps, rips, or gets foreclosed on—it's all okay. Because it ain't nothin' but a thing.

Dorsey P. Leonard

The Pentagon, 9/11

April Gallop

Military
Woodbridge, Virginia

September 11, 2001, changed my life and the life of my son, Elisha Zion. It was my first day back at the Pentagon after maternity leave from my job with the Army. Elisha, who was only two and a half months old, was strapped safely in his stroller. I had stopped by my desk to get a document for my commanding officer before taking Elisha to the child care center. We never made it there. When the plane slammed into the Pentagon, the blast was so strong that my son was completely blown out of his stroller. I was thrown across the room, too, and ended up trapped beneath a heap of concrete, collapsed walls, and ceiling.

I was unconscious for a few moments, then woke to the sound of Elisha's crying. I felt no physical pain and operated solely on instinct, relying on inner strength—or something from the heavens—to get me out from under the enormous pile of debris. I heard the moans and screams of co-workers who were still trapped. Wreckage continued to fall all around us—I couldn't believe what I was seeing. There was complete hysteria.

How do I find my child? I thought. I desperately reached down into the rubble and felt him. I grabbed hold of him, pulled him out, and slung him over my shoulder. He had stopped crying, and I thought for a moment that he was dead. Even in the midst of my panic, I felt torn. *Do I just think of my son, and get out of here, or do I try to save the others, too?*

I ended up climbing through the mess and carrying Elisha to safety, helping as many others as I could along the way. Minutes later, I was lying on the ground not far from the site of the crash, waiting for medical care. Like a floodgate opening, the pain suddenly kicked in, and I began to scream.

Elisha was the only child to survive the terrorist attack on the Pentagon. He suffered hearing loss and developmental delays as a result of his head injuries. Once a healthy little boy, he'll now be under a doctor's supervision until he is 18 years old.

I, too, was hurt in the blast and still suffer from chronic migraines, backaches, and spasms. Elisha's and my road to recovery hasn't exactly been filled with flowers. Charities that promised to help us never did; and some people have actually told me that because my injuries were not severe, I should "suck it up and drive on." At times I've allowed all of this to get to me, to tear open my wounds.

In the days and weeks following the attack, I would rub Elisha's back, tell him how much I loved him and that he was going to be all right. I did this every day, despite the fact that many people believed he would never walk or run again.

The initial shock of that terrible day took a long time to wear off. The vivid images were etched so strongly in my memory that they would replay over and over in my head like an endless loop. One particular day, they just wouldn't stop. That's when the full impact of September 11th finally hit. Until that moment, I had promised myself that I would never let my son see me cry about what happened to us on that terrible day. But now I cried like a newborn baby—loud, hard, and without shame.

By this time Elisha was two years old, and he'd never seen me like this before. But that didn't seem to scare him. Instead, he grabbed my head in his tiny hands and began to stroke my hair.

"Mommy, you be awright."

"Why? How do you know?" I said. Naturally, I didn't expect him to respond. I was just talking out loud. But Elisha *did* answer.

"'Cause I love you," he said, sounding like he knew exactly what he was talking about and exactly what I was feeling. He pointed to my tear-filled eyes and said, "Eyes hurt?" Then he kissed them, just like I kiss him when he's hurting. Kiss the spot and make it all better.

I stopped crying and felt a great weight lifting. For all that we'd been through together—the horror of the attack, the pain of recovery, the frustration of trying to begin living a normal life again—Elisha was the first and only person to bring me a sense of inner peace. Drawing from the few words he understood, he let me know that I would be okay because of his love.

Later that night, I cuddled with Elisha at bedtime. Watching his beautiful face as he drifted to sleep, I pulled him closer. I thought to myself, *My son is now carrying me to safety.*

Lipie D Hallop

Keep It in Your Head

Marne Benedict

Retired Teacher
Eugene, Oregon

When my sister and I were growing up, our home life was simple. Material things were kept to a minimum, and my mother never failed to stretch a penny. She bought chicken necks by the bucket to make soup for us; and cheaper, broken cookies from bins, that we'd crumble up into a glass of milk and eat with a spoon. She canned her own food—green beans and peaches and beets—that she grew in her giant garden. And instead of buying our clothes at the department store, she got them from the Goodwill.

But my sister and I never felt shabby or impoverished in any way. We went to a good school; took tap dance, piano, and baton lessons; and belonged to the Campfire Girls. It was a given that we could participate in any activity we wanted to, provided that it enriched our minds.

"If I put it on your back, someone can take it away from you," my mother would say. "If I put it in your head, no one can."

These words were important to my mother. She was born in a sod house on the prairie in South Dakota in 1906 and raised as a child of the Depression. She was the second daughter of parents who didn't feel it was important for her to finish high school. Instead, she was expected to stay home and care for her five younger siblings.

Still, my mother was determined to get an education, so she went to classes whenever her chores were done. She didn't graduate from high school until she was 21. Her next dream was to go to nursing school, and she carefully saved $75 over the years to pay for her tuition. But when the banking system collapsed, she lost every cent.

Not one to surrender to defeat, Mother started over. She went to work in town for a doctor; she took in washing and ironing. Eventually, she saved up that $75 tuition again and this time got herself out of South Dakota and on to Omaha for nursing school.

After becoming a nurse, Mother got married and moved to New York. Her husband was an electrical engineer, and when he lost his job he suffered a complete mental breakdown. He had to be committed to Bellevue for the rest of his life. By then my mother had a little boy—my half brother—to support, so she cleaned houses and took in laundry, charging five cents a shirt. She also sold paper roses that she made by hand. (I still have the kit she used—it must be over 70 years old.)

Around this time she began writing letters to my dad, whom she'd met back in Omaha. Their correspondence lasted for two years. One day, he wrote, "If I send you the money to take the train from New York to Omaha, will you marry me?" My mother was barely off the train in Nebraska before they married.

My parents' attitudes about money couldn't have been more different. Dad worked for the railroad as an engineer and gave out loans to whoever needed them. He spent all the money that came in, mostly on new cars and gadgets. When my mother insisted on buying a house, Dad didn't want to. Finally, he gave her $200 a month and said, "If you can put food on the table and buy clothes for the girls and *still* figure out how to buy a house with that, go do it." She did.

Despite my mother's efforts to save money, by the time my father died we were bankrupt. I was 12 years old.

"Don't open the door to anybody!" Mother would shout, as people came to our home right and left to repossess things. But we never lost the house because it was in my mother's name. She went back to nursing—she was 51—often doing double shifts at night, so she could garden and can food and drive us to all our activities during the day. She didn't stop working until she was 70.

When my mother died in 1993 at the age of 86, she was still living in the home my dad didn't want her to buy. Cleaning out the house, my sister and I couldn't believe her collections. She'd saved a drawer full of cut-off girdle clips for nylons, in case she needed them someday, and a drawer full of little trash bag twisties, divided by yellow, red, and green—all very clean and organized.

It was only then that we began to appreciate how hard our mother had worked to provide for us—the scrimping and saving she'd done; the sacrifices that she made. The only reason we'd been able to take dance lessons, we learned, was because Mother went to the school at night and, on her hands and knees, scraped the black scuff marks from the studio floor.

Suddenly those words she used to say to us made more sense. *If I put it on your back, someone can take it away from you. If I put it in your head, no one can.* Our clothes may not have been store-bought, but our lives had been enriched. We had confidence and intelligence and a sense of family. These are things that can never be repossessed.

Marne Benedict

The Broken Lamp

Tim O'Driscoll

Lawyer
Burlington, Ontario, Canada

My friendship with Mark was factory-forged during seven summers in a packaging plant. I was a university student exchanging spare holiday time for money to burn each school term; he was putting food on the table for his growing family. Mark was one of a vanishing breed of unionized factory employees who believed—much to the chagrin of some co-workers—that in return for a hard-bargained hourly rate, one should put in a solid eight hours of work, whistle to whistle.

I took a somewhat less dedicated approach to my workday, spending most of my time playing hide-and-seek with a foreman unknowingly designated "It." Despite our different perspectives—or perhaps because of them—Mark and I formed a solid bond.

So when a call from Mark came from out of the blue, asking me to help him move into his new place, I was more than happy to lend a hand. After years of apartment dwelling, he had purchased a house for himself, his wife, and their boisterous trio of young boys.

For me, pitching in on moving day wasn't the usual grunt work. I actually enjoyed helping Mark open all of those storage boxes and sift through mounds of good stuff he hadn't been able to fit in his apartment. Most of the belongings were home furnishings that Mark had patiently stored since moving to Canada from his West Indian homeland. As we removed each treasured item, the eyes of his two eldest sons opened wide. Gradually the living room took on a new Caribbean flavor.

"There," said Mark, carefully placing the lamp on the end table. It wasn't exactly my cup of tea, but for him the lamp was obviously a source of great pride. It had a Chinese-red base, a matching lampshade with mustard-colored pompoms ringing the bottom edge, and a tassel attached to the pull-cord. Its twin had just been installed on the table at the opposite end of the couch, and together the two cast a warm, rosy glow on the sunset scene that hung on the wall between them.

On our way to the kitchen for some cold beer, Mark and I crossed paths with his youngest child, Lorne, a toddler who was weaving a wobbly path through the new home like a drunken sailor on shore leave. Lorne hadn't yet explored the newly arranged living room and was headed in that direction for a look. The crash of the lamp hitting the floor coincided with the snap of the first beer can. Mark and I ran down the hall to the living room, and there was Lorne, still holding the tassel, the broken lamp at his feet.

Mark's rush of anger and frustration came suddenly and unexpectedly. Grabbing the broken lamp and laying it across the couch, he turned to discipline his child, wearing a mask of fury.

To this day I don't know what made me say it. I wasn't trying to be profound; it was just something that popped out of my mouth as I leaned in and quietly tried to calm Mark down. My simple question stopped Mark cold as he registered what I'd said.

"You're absolutely right—thanks," he said in response with an embarrassed grin, his anger subsiding as quickly as it had erupted. He then administered a gentle bear hug to the frightened child and assured him that all was well, accidents happen, and the lamp could be fixed. We spoke no more about the question I'd asked him. We didn't need to.

Mark and I diagnosed the damage while sipping on the cold beers—it was a clean break in the base, straight across one of its lathe-turned grooves—and prescribed some epoxy glue and a little bit of matching red nail polish to hide the telltale white line of the crack. The day ended on a contented note, with Calypso music and barbecued hot dogs.

I bumped into Mark a few months later in a store and of course inquired as to the state of the house, the wife, the kids. I was stunned when he related the tragic news of Lorne's death: Shortly after the move, the toddler had contracted and succumbed to a serious illness. Words failed me.

A couple of years later Mark was blessed with another boy, and I dropped in on him for a visit. He ushered me into the living room and headed to the kitchen to fetch us each a beer. My eyes were immediately drawn to the lamp. It was in one piece, but the white of the crack was still clearly visible, no nail polish having ever been applied. When Mark returned to the room, he noticed what held my gaze (how long had I been staring?) and I turned to face him with a sheepish look.

"Remember that question you asked when he broke the lamp?" Mark said in a barely audible voice. "We'll never cover up that crack."

As I left the house a while later, the vision of Lorne—tassel in his hand, broken lamp on the floor—followed me down the sidewalk to my car. I couldn't help but wish that the lamp could somehow still be in storage, my rhetorical question never having been asked, its answer therefore never needed.

A decade later, with six years of parenthood under my belt, I wipe the crayon marks off the walls and ballpoint pen doodles from the leather couch only half annoyed. Then I breathe a silent prayer that more juvenile vandalism will inevitably follow. And all the while, my question to Mark echoes soundlessly through the house.

"Hey, what would you rather have, an unbroken lamp or a beautiful child?"

Surviving Mom

Ann Hite

Freelance Writer
Smyrna, Georgia

Where do you find the time to accomplish so much? What drives you? If I've heard these questions once, I've heard them a thousand times—from fellow employees, friends, even my family. I smile, shrug, and go about my business.

But, always, I think back to that March day in 1971 when one sentence changed my life forever.

It was a Sunday night, and my mother burst through my bedroom door carrying a belt. She beat me until I prayed to die. Mom suffered from mental illness, but at the time, I didn't know this. I was 13 years old and thought she was perfect. In fact, I believed I was the one with the defective mind.

Most people outside of our home thought she was a wonderful mom. She was divorced from my father, and by all appearances, doing a fine job raising my brother and me on her own.

But behind closed doors was another story. Her wild inconsistencies, her violent reactions to anything negative said about her, her chronic paranoia—all of them sure signs of severe imbalance. Still, I kept her rampages to myself. Back then, privacy was practically a religion in the Deep South. Besides, what do you say? "Oh, by the way, my mom beats me for no reason"?

So on it went, the verbal abuse, the emotional abuse, and the regular beatings with whatever object she found available.

But everything changed after that Sunday beating. The next day, I didn't wear short sleeves or a skirt to school because of all the bruises on my arms and legs. A 13-year-old girl doesn't want her peers or teachers to see that sort of thing. But as I was changing for gym class that day, my Phys Ed coach spotted me putting on long pants and insisted that I wear my shorts and T-shirt.

"You either dress properly or go to the principal's office!" she said, her loud voice drawing the attention of my classmates. Because she was one of those mean types—always yelling, never listening—I quickly changed into my shorts, and that's when she noticed the bruises.

"What're those?" she asked in front of the 20 other girls. Obviously I couldn't reveal that my mother had caused the marks, so I said that I'd fallen down the stairs in my apartment building.

Next thing I know, my coach had gone to the principal's office, and the two of them returned to the gym together and watched the class play Battle Ball. I could feel the principal's eyes on me. Obviously he understood what was going on. For the first time, an adult was seeing what my mother had done to me. And he seemed shocked.

The school mandated that my mother and I attend family counseling.

This was not as common a practice as it is now, especially in the small Atlanta suburb where I lived. We were told that during our first appointment, the therapist would evaluate both my mom and me. Mother voiced her opinion about that all the way to the office.

"If you hadn't opened your mouth, I wouldn't be going through this," she barked, staring hard at the road. Then she announced, "You're my child. I can raise you like I want."

Once we arrived at the counselor's office, Mother was called in to see the doctor first, while I pretended to read *Teen* in the waiting room. Thirty minutes later, I was escorted back to a small room, with only a desk and a single window that looked out onto a playground.

I was distracted. Somewhere within the building, I imagined I heard my mother's voice crackling with anger. Before long, a young woman dressed in jeans walked into the office. I remained silent for an entire minute. The therapist watched me, and I watched her like an animal afraid for its life. Finally, she held out her hand.

"I'm Dr. Baker," she said, "but you can call me Val if you like."

What I remember most was her soft expression, and the way I could still see children playing on the slide outside.

"I've just met with your mother," Val continued, "and what I'd like from you is a truthful explanation of exactly how you received those terrible bruises—the ones you're trying to hide with long sleeves on such a warm spring day."

I don't know if it was the tenderness of her voice or the need just to come clean, but I told this woman what happened—in detail. I explained to her how I was a bad person, how I'd caused Mother to lose her temper. Val listened in complete silence. When I finally ran out of steam, she stood and turned toward the window. She watched the children play for a while, and then she turned to me and spoke.

"Ann," she said, "did you ever think your mother is wrong?"

Her words rushed through my mind. Wrong? My mother? You've got to be kidding. But as the idea began to sink in, I swear the sun grew brighter outside.

Val was still waiting for an answer, but I could only shake my head in disbelief. Up until that moment, my mom was my life. I needed to believe in her in order to survive. But those simple words from Val told me that I was going to make it through this. It was the defining moment of my life.

I left the office that day knowing that life could be different, that there *are* good adults out there. I began to replay in my head countless scenes from the past. Everything began to fit together, like a giant thousand-piece puzzle. I was a kid, but I wasn't a *bad* kid. Someone had helped me to know that my mother was wrong.

Mom stopped going to counseling, but I continued to see Val weekly for another six or seven months. I would take the school bus to the very last stop, then walk the extra mile to Val's office. She would see me without charge.

I wish I could say Mother became better after that, or that the state stepped in and put me in a different home, but neither happened. However, something more important occurred: I developed a sense of survival within me, a sense of self-worth.

Today, whenever I'm down on myself, I remember the time someone told me my mother was wrong. And I know I'm going to be all right.

Ann Hite

Waiting for My Real Life to Begin

Maureen Ryan Griffin

Writing Instructor and Coach
Charlotte, North Carolina

Busy, that's me. Seems like I've been busy my whole life. And much of the time, what I've been busy with is wishing my real life would start.

I couldn't wait to get into high school and leave behind all the things I didn't like about grade school. But before I knew it, I couldn't wait to get out. My life would really be good, I bargained, when I left Mercyhurst Prep behind, and my whole hometown of Erie, Pennsylvania, along with it.

Once I was in college, those years also became just a time to get through. They were only stepping stones, I thought, to the day when I'd have my own apartment and a real job. And then someday, a husband. Maybe kids, too.

And on it went. Each new chapter of my life only made me wish for the next one to begin. I couldn't wait to start that perfect life I was supposed to be living.

A decade went by, and there I was, in my mid-thirties, living with a husband, two stepchildren, and two children of my own. And still, somehow I always felt like there was something better out there. My house was constantly cluttered, I was always tired, and the mounds of laundry never seemed to go away. I felt like a riptide was pulling me under.

I spent my days waiting. Waiting for when all the kids were in school. When no one wet the bed anymore. When I had a new house with a big laundry room. That's when life would get good, right?

Things might have gone on that way forever if it hadn't been for the poet Li-Young Lee. I'd seen Li-Young reading and discussing his work with Bill Moyers on public television and actually met him once at a writer's conference.

One day, in between laundry loads and diaper changes, I was reading "Braiding," a poem Li-Young had written about braiding his wife's hair. I was particularly enjoying his references to Pittsburgh, where I'd lived while I was student-teaching. He mentioned the dark winter mornings that I remembered so well, and even the 71 Negley, a local bus I'd ridden.

Then I got to the lines:

> *How I wish we didn't hate those years*
> *while we lived them.*

How could Li-Young and his wife have hated their years in Pittsburgh? Sure, it was cold, but Pittsburgh is a great city. Hadn't I loved my time there? Didn't I enjoy spending the day with my third-grade students in Squirrel Hill, riding the 71 Negley, and going to the art museum on Sunday afternoons?

No. The more I thought about it, the more I had to admit that I spent a fair amount of time there, as usual, wishing I was somewhere else—getting on with my *real* life, the one I was going to love.

Well, here I was again, ten years later, not appreciating *this* life, either.

Li-Young's poem made me stop and think. This is the only life I have, and these years are filled with shining moments that I will miss if I don't pay attention. Moments like my daughter catching fireflies to share with her baby brother. Or afternoons spent cuddling while we all read a favorite picture book together. Or my stepson's wonderful sense of humor. Every day offers its own little gems.

Why hadn't I realized before that, strung together, all of these moments make up a life? A good life.

I vowed then and there that I was finished not loving my life. I created a new mantra for myself: *How she loves these years as she is living them.* I said it to myself all day long, smiling a little more with every repetition. I even put up a copy in my laundry room.

What a great gift Li-Young gave me—the gift of loving my life as I live it.

Coda

Gregory Fouts

Education and Training
Hendersonville, North Carolina

The phone call was from a former student of mine, now a psychologist working with end-of-life patients and their families. Helen was contacting me to discuss one of her clients, who was currently in a hospice. As she spoke, I remembered how much I'd admired her compassion as a student. I hadn't seen her for several years.

Helen described her client's ordeal. At 92, Mrs. M. was terminally ill. She'd been in the hospital for many weeks; and after several efforts to stabilize and improve her condition, she and her family—along with their physician—elected to remove the tubes, stop the medication, and move Mrs. M. into a nearby hospice so she would not have to spend her last days in a hospital ward. Her doctors felt she would not last more than a few days, but she did. In fact, it had been two months since the move.

That was the reason Helen had called. From her experience, she was worried that Mrs. M. was having difficulty "letting go."

As a psychology professor at a large university, I had, for years, discussed "connectedness" with my students and how we experience and express it throughout our lives. Depending on the individual, this connectedness could be with a variety of things—from nature to the arts to, perhaps, a higher power. I wondered out loud to Helen whether Mrs. M. needed to experience her own way of connecting in order to let go. Helen asked if I could visit Mrs. M. and her family that afternoon. I agreed.

The room was cheery. From her bed, Mrs. M. could look through the window at the trees and summer sunshine outside. A pot of yellow mums sat on her nightstand; an old teddy bear, worn from years of love, lay beside her, her left hand gently resting on it. When I entered, her daughter was reading aloud from one of her mother's favorite novels.

Not long into my visit, I started to get a sense of who Mrs. M. was— what she loved, and how she'd lived her life. Music was her passion. She'd taught it in public schools for many years, given private piano lessons, and listened to it almost every day of her adult life. She had also handed down her appreciation of music to her children and grandchildren, and her son had been a professional musician for a few years.

As I spoke with her daughter about music, Mrs. M. opened her eyes. We looked at one another and smiled. It was then that I realized how the absence of music in her life for the past several months must have been unbearable for her. I leaned over the side of the bed and spoke to her.

"Do you miss music?" I asked.

Mrs. M. tried to answer, her lips trembling, her eyes glistening. She nodded and mouthed a word, but no sound came out. She tried again, and this time her voice was clear.

"Brahms," she said. "I like Brahms."

I turned to her daughter, who recalled that her mother had a favorite tape of Brahms's piano concertos that she played all the time before becoming ill. I asked if she knew where it was.

"I guess it's with Mom's things in her room at home," she said. At that moment, we both knew what had to be done. She put her hand on her mother's forehead and said, "Mom, I'll be back in a while. I have an errand to run."

That evening, Mrs. M.'s daughter, son-in-law, and a grandson were in the room as I entered. It was a warm, summer night. Streaks of orange were collecting on the horizon, and we could hear birds through the open window.

Her daughter put a small cassette player on the nightstand next to the mums. Mrs. M. had just eaten dinner and was wide awake. She was talking, with some effort, about how birds reminded her of music. Smiling and alert, she showed more energy than she had earlier in the afternoon.

"I brought some music for you, Mom," her daughter said. "It's your favorite—Brahms! Would you like to listen for a while?"

Without waiting for an answer, her daughter turned on the cassette player. "Loud enough, Mom?" she asked. Mrs. M. nodded.

Brahms began to fill the room, and Mrs. M. closed her eyes to listen. A sense of peace tiptoed over her face—no pain or tension, just a look of deep bliss. Suddenly, Mrs. M. opened her eyes and looked at me. I could see the little girl she had been decades before, innocent and beautiful. She motioned for me to come nearer. As I did, she reached out to touch my face.

"Thank you," she said in a clear voice. She peered into my eyes and continued, almost insistently. "My life has been like a piece of great music, you know. There have been a lot of good notes, but mostly, it's living in the spaces between the notes that's been important to me."

I nodded. Her eyes glowed as I held her frail hand in both of mine.

Mrs. M.'s daughter climbed onto the bed and lay next to her mother, listening to the music as she had done as a child. I left them alone. When I returned a half hour later, the music was still playing. Her daughter was talking softly to her mother as tears ran down her cheeks.

"Mom's left us," she said.

The sky was dark by the time I got to my car. I'm not sure why, but rather than drive, I put the car keys back into my pocket and headed for home on foot. I spent the two-hour walk thinking about Mrs. M. and how grateful I was to have gotten to know her in these last hours of her life. I thought about the power of the words she had spoken to me and began to wonder: Was this moment—right now—a note in my life? Or was it a space between the notes?

Gregory Jantz

PART THIRTEEN

A St. Jude Story

A Regular Kid

Lindsey Wilkerson

Event Coordinator, St. Jude Children's Research Hospital
Cordova, Tennessee

In the fall of 1991, I was just your average ten-year-old girl, living in a small town in Missouri. My biggest worry was about where the next sleepover would be on the weekend. What I didn't know is that I was becoming critically ill, and that my life was about to change forever.

No one seemed to notice anything particularly wrong about me even though I started losing my appetite. Then I began noticing bruises all over my body. I liked school a lot, but I was falling asleep in class and even became too tired to play with my friends during recess. Everyone thought I was just under the weather.

Then on the morning of November 11, 1991, when my mother woke me up, she was alarmed because I looked as gray as a corpse. She and my father immediately took me to the doctor, fully expecting to hear that I had a bad case of the flu. But the doctor did a bone marrow aspiration that revealed that I had cancer. It was called Acute Lymphoblastic Leukemia.

Suddenly time began to move in slow motion. I associated that word—*cancer*—with people dying. My great-grandmother had died from a brain tumor, so when I heard the doctor tell me that I had cancer, too, I was scared like I didn't even know a person could get. I looked over at my parents to watch their reaction to the news. They fell apart—and so I started to cry myself. Our world was turned upside down.

Here I was, just a child, facing the possibility that I would never grow up, finish school, get married, or see any of my dreams come true. I'd been given a death sentence before I'd ever had a chance to really live. In a matter of minutes, I had lost all hope.

That's when my pediatrician told us that the best place for me to go was St. Jude Children's Research Hospital in Memphis, Tennessee. "It's a place of hope," he said. But we needed to get there quickly. My blood count was so high, and my body under such stress, that if I didn't receive treatment within 48 hours I could die.

My parents and I raced home and frantically packed our things. I hugged my two brothers good-bye, then headed off with my mom, dad, and grandmother to Memphis. I slept for most of the five-hour ride, but by the time we arrived at St. Jude I was terrified. Back home, my mother had helped raise money for St. Jude, and I'd even ridden in bike-a-thons for the hospital. But neither of us had ever imagined this would happen to me. It was always, *Oh, those poor kids.*

Now I was one of them.

The only thing I remember of that first month at St. Jude was that my initial chemotherapy treatments made me feel sicker than I'd ever felt before. It was an all-out assault on the disease in my body. I started losing my hair, and at times I was so weak I couldn't even walk. Then one day, a few months into treatments, it all became too much. The chemo. The needles. The nurses. I was tired of it all, and I didn't understand why I had to go through any of this, or how it was saving me.

The nurse who was taking care of me that day—Nurse Swofford—tried to administer yet another IV, and I began to cry. By now my veins were so weak they could barely sustain another needle; and as Nurse Swofford searched for a new vein, I stopped cooperating. I wouldn't lay still and actually began fighting against her.

"I'm going to fire you!" I yelled at her, crying all the while. But Nurse Swofford continued to be patient with me, patting my arm lovingly.

"It's okay, Lindsey," she said, gently taking my hand. "I understand what you're going through."

"How would you know?" I asked angrily.

"Because I was a patient at St. Jude, too."

I was completely surprised. I'd never seen a childhood cancer survivor before, and here was one for real, standing right at my side, as a happy and healthy adult. It was a humbling moment, even for a ten-year-old.

Nurse Swofford's gentle and calming words touched me in a very personal way. *If she can make it,* I thought to myself, *then why can't I?* I had a whole new perspective on my future.

Until that moment, I had never thought of myself as a possible survivor. I'd been so lost in my own struggle, I'd only noticed the children around me who *didn't* survive, and the way shockwaves would go through the hospital whenever a child lost his or her battle. *Will I be the next one to go?* I'd think.

But that day, Nurse Swofford's words of comfort—and the example that she set—gave me the strength and determination not only to make it through my treatments, but to become a survivor myself!

Nurse Swofford had loved me even though I was being so awful, and I soon realized that everyone who worked at St. Jude was the same way. They became a part of each child's battle and did all they could to let us know that we were not alone. They were our personal warriors, and through their support we found strength.

As I progressed through three more years of intense chemotherapy, it was this compassion that would make all of the difference.

When I graduated high school in 1999, I savored every moment of that special day because, years earlier, I was sure I would never make it that far. I felt the same sense of gratitude when I got married three years ago, as all of the doctors and nurses who had saved my life were there to watch me walk down the aisle. It was a beautiful day.

It has been ten years since I went off treatment, and now I am "a lifer" at St. Jude. Once I learned that I would become a survivor, I knew I wanted to come back and work with the children as a healthy adult—someone who'd *been there* and knew what it felt like. It was always my dream to give back to another child what Melinda Swofford, my nurse and guardian angel, had given to me.

When I was 11 and undergoing treatment, I wrote a poem that expressed my feelings, and the feelings of the other kids who were there with me at that time. I'm sure all the children who are at St. Jude now are feeling the same way, too.

> *I want to be a regular kid*
> *Laugh and play like you and me did.*
> *I want to know why can't I*
> *I want to know why oh why*
> *Why do kids have to cry?*
> *Why do kids have to die?*
> *Why oh why can you tell me why?*
>
> *But I know I'm going to make it*
> *Just you wait and see*
> *So don't you be worrying about me.*

Lindsey Wilkerson

The children of St. Jude Children's Research Hospital

*Memphis, Tennessee
February 2006*

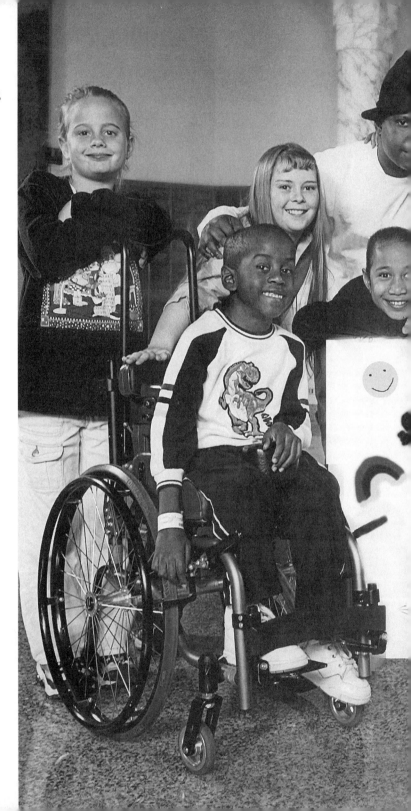

*For more information on the Right Words
project, and how you can share your own story,
log on to www.rightwordsbooks.com.*